T0392625

Democratic Innovations in Central and Eastern Europe

Democratic Innovations in Central and Eastern Europe expands research on democratic innovations by looking specifically at different forms of democratic innovations in Central and Eastern Europe.

The book covers direct democracy (referendums in particular), deliberative democracy practices and e-participation – forms which are salient in practice because they match the political realities of our time. Expert contributors show how the recent actions of ordinary citizens in several Central and Eastern European countries have challenged the contemporary political order, and grassroots movements and diverse forms of mobilization have challenged the notion of weak civil societies in the East. The empirical evidence presented attempts to deepen citizen involvement in political contexts sometimes quite different from the democratic political systems in the Western world. Using lessons from a still largely underexplored part of Europe, the book both complements and revises theoretical approaches, or complements empirical results in existing studies on democratic innovations.

Democratic Innovations in Central and Eastern Europe will be of great interest to scholars working on democracy, political systems, political engagement, and Central and Eastern European politics. The chapters originally published as a special issue of *Contemporary Politics*.

Sergiu Gherghina is a Lecturer in Comparative Politics in the Department of Politics at the University of Glasgow, Scotland. His research interests lie in party politics, legislative and voting behavior, democratization, and the use of direct democracy.

Joakim Ekman is a Professor of Political Science, with a special focus on the Baltic Sea Region and Eastern Europe, at the Centre for Baltic and East European Studies (CBEES) at Södertörn University, Sweden. His research interests comprise democratisation, public opinion and political participation.

Olena Podolian is a Ph.D. candidate at Södertörn University in Stockholm, Sweden. She holds an M.A. in Political Science from the Central European University in Budapest, Hungary, and an M.Sc. in Russian, Central and East European Studies from the University of Glasgow.

Democratic Innovations in Central and Eastern Europe

Edited by
**Sergiu Gherghina, Joakim Ekman
and Olena Podolian**

Routledge
Taylor & Francis Group

LONDON AND NEW YORK

First published 2020
by Routledge
2 Park Square, Milton Park, Abingdon, Oxon, OX14 4RN

and by Routledge
52 Vanderbilt Avenue, New York, NY 10017

Routledge is an imprint of the Taylor & Francis Group, an informa business

© 2020 Taylor & Francis

British Library Cataloguing in Publication Data
A catalogue record for this book is available from the British Library

ISBN13: 978-0-367-42167-0

Typeset in Myriad Pro
by Newgen Publishing UK

Publisher's Note
The publisher accepts responsibility for any inconsistencies that may have arisen during the conversion of this book from journal articles to book chapters, namely the inclusion of journal terminology.

Disclaimer
Every effort has been made to contact copyright holders for their permission to reprint material in this book. The publishers would be grateful to hear from any copyright holder who is not here acknowledged and will undertake to rectify any errors or omissions in future editions of this book.

Contents

Citation Information   vi
Notes on Contributors   viii

1   Democratic innovations in Central and Eastern Europe: expanding the
    research agenda   1
    Sergiu Gherghina, Joakim Ekman and Olena Podolian

2   The role of partisan cues on voters' mobilization in a referendum   11
    Miroslav Nemčok, Peter Spáč and Petr Voda

3   And yet it matters: referendum campaigns and vote decision in Eastern Europe   29
    Sergiu Gherghina and Nanuli Silagadze

4   'Never just a local war': explaining the failure of a mayor's recall referendum   47
    Sergiu Mişcoiu

5   Direct democracy in an increasingly illiberal setting: the case of the
    Hungarian national referendum   62
    Zoltán Tibor Pállinger

6   Deliberative democracy and trust in political institutions at the local
    level: evidence from participatory budgeting experiment in Ukraine   78
    Dmytro Volodin

7   Attrition in long-term deliberative processes. The neighbourhood
    consultative councils in Timisoara   94
    Adrian Schiffbeck

8   Democratic innovations in Serbia: a misplaced trust in technology   111
    Ivana Damnjanović

Index   128

Citation Information

The chapters in this book were originally published in *Contemporary Politics*, volume 25, issue 1 (February 2019). When citing this material, please use the original page numbering for each article, as follows:

Chapter 1
Democratic innovations in Central and Eastern Europe: expanding the research agenda
Sergiu Gherghina, Joakim Ekman and Olena Podolian
Contemporary Politics, volume 25, issue 1 (February 2019) pp. 1–10

Chapter 2
The role of partisan cues on voters' mobilization in a referendum
Miroslav Nemčok, Peter Spáč and Petr Voda
Contemporary Politics, volume 25, issue 1 (February 2019) pp. 11–28

Chapter 3
And yet it matters: referendum campaigns and vote decision in Eastern Europe
Sergiu Gherghina and Nanuli Silagadze
Contemporary Politics, volume 25, issue 1 (February 2019) pp. 29–46

Chapter 4
'Never just a local war': explaining the failure of a mayor's recall referendum
Sergiu Mișcoiu
Contemporary Politics, volume 25, issue 1 (February 2019) pp. 47–61

Chapter 5
Direct democracy in an increasingly illiberal setting: the case of the Hungarian national referendum
Zoltán Tibor Pállinger
Contemporary Politics, volume 25, issue 1 (February 2019) pp. 62–77

Chapter 6
Deliberative democracy and trust in political institutions at the local level: evidence from participatory budgeting experiment in Ukraine
Dmytro Volodin
Contemporary Politics, volume 25, issue 1 (February 2019) pp. 78–93

Chapter 7

Attrition in long-term deliberative processes. The neighbourhood consultative councils in Timisoara
Adrian Schiffbeck
Contemporary Politics, volume 25, issue 1 (February 2019) pp. 94–110

Chapter 8

Democratic innovations in Serbia: a misplaced trust in technology
Ivana Damnjanović
Contemporary Politics, volume 25, issue 1 (February 2019) pp. 111–127

For any permission-related enquiries please visit:
www.tandfonline.com/page/help/permissions

Notes on Contributors

Ivana Damnjanović is an Assistant Professor in the Faculty of Political Science at the University of Belgrade, Serbia.

Joakim Ekman is a Professor of Political Science at the Centre for Baltic and East European Studies (CBEES) at Södertörn University, Sweden.

Sergiu Gherghina is a Lecturer in Comparative Politics in the Department of Politics at the University of Glasgow, Scotland.

Sergiu Mișcoiu is a Professor of International Relations and German Studies at Babes-Bolyai University, Romania.

Miroslav Nemčok is a Research Specialist at Masaryk University, Czech Republic.

Zoltán Tibor Pállinger is Head of the Department of Political Theory and European Democracy Research at Andrássy University, Hungary.

Olena Podolian is a Ph.D. candidate at Södertörn University in Stockholm, Sweden.

Adrian Schiffbeck is a Ph.D. candidate in the Faculty of Arts and Humanities at the University of Passau, Germany.

Nanuli Silagadze is a Ph.D. candidate at Åbo Akademi University, Finland.

Peter Spáč is an Associate Professor in the Department of Political Science at Masaryk University, Czech Republic.

Petr Voda is an Associate Professor in the Department of Political Science at Masaryk University, Czech Republic.

Dmytro Volodin is a postgraduate researcher in the Graduate School for Social Research at the Polish Academy of Science, Poland.

Democratic innovations in Central and Eastern Europe: expanding the research agenda

Sergiu Gherghina (ID), Joakim Ekman and Olena Podolian

ABSTRACT
Democratic innovations have recently gained momentum throughout the world. An increasing number of such practices takes place and coincides with a visible grow in the number of analyses focusing on the forms, functioning and effects of democratic innovations. In spite of these developments, a great deal of research on democratic innovations have largely neglected Central and Eastern Europe. This special issue of *Contemporary Politics* adds to the existing literature on democratic innovations by focusing on such attempts to deepen citizen participation in the political decision-making process in Central and Eastern Europe. Its attempt to expand the research agenda relies on new empirical evidence relative to three major forms of democratic innovations (direct democracy, deliberative democracy and citizens' involvement with the aid of ICTs).

Introduction

In recent decades the process of political representation has faced several challenges and problems (Ruth, Welp, & Whitehead, 2016). According to most conventional assessments, citizens have become increasingly discontent and gradually abandoned the traditional forms of political participation: electoral turnout is in decline, party membership shrinks, and the amount of loyal voters seemingly decreases from year to year. On top of all of that comes a general lack of trust in political institutions, parties and political leaders (Amnå & Ekman, 2013; Dalton, 2008; Norris, 1999, 2011; Putnam, 2000; Skocpol & Fiorina, 1999). Scholars and politicians pin their hopes on participatory innovations as a means to cure this democratic malaise (Geissel & Newton, 2012). Several governments in established democracies at both national and local levels have gone down the participatory route and implemented various kinds of democratic innovations that allow citizens to make their voices heard (Altman, 2011; Buss, Redburn, & Guo, 2016; Geissel & Joas, 2013; Gherghina & Groh, 2016; Kriesi, 2005; LeDuc, 2003; Smith, 2009). Such innovations range from direct democracy (e.g. referendums, agenda initiatives, and recall procedures) to deliberative practices like deliberative polling, consultative mini-publics, or participatory budgeting (Geissel & Gherghina, 2016; Gronlund, Bachtiger, & Setala, 2014; Sintomer, Traub-Merz, & Zhang, 2012) – in offline as well as online settings (Knobloch & Gastil, 2014; Tomšič & Kleindienst, 2017). In addition to direct and deliberative (or dialogue oriented) procedures, the literature also identifies a third form, which is usually a mixture between the two. This third category is very broad and a large variety of innovations are included as long as they provide an avenue for citizens' involvement that is complementary to the current system of political representation.

As for more specific definitions, democratic innovations may be understood in the following way: they are institutions that have been specifically designed to increase and deepen citizen participation in the political decision-making process. Such institutions are 'innovations' since they 'represent a departure from the traditional institutional architecture that we normally attribute to advanced industrial democracies' (Smith 2009: 1). Sometimes cooperation between state actors and non-state actors (like civil society) is also seen as a way of involving citizens to a higher extent into the political process (Geissel & Joas, 2013), and it has moreover been claimed for a long time that participation in deliberative procedures would improve citizens' political efficacy (Elstub & McLaverty, 2014; Geissel & Hess, 2017).

To better understand the complexity of this picture, a closer look at the forms, functioning and effects of these democratic innovations in different contexts is necessary. In particular, this special issue of *Contemporary Politics* adds to the existing literature on democratic innovations by focusing on such attempts to deepen citizen participation in the political decision-making process in Central and Eastern Europe. There are three general forms of democratic innovation addressed by the articles of this special issue: direct democracy, deliberative practices and citizen involvement with the aid of technology. These forms are the ones usually agreed by the literature (see above). The analyses include a broad variety of countries ranging from new democracies (Bulgaria, Poland and Slovakia) or countries under the threat of de-democratization (Hungary and Romania) to democratizing or transition countries (Moldova, Serbia and Ukraine). We get back to these in detail when describing the contribution brought by this collection to the state of the art. Before that, the following section provides an overview of the state of the art of democratic innovations in Central and Eastern Europe.

Central and Eastern Europe: a relatively neglected region

It has often been noted that research on political participation and civic engagement – a vast and constantly growing research field (Adler & Goggin, 2005; Barrett & Zani, 2015; Berger, 2009; Ekman & Amnå, 2012; van Deth, Montero, & Westholm, 2007) – has for a long time focused mainly on Western democracies, and that citizen involvement in politics as voters, activists or protesters have for a long time been regarded as a marginal phenomenon in Central and Eastern Europe (Bernhagen & Marsh, 2007; Hooghe & Quintelier, 2013; Howard, 2003; Kostelka, 2014; Vrablikova, 2013). This notion has been challenged in recent years, in studies on civic activities and political interest in Eastern Europe (Ekman, Gherghina, & Podolian, 2016; Marchenko, 2016), in research on social movements and post-communist civil society mobilization (Jacobsson, 2015), and in studies on radical political movements in Central and Eastern Europe (Wennerhag, Fröhlich, & Piotrowski, 2018). Still, the general consensus in the literature on citizen participation has for a long time been that levels of political participation are generally lower and civil society is typically weaker in Central and Eastern Europe, compared to Western Europe and Scandinavia.

That may be one reason for which research on democratic innovations has largely neglected the Central and Eastern European region. For example, Smith's seminal *Democratic innovations* (2009) draws on empirical observations from Brazil, Canada, the US and Switzerland, Geissel and Joas' *Participatory democratic innovations in Europe* (2013) focuses mainly on Western and Northern Europe, and Knobloch and Gastil's 'Civic (re) socialisation: The educative effects of deliberative participation' (2014) on Australia and the US. The same goes for *Evaluating democratic innovations* by Geissel and Newton (2012) and, in a similar way, Setälä and Schiller's volume on *Referendums and representative democracy* (2009) features case studies on Ireland, Canada, California, Israel, Southern Europe, the Nordic countries and the Netherlands.

The assumption, as it were, seems to have been that 'democratic innovations' are not really what you would expect to find in Central and Eastern Europe. And for sure, a lot of studies in recent years have focused on challenges to democracy rather than on democratic innovativeness. Following the 2004, 2007 and 2013 Eastern enlargements of the EU – sometimes described as a 'return to Europe' following decades of communist rule – we have throughout the post-communist region witnessed what has sometimes been labelled 'democratic backsliding', Euroscepticism, the rise of radical right populism, the spread of corruption, an authoritarian backlash and the rise of xenophobia and chauvinism. At the same time, this development has not followed a singular course in Central and Eastern Europe, and not everybody agrees that we should talk about a general backlash or democratic backsliding in the region. For the present special issue, the crucial point is that depicting Central and Eastern Europe as democratically backward is not the full story. In fact, after undergoing the regime change or (re)gaining state independence in the early 1990s, the post-communist countries in the region swiftly adopted many provisions and regulations about democratic innovations in general and direct democracy in particular (Gherghina, 2017a; Walter-Rogg, 2008).

To date, there is still only a limited amount of studies that have reflected on post-communist examples of democratic innovations. Even the handful of studies that have in fact included the region, have done so in a quite general manner rather than closely investigating the processes and mechanisms. When referring to direct democracy in the region, one approach has been to include it in broader comparisons with other parts of the world or of the continent, in particular when it comes to referendums. For example, in their account of the referendum and initiative process in Europe, Kaufmann and Waters (2004) conduct an analysis of EU member states and thus explicitly compare the Western and Eastern European countries in a historical perspective. In a similar way, both Buttler and Ranney (1994) and Qvortrup (2014) seek to provide an overview of the strengths and weaknesses, as well as the increased popularity, and the use of referendums around the world. They both have a chapter dedicated to the former Soviet Union and Eastern Europe in their studies. Moreover, Silagadze and Gherghina (2018) seek to understand when the policy subjected to popular vote is accepted by the population and focuses on the top-down referendums organized in Europe between 2001 and 2013. Gherghina (2017a) further compares the forms of direct democracy available in Western and Eastern Europe and concludes that the countries belonging to the latter category had earlier provisions both at local and national level. The results show that referendums proposed by a large parliamentary majority or with clear messages from political parties during campaign are likely to be successful, a conclusion that is valid across the investigated countries without regional specificity. In his overview of the referendums organized in 11 East European countries, Gherghina (2017b) reveals the existence of important differences before and after the accession. Findings indicate that in the most recent decade the number of citizen-initiated referendums has increased, more referendums have taken place, but the turnout has slowly decreased.

The literature on referendums – as one form of democratic innovations – has thus included Central and Eastern Europe, since the EU Eastern enlargement and the accession referendums attracted a lot of scholarly attention. Other forms of democratic innovations in Central and Eastern Europe have been less studied, for example, innovations relating to deliberative democracy. One general perspective has been provided by Folscher (2007), who focuses mainly on the context in which participatory budgeting takes place in Central and Eastern Europe, in order to present policy-related lessons from such deliberative practices. Also, there are some single-case studies of deliberative practices in the region, that typically provide extensive descriptions of the processes, with rich details that can form the basis for further research. One of the studies that pursue an in-depth analysis of deliberative practices refers to the legitimacy of the constitutional forum organized in Romania in 2013 (Gherghina & Miscoiu, 2016). The authors use a tri-dimensional approach of legitimacy and their results indicate that while input legitimacy was achieved, output legitimacy is mostly absent due to the lack of action from political parties.

Furthermore, there are a few case-studies on E-participation initiatives in the region. For example, Tomšič and Kleindienst (2017) have analyzed E-participation and E-democracy in Central and Eastern Europe, and more specifically, mechanisms initiated in order to enhance political engagement and political knowledge among citizens in Estonia, one of not only the region's but also the world's leaders in E-democracy (Jonsson, 2015). More studies are likely to emerge in the years to come. For example, the 2017 edition of the *Governance Report*, produced by the Hertie School of Governance in Berlin, focuses on democratic innovations: innovative policies and initiatives meant to address the causes of democratic malaise, to foster democratic resilience, and to enhance citizen participation. In the 2017 report, Smilov (2017) addresses democratic innovations and lessons from Eastern Europe.

This literature review indicates that most of the crucial elements of democratic innovations are at least touched upon in studies that include Central and Eastern Europe, at least when it comes to referendums. However, mere overviews of innovations and general descriptions of how they work are not sufficient to provide comparable empirical evidence; more systematic studies are needed. Thus, the ambition with this special issue is to expand the research agenda, by looking specifically at different kinds of democratic innovations in Central and Eastern Europe. We have made a point here to include not only direct democracy referendums, but also the two most frequently debated types of democratic innovations found in the research literature, namely deliberative democracy practices and E-participation (Geissel & Gherghina, 2016; Gronlund et al., 2014; Knobloch & Gastil, 2014; Sintomer et al., 2012; Tomšič & Kleindienst, 2017).

In addition to expanding the research literature by covering more empirical cases, this is also in many ways a timely issue. Very recently, we have witnessed a number of relevant developments in the politics of the region, like, for example, the 'Black Protest' marches in Poland, that started in the fall of 2016, when a massive number of people took to the streets in order to protest against the proposed total ban on abortion. Since then, similar marches have been organized by e.g. women's rights activists, in Poland and else-where. The large anti-corruption protests in Budapest, in the spring of 2017, is another case in point. When the Central European University (CEU) in Budapest, Hungary, was attacked by Viktor Orbán, tens of thousands of people took to the streets, in protests that resonated worldwide. Thus, the actions of ordinary citizens in Central and Eastern Europe have in some places challenged the contemporary political order, and grassroots movements and diverse forms of mobilization have challenged the notion of weak civil societies in the East. In fact, some scholars have argued that what we have witnessed in recent years in a number of places in the region represents nothing short of a new phase in the development of civil societies in Central and Eastern Europe (Jacobsson, 2015). Consequently, we are well advised not to keep neglecting the potential power of ordinary citizens in Central and Eastern Europe, and we thus also need to pay closer atten-tion to constitutional and institutional arrangements designed to deepen citizen partici-pation in the political processes in the post-communist countries.

The contribution of this special issue

This special issue of *Contemporary Politics* adds to the existing body of literature on demo-cratic innovations by including examples from a number of countries in Central and Eastern Europe. This entails providing new empirical evidence that illustrates attempts to deepen citizen involvement in political contexts sometimes quite different from the democratic pol-itical systems in the US, South America, Western Europe and Scandinavia. Here, the idea is thus to use lessons from a still largely underexplored part of Europe in order to complement or revise theoretical approaches or complement empirical results in existing studies on democratic innovations. Our hope is that the contributions of this special issue will present new empirical findings and theoretical insights that will go beyond the compara-tive study of Central and Eastern Europe, and have broader implications for the study of citizen behavior and democratic innovations in political systems all over the globe. The articles are clustered in three main categories of innovations: direct democracy, citizen involvement with the aid of technology and deliberative democracy.

The direct democracy is reflected through three different approaches in the special issue. First, its most common form is the referendum and two articles look at crucial elements: the relationship between parties, citizens and the role of referendum campaigns in voting decision. Second, the recall procedure is quite rare in practice and the article about the recall of the mayor from the capital city of Republic of Moldova provides useful insights into the subject matter. Third, the use of direct democracy, seen as broadly complementary to representative democracy, is closely analysed in Hungary. To begin with the contributions on referendums, Nemčok and Spáč examine the role of par-tisan cues on voter mobilization in the 2015 'Family' referendum in Slovakia, dealing with the rights of sexual minorities. Conventional wisdom tells us that distinct partisan cues are of central importance for the way people will vote in a referendum, but less is known about partisan cues and the decision to vote or not in a referendum, which is certainly a crucial issue. Indeed, the very act of *not* turning up to vote in a referendum may in some cases be regarded as a strategic decision, in order to invalidate or de-legitimize the referendum as shown by Gherghina and Miscoiu (2013). Drawing on a pre-referendum survey, Nemčok and Spáč show that clear party cues about turning up to vote or not seem to work, in the same way as party cues on which side to vote for. Moreover, as the Slovak case illustrates, in certain institutional settings the mobilization recommendations from parties can have an even stronger impact on voters than cues about which side to vote for.

Referendum campaigns are central to Gherghina and Silagadze's contribution. Referendum campaigns typically differ from election campaigns, in a number of ways. Party positions are not seldom less clear, since the parties may be internally divided over the issue at stake. Also, referendums may be perceived by voters as less important and/or as more demanding than regular elections (i.e. the notion of second-order elections). In the literature on the way citizens vote in referendums, surprisingly little attention has been paid to the actual campaigns themselves, as explanatory variables for the outcome. To fill this gap in the literature, Gherghina and Silagadze argue that the actual referendum campaign is an important predictor of the voting decision. Three referendums are used to demonstrate this point, organized in 2015–2016 in different East European countries (Bulgaria, Poland and Slovakia).

Moving on to the recall procedure, Miscoiu analyses the failure of such a vote in Republic of Moldova. Although it happened at local level, in the capital city Chisinau with the aim to dismiss the mayor from office, this was not limited to local politics. Instead, the vote was cast on broader issues and the symbolic or perceived stakes were much greater than the office itself. The contribution illustrates the limits of democratic innovations and how they can challenge the playing field set up by the political elites. The qualitative evidence from the focus groups conducted by the author at the end of 2017 reveals complex mechanisms behind the voters' decision to support the mayor. This type of information nuances earlier research focusing on the determinants of voting in referendums.

The general approach to direct democracy rests on the notion of a democratic malaise or crisis. This is the point of departure for Pallingér's contribution in this special issue. While democracy in a manner of speaking is 'always' in crisis since it always needs to be reformulated, the situation in contemporary Central and Eastern Europe still seems to be more serious than in Western Europe. Recently, instances of corruption, the abuse of power, the repression of the media, and attempts to break the constraints of checks and balances and to centralize executive power has gone hand in hand with the intensification of nationalist and populist politics in a number of countries in the region. In this context, Hungary seems to represent a special case: 'The case of Hungary remains the most puzzling. While it was set as a model of democratic consolidation in the EU's post-communist space, it also experienced the most severe challenges to democratic institutions that have taken place in the region since the end of communism' (Herman, 2006, p. 258). In this situation, when the room for maneuver of the opposition is limited and where the governing parties are also dominant in the media, what about the role of referendums to reach out to the wider public? Pallingér's contribution explains why the opposition in Hungary has *not* followed such a strategy, pointing to logic of the Hungarian political system. The existing instruments of direct democracy are in the hands of the political elite, as a tool to mobilize their supporters and to crowd out the opposition. This illustrates certain limitations of democratic innovations that could be of relevance to consider in cases outside of Central and Eastern Europe as well.

Deliberative democracy is approached from two different angles in this special issue. On the one hand, it brings empirical evidence according to which the involvement of people in participatory budgeting, one of the most popular forms of deliberation, pro-duces attitude changes in society. On the other hand, it provides a nuanced discussion about reasons for which people stop engaging in citizens' councils and the consequences such a decision has for the local community. To begin with the first approach, Volodin's article focuses on participatory budgeting, using Ukraine as a case to illustrate the relation between deliberative practices and citizens' trust in political institutions. Even in a critical case like Ukraine, being a hybrid regime, deliberative practices may in fact foster insti-tutional trust among citizens, at least at the local level. Volodin's contribution also under-lines the need for fair procedures: as long as the process of participatory budgeting has a clear legal mandate, its results may be perceived as fair, transparent and legitimate. The outcome of participatory budgeting, also in least likely cases, may thus function well as a democratic innovation.

The second approach is illustrated in Schiffbeck's article that seeks to understand why citizens withdraw from a deliberative setting that was praised and brought opportunities for popular involvement in decision-making in a Romanian large city. His findings support those of earlier research conducted in Western Europe, thus illustrating that overall the barriers for democratic innovation are quite similar across countries. There is also empirical evidence about how some context specific factors played a role in the withdrawal of people; these findings are meant to nuance and contribute to the fairly limited literature about causes for defection.

The third form of democratic innovations, the use of information and communication technologies (ICTs), is reflected in an article about the potential effects on citizenry. Damn-janović compares the results of three projects from Serbia, which share the assumption that the power of ICTs can improve communication between the government and the citi-zens and increase, at least to some extent, citizen participation. However, as the Serbian democratic innovations under review demonstrate, neither of these projects can be unequivocally seen as a success, although they fail in different ways and to various degrees. These results are still important to us, as they will help to identify general factors of success (or failure) of this type of technologically based democratic innovations in a post-communist setting.

Conclusion

The discussion above suggests the existence of a discrepancy between the limited scho-larly attention paid to democratic innovations and reality in Central and Eastern Europe. The evidence presented in this special issue indicates that three major forms of democratic innovations – direct democracy, deliberative democracy and citizens' involvement with the aid of technology – have been taking place in the region. The countries in the region adopted regulations regarding the existence of democratic innovations fairly early in their transition to democracy. Their existence in practice reflects that some of those regulations were implemented. The general findings of the contributions to this special issue reflect some tendencies that have been already documented for the Western democracies. The logic behind the use of democratic innovations and the conse-quences produced within the political system or society are fairly similar. In this sense, the general lines along which these are developed are known and Central and Eastern Europe provides supplementary evidence to strengthen existing observations. At the same time, some of these cases provide relevant nuances that enrich our knowledge about the topic. More precisely, they introduce new explanations for the variation in the outcome of democratic innovations. These explanations can be, for example, the importance of the regime like in Hungary and Ukraine or contextual factors like in Moldova, Romania or Serbia.

These observations open the floor for further investigations about other forms of democratic innovations in Central and Eastern Europe. Recently, several countries witnessed the emergence of citizens' initiatives, one form of direct democracy, and of mini-publics, a popular form of deliberative democracy, as a means to promote citizens' engagement in politics. At a local level, an increasing number of democratic innovations have emerged and developed throughout the entire region. Central and Eastern Europe remains a fertile soil for future investigation especially with the new obstacles to representative democracy raised by some of the national governments.

Disclosure statement

No potential conflict of interest was reported by the authors.

ORCID

Sergiu Gherghina ⓲ http://orcid.org/0000-0002-6627-5598

References

Adler, R. P., & Goggin, J. (2005). What do we mean by 'civic engagement'? *Journal of Transformative Education, 3*(3), 236–253.

Altman, D. (2011). *Direct democracy worldwide.* Cambridge: Cambridge University Press.

Amnå, E., & Ekman, J. (2013). Standby citizens: Diverse faces of political passivity. *European Political Science Review, 6*(2), 261–281.

Barrett, M., & Zani, B. (Eds.). (2015). *Political and civic engagement: Multidisciplinary perspectives.* New York, NY: Routledge.

Berger, B. (2009). Political theory, political science and the end of civic engagement. *Perspectives on Politics, 7*(2), 335–350.

Bernhagen, P., & Marsh, M. (2007). Voting and protesting: Explaining citizen participation in old and new European democracies. *Democratization, 14*(1), 44–72.

Buss, T. F., Redburn, S., & Guo, K. (Eds.). (2016). *Modernizing democracy: Innovations in citizen participation.* London: Routledge.

Butler, D., & Ranney, A. (Eds.). (1994). *Referendums around the world: The growing use of direct democracy*. Basingstoke: Macmillan.

Dalton, R. J. (2008). *Citizen politics. Public opinion and political parties in advanced industrial democracies* (5th ed.). Washington, DC: CQ Press.

Ekman, J., & Amnå, E. (2012). Political participation and civic engagement: Towards a new typology? *Human Affairs, 22*(3), 283–300.

Ekman, J., Gherghina, S., & Podolian, O. (2016). Challenges and realities of political participation and civic engagement in central and eastern Europe. *East European Politics, 32*(1), 1–11. https://doi.org/10.1080/21599165.2016.1141091

Elstub, S., & McLaverty, P. (Eds.). (2014). *Deliberative democracy. Issues and Cases*. Edinburgh: Edinburgh University Press.

Folscher, A. (2007). Participatory budgeting in Central and Eastern Europe. In A. Shah (Ed.), *Participatory budgeting* (pp. 127–155). Washington, DC: World Bank.

Geissel, B., & Gherghina, S. (2016). Constitutional deliberative democracy and democratic innovations. In M. Reuchamps & J. Suiter (Eds.), *Constitutional deliberative democracy in Europe* (pp. 75–92). Colchester: ECPR Press.

Geissel, B., & Hess, P. (2017). Explaining political efficacy in deliberative procedures: A novel methodological approach. *Journal of Public Deliberation, 13*(2), 1–25.

Geissel, B., & Joas, M. (Eds.). (2013). *Participatory democratic innovations in Europe. Improving the quality of democracy?* Opladen: Barbara Budrich.

Geissel, B., & Newton, K. (Eds.). (2012). *Evaluating democratic innovations: Curing the democratic malaise?* London: Routledge.

Gherghina, S. (2017a). Direct democracy and subjective regime legitimacy in Europe. *Democratization, 24*(4), 613–631.

Gherghina, S. (2017b). The use of referendum in Central and Eastern Europe after EU accession. In T. Hashimoto & M. Rhimes (Eds.), *Reviewing European Union accession. Unexpected results, spillover effects, and externalities* (pp. 41–56). Leiden: Brill.

Gherghina, S., & Groh, A. (2016). A poor sales pitch? The European citizens' initiative and attitudes toward the EU in Germany and the UK. *European Politics and Society, 17*(3), 373–387.

Gherghina, S., & Miscoiu, S. (2013). The failure of cohabitation: Explaining the 2007 and 2012 institutional crises in Romania. *East European Politics & Societies, 27*(4), 668–684.

Gherghina, S., & Miscoiu, S. (2016). Crowd-sourced legislation and politics: The legitimacy of constitutional deliberation in Romania. *Problems of Post-Communism, 63*(1), 27–36.

Gronlund, K., Bachtiger, A., & Setala, M. (2014). *Deliberative mini-publics. Involving citizens in the democratic process*. Colchester: ECPR Press.

Herman, L. E. (2006). Re-evaluating the post-communist success story: Party elite loyalty, citizen mobilization and the erosion of Hungarian democracy. *European Political Science Review, 8*(2), 251–284.

Hooghe, M., & Quintelier, E. (2013). Political participation in European countries: The effect of authoritarian rule, corruption, lack of good governance and economic downturn. *Comparative European Politics, 12*(2), 209–232.

Howard, M. M. (2003). *The weakness of civil society in post-communist Europe*. Cambridge: Cambridge University Press.

Jacobsson, K. (Ed.). (2015). *Urban grassroots movements in Central and Eastern Europe*. Farnham: Ashgate.

Jonsson, M. E. (2015). Democratic innovations in deliberative systems – the case of the Estonian citizens' assembly process. *Journal of Public Deliberation, 11*(1), 1–29.

Kaufmann, B., & Waters, D. (Eds.). (2004). *Direct democracy in Europe: A comprehensive reference guide to the initiative and referendum process in Europe*. Durham: Carolina Academic Press.

Knobloch, K. R., & Gastil, J. (2014). Civic (re)socialisation: The educative effects of deliberative participation. *Politics, 35*(2), 183–200.

Kostelka, F. (2014). The state of political participation in post-communist democracies: Low but surprisingly little biased citizen engagement. *Europe-Asia Studies, 66*(6), 945–968.

Kriesi, H. (2005). *Direct democratic choice. The Swiss experience*. Plymouth: Lexington Books.

LeDuc, L. (2003). *The politics of direct democracy: Referendums in global perspective.* Toronto: Broadview Press.

Marchenko, A. (2016). Civic activities in Eastern Europe: Links with democratic political culture. *East European Politics, 32*(1), 12–25.

Norris, P. (Ed.). (1999). *Critical citizens: Global support for democratic government.* Oxford: Oxford University Press.

Norris, P. (2011). *Democratic deficit: Critical citizens revisited.* Cambridge: Cambridge University Press.

Putnam, R. D. (2000). *Bowling alone: The collapse and revival of American community.* New York, NY: Simon & Schuster.

Qvortrup, M. (2014). *Referendums around the world. The continued growth of direct democracy.* Basingstoke: Palgrave Macmillan.

Ruth, S. P., Welp, Y., & Whitehead, L. (Eds.). (2016). *Let the people rule? Direct democracy in the twenty-first century.* Colchester: ECPR Press.

Setala, M., & Schiller, T. (Eds.). (2009). *Referendums and representative democracy. Responsiveness, accountability and deliberation.* London: Routledge.

Silagadze, N., & Gherghina, S. (2018). When who and how matter: explaining the success of referendums in Europe. *Comparative European Politics, 16*(5), 905–922.

Sintomer, Y., Traub-Merz, R., & Zhang, J. (Eds.). (2012). *Participatory budgeting in Asia and Europe. Key challenges of participation.* Basingstoke: Palgrave Macmillan.

Skocpol, T., & Fiorina, M. P. (Eds.). (1999). *Civic engagement in American democracy.* Washington, DC: Brookings Institution Press.

Smilov, D. (2017). *Democratic innovation and the politics of fear: 25 lessons from Eastern Europe.* In *Governance Report 2017* (Hertie Sch, pp. 25–42). Oxford: Oxford University Press.

Smith, G. (2009). *Democratic innovations. Designing institutions for citizen participation.* Cambridge: Cambridge University Press.

Tomšič, M., & Kleindienst, P. (2017). E-participation, e-democracy and political engagement of the citizenry in Central and Eastern Europe. In B. Rončević & M. Tomšič (Eds.), *Information society and its manifestations: Economy, politics, culture* (pp. 117–134). Frankfurt am Main: Peter Lang.

van Deth, J. W., Montero, J. R., & Westholm, A. (Eds.). (2007). *Citizenship and involvement in European democracies: A comparative analysis.* New York, NY: Routledge.

Vrablikova, K. (2013). How context matters? Mobilization, political opportunity structures, and none-lectoral political participation in old and new democracies. *Comparative Political Studies, 47*(2), 203–229.

Walter-Rogg, M. (2008). Direkte demokratie. In O. W. Gabriel (Ed.), *Die EU-Staaten im Vergleich. Strukturen, Prozesse, Politikinhalte* (pp. 236–267). Wiesbaden: VS, Verl. für Sozialwissenschaft.

Wennerhag, M., Fröhlich, C., & Piotrowski, G. (Eds.). (2018). *Radical left movements in Europe.* London: Routledge.

The role of partisan cues on voters' mobilization in a referendum

Miroslav Nemčok (iD), Peter Spáč (iD) and Petr Voda (iD)

ABSTRACT
Even though partisan cues are widely recognized as a primary force shaping voter behaviour in a referendum, their effect on a decision whether to attend or abstain from voting has not yet been carefully studied. Our analysis of the pre-referendum survey data gathered before the 2015 citizen-initiated referendum in Slovakia leads to two important conclusions: First, parties' recommendations whether to attend or abstain from voting influence voters' behaviour in a similar fashion as their suggestions for which side to vote for. Moreover, in certain institutional settings, the partisan cues related to mobilization have an even stronger impact on voters than endorsements for who or what to vote for. Second, the provided party recommendations must be unambiguous and clear. Lower clarity cues are reflected in voters' behaviour to a lesser extent.

Introduction

The complexity of every referendum issue goes far beyond the question stated on the ballot. Therefore, voters often gladly respond to cues from familiar political parties and let the cues guide them through a complex, information-rich environment to a simple 'yes' or 'no' answer on the ballot (De Vreese & Semetko, 2004; Lupia & McCubbins, 1998; Zaller, 1992). The influence of voting recommendations made by a preferred party on a voter's decision of which side to vote for has been empirically documented by numerous studies (Cini, 2004; Franklin, Marsh, & McLaren, 1994; Franklin, Marsh, & Wlezien, 1994; Hobolt, 2006, 2007; Hug & Sciarini, 2000; Pierce, Valen, & Listhaug, 1983). Moreover, partisan cues seem to influence voters' behaviour across various contexts to a sufficient degree that they can substantially contribute to a referendum's success (Sila-gadze & Gherghina, 2017).

However, while the impact of partisan cues on voting has been extensively studied, their influence on voters' decisions to turn out has remained excluded from the focus of researchers. This is rather surprising, given the fact that in some institutional settings, the decision to abstain from voting may be a strategic choice and effective means to inva-lidate a referendum, which was e.g. the case of the 2012 referendum in Romania (Gher-ghina & Miscoiu, 2013).

ⓑ Supplemental data for this article can be accessed at https://doi.org/10.1080/13569775.2018.1543753

Especially in the CEE region, parties are willing to 'hijack' the referendums to improve their own position in political struggles instead of using them as a way to increase the public engagement of citizens in the democratic system (Gherghina, in press). Therefore, it is relevant to study the impact of partisan cues because they may largely determine the outcomes of a popular vote, which may serve as a means for parties to achieve their selfish goals and expand their own power.

This article seeks to partially fill this gap by analysing the 2015 'Family' referendum held in Slovakia. The choice of country lies in both in its rich experience with referendums as well as in its institutional setting. Since its emergence in 1993, Slovakia has held eight referendums. Its legal rules require a fifty percent turnout for a referendum to be valid. Given such a threshold, opponents of a referendum have utilized a strategy of demobilizing their supporters, and have thus effectively lowered the turnout. Hence, turnout is the crucial factor in Slovak referendums, and only one has successfully passed so far (Nemčok & Spáč, 2018).

The 2015 Slovak referendum issues, initiated by a non-party actor, dealt with the rights of sexual minorities. The highly religious Slovak society was clearly polarized by this issue, as three out of every four people identify with some religious denomination, while a considerable majority (roughly 62%) of the whole population consider themselves Catholics (Statistical Office of the Slovak Republic, 2011). But the topics related to sexual minorities do not clearly divide the Slovak political representation and therefore a variation in the degree to which political parties provided voters with straightforward recommendations about how and if to turn out to vote could be observed. Some political parties took a clear stance, while others were hesitant to do so and provided little if any recommendation. These varying levels of clarity in parties' endorsements unlocked an opportunity to study how the level of clarity influences the impact of partisan cues when it comes to a voter's decision to attend or abstain from voting in a referendum.

This paper uses the data collected in an original pre-referendum representative survey. Through a series of statistical tests, it aims to study the effect of partisan cues on the mobilization of voters in a referendum and how the effect varies in relation to the ambiguity of an endorsement. Our results suggest that the party cues related to mobilization influence voters in a similar fashion compared to cues recommending which side to vote for. Moreover, the clearer the cue, the bigger its influence. But most importantly, voters who vote are more autonomous of their party's recommendation. Therefore, a party's call to mobilize constitutes a critical force in shaping referendum outcomes, because it influences the behaviour of voters who are more inclined to follow the cues put forth by their preferred party.

The next section sums up the recent knowledge about the impact of partisan cues and the conditions which determine their effects. Subsequently, the research design and data employed, as well as the context of the 2015 Slovak 'Family' referendum, are presented. The last section contains the results of the empirical analysis. The section is followed by a discussion about the institutional regulations that determine when the party's call to attend or abstain from voting becomes more popular than the recommendation of which side to vote for.

Complexity of referendum issues and the role of cues

Voting in a referendum means choosing an answer from two dichotomous options provided on a certain question. As an act, it seems quite simple. However, behind a ballot paper, there are hidden comprehensive dilemmas which require a fair deal of intermediate sub-decisions in order to arrive at a simple-looking 'yes' or 'no' (De Vreese & Semetko, 2004; Lupia & McCubbins, 1998). Referendums deciding about the issues related to the European Union represent great examples. In the case of the Brexit referendum, the question itself consisted of sixteen words. However, for a qualified decision one needed to understand a colossal number of agendas influenced by the European Union as well as the possible impacts on the future economic, political and societal development of the United Kingdom. Indeed, not all referendums are as comprehensive as the European ones, and the referendum about family analysed here is an example, but every single one expects that a voter is familiar with issues reaching far beyond the actual referendum question (Altman, 2011; Hobolt, 2007, p. 155; LeDuc, 2009; Lupia & Johnston, 2001).

The complexity of the topic may easily become a source of confusion and uncertainty for voters. Pre-referendum discourse packed with contradictory messages and mutually exclusive projections of future development even worsen the whole situation. Therefore, it is unsurprising that voters gladly grab the familiar cues and allow them to guide their decision-making process (Lupia & McCubbins, 1998). The endorsement of a certain referendum outcome by a preferred party (or its leader) is exactly the kind of cue that provides the electorate with clear directions through a confusing media space and hard-to-predict policy implications.

Kriesi (2005) and Sager and Bühlmann (2009) confirmed that the higher familiarity of voters with the referendum topic increases the probability of their turnout at the polls. The reason is that the cues increase the availability of information in the public space and make it easier for voters to make up their minds (Font & Rodríguez, 2009). Therefore, if parties approach a referendum actively, clearly formulate their stances and add the ideological bases to the referendum topic, their activities make the voters' decision-making processes less demanding, which increases the probability that voters will turn out to vote. On the contrary, lack of partisan cues and blurred ideological standpoints result in high volatility (LeDuc, 2009) and poor party performance in mobilizing its own supporters (De Vreese & Semetko, 2004).

It may be argued that the story is rather the other way around and it is not a partisan cue that comes first and drives the voters' behaviour, but it is instead popular demand that determines the cues, because parties want to stay consistent with the preferences of their supporters. However, this is highly unlikely. The thing is that voters tend to enter already initiated referendum campaigns with 'relatively weak predispositions and low levels of information' (LeDuc, 2009, p. 158). Therefore, it is basically impossible for parties to have sufficiently accurate estimates of their supporters' positions on the issue to position themselves before the campaign starts (Pierce et al., 1983). Moreover, while parties hold their positions more or less constant throughout the whole campaign, voters are more likely to shift their opinion in order to follow a partisan cue (Jenssen & Listhaug, 2001, p. 190). Furthermore, a canon of case studies confirms that partisan attachments serve as a primary force in referendum voting and constitute a strong and consistent predictor of a voter's final decision (Cini, 2004; Franklin, Marsh, & McLaren, 1994; Franklin, Marsh, & Wlezien, 1994; Hug & Sciarini, 2000; Pettersen, Jenssen, & Listhaug, 1996; Pierce et al., 1983). Therefore, following the literature, we also expect that the cues are closer to being the independent factor influencing voter behaviour in a referendum campaign.

Factors determining the impact of partisan cues

Even though the influence of partisan cues on voter behaviour has been widely recognized for quite some time, the field has undergone substantial development. During the 1970s, partisan cues were considered to be a direct power influencing voter mobilization and choices to a very large extent (e.g. McKelvey & Ordeshook, 1986). However, as time goes by, further contextual conditions are being added – such as political environment and the characteristics of actors giving and receiving the cue (e.g. Lupia & McCubbins, 1998), and the link between a cue and a voter has become less straightforward and more blurred (Hug & Sciarini, 2000). The following section presents the development and describes the additional factors that facilitate the actual impact of party cues on a voter's decision to attend or abstain from a referendum voting.

Individual determinants

Quite naturally, the impact of a cue on the decision to attend or abstain from voting does not have constant impact across the whole electorate. Even though a cue can in theory influence any voter, it is the power of partisanship that facilitates its actual impact. As argued by Borges and Clarke (2008, p. 445), it is 'the interaction with political predisposition towards a cuing party or political leader that generates theoretically plausible and statistically significant results'. Therefore, partisans and party supporters are exactly those actors, in particular, whose decisions about participation and voting are primarily driven by cues provided by the parties and leaders they prefer (Borges & Clarke, 2008; Zaller, 1992).

However, it may be expected that some of an individual's characteristics that influence the decision-making process could be triggered by the referendum topic and override the impact of partisan cues. This is especially the case for controversial issues related to e.g. the rights of sexual minorities, which can stimulate personal prejudices such as homophobia and can impact how an individual will vote. However, the link between prejudices and voting does not seem to be straightforward and nor does it completely override the cues. Empirical research studying same-sex marriage referendums in the USA identified, on an aggregate, a strong link between party affiliation or party vote shares and support for same-sex marriage (Camp, 2008; McVeigh & Diaz, 2009). The same holds true for the 2013 Croatian Referendum on the Constitutional Definition of Marriage, whose cultural context is much closer to the case of the Slovak 'Family' referendum. Based on originally collected aggregate-level data from the 2013 referendum in Croatia, Glaurdić and Vuković concluded (2016, p. 803) that '[c]ontrary to popular interpretations, [...] the referendum results primarily reflected the pattern of support for the two principal electoral blocs, rather than communities' traditionalist characteristics or grievances stemming from economic adversity'. These studies indicate a strong connection between partisanship and support for or voting in a referendum. Thus, we may reasonably expect that if prejudices influence the impact of partisan cues, it happens in the beginning by determining voters' partisanship inclinations. As an intervening factor, the partisanship mediates the connection between prejudices and voting by making voters more attentive to the cues sent by the preferred party, which therefore have more influence on voter decisions.

In addition to interacting with partisanship, cues also affect a voter's political awareness. The voters with a high level of political awareness tend to be more independent of the partisan cues and prioritize their own attitudes towards a topic (Hobolt, 2005). On the contrary, the ill-informed voters tend to be more inclined to follow the parties' recommendations, even though it can drive them to cast a vote that is further away from their own preferences (Hobolt, 2007). Even though both of Hobolt's (2005, 2007) above-mentioned conclusions were actually related to voting, her observations are important for referendum turnout as well. Even among partisans, we should expect that higher levels of a voter's political knowledge will result in greater decision-making autonomy. Hence, a cue recommending (de)mobilization has a bigger impact among less politically knowledgeable partisans compared to their counterparts with higher levels of political awareness.

Clarity

Like voters, partisan cues are far from being uniform. While some parties unambiguously and repeatedly state their recommendations on whether to attend a plebiscite or not, others can be internally divided, which may result in a tentative or not-entirely-clear recommendation. The literature specifically mentions that '[…] for partisanship to have maximum impact, the parties must take clear and uniform positions on the issue at stake. When the parties divide, so do their followers' (Pierce et al., 1983, p. 61). With the mixed or unclear messages, parties perform poorly in mobilizing their own supporters, not to mention the rest of the electorate (De Vreese & Semetko, 2004).

However, the level of a cue's clarity must be perceived as a party's conscious strategy. It's decision to emphasize or blur its recommendation simply reflects intra-party struggles, heterogeneity of the party's electorate in relation to the referendum topic or the party's position on issue dimensions within the political competition (Rovny, 2012). Since voters gladly consume easily available information in the referendum campaign (Font & Rodríguez, 2009), which cues clearly are, it is the strategic blurring and ambiguous recommendations that partially cause voters to often complain of there being 'insufficient information' throughout the referendum process (LeDuc, 2009) and that they lack an important guide through the referendum campaign (Hobolt, 2006).

Therefore, a clear cue is more efficient in facilitating a voter's orientation in a pre-referendum campaign and influencing a voter's decision whether to attended or abstain from voting in a referendum to a higher degree compared to an ambiguous recommendation.

Institutional determinants

Regardless of the issue, a referendum is part of politics and, consequently, must be perceived as a struggle among political actors. Therefore, a referendum that manages to mobilize a sufficient portion of the electorate in order to become valid, not only has implications for the future development of a common polity, but moreover divides parties into winners and losers in accordance with their initial pre-referendum position. This is how referendums are perceived from the 'second-order' perception (Silagadze & Gherghina, 2017), which claims that they constitute an additional means for voters to punish or reward the parties for their performance (Franklin, Marsh, & McLaren, 1994; Franklin, van der Eijk, & Marsh, 1995). Therefore, satisfaction with elected representatives is another key factor determining whether voters turn out the vote, if (de)mobilization is already a legitimate means of expressing one's (dis)satisfaction.

According to Hug and Sciarini (2000), there are three institutional features which mediate the impact of partisanship on mobilization and voting behaviour and therefore influence the strength of partisan cues: '[1] whether the referendum is required, [2] whether the people's decision has a binding character or [3] which government coalition is presently in power'. These aspects mainly determine the importance of a referendum and, consequently, (de)mobilization can reflect the condemnation of or a 'vote of confidence in' the government/political representation.

Research design

The 2015 'Family' Referendum in Slovakia constitutes a great case to study the effect of partisan cues on voters' behaviour mainly for three reasons: First, the referendum was initiated through a plebiscite and by a non-party actor. Moreover, thanks to rather controversial topics regarding the rights of LGBT community, none of the parties tried to 'kidnap the plebiscite' in order to steal the spotlight and gain popular support. The referendum did not turn into an inter-party clash that could significantly shape the perception of the referendum among voters (Cini, 2004), but remained an act initiated by an NGO with no direct affiliation to any political party. Second, given its topic, the 'Family' referendum was non-required, with basically no biding incentives for any of the political actors. In this aspect, the plebiscite dealt only with the initial topic. Therefore, voters had basically no reason to perceive the referendum as a 'second-order' opportunity to punish or reward the parties. These two aspects ensure that the above-stated institutional determinants remain constant and allow us to study the general impact of partisan cues on mobilization in a referendum. Third, the political parties decided to implement low profile strategies in the campaign (Rybář & Šovčíková, 2016). Therefore, if we can find substantive evidence confirming the impact of partisan cues on mobilization where parties kept a low profile, there is no doubt that an even stronger impact can be expected in cases of referendums where parties played a more significant role.

Besides that, the controversial topic had additional positive externality: alongside those who openly declared their recommendations for voting behaviour, there were parties hesitant to take a clear stance because their electorates came from Christian clusters as well as from more liberal segments of society. This also provided us with a variation in the ambiguity of parties' endorsements and allowed us to study another important attribute of cues specifically emphasized by Pierce, Valen, and Listhaus (1983) – the clarity of the recommendation.

Data and methods

The effect of partisan cues on mobilization in a referendum is tested on the dataset resulting from a public survey which was conducted by FOCUS Agency on behalf of the Slovak Daily newspaper SME. Data collection took place between 20 and 26 January 2015, i.e. roughly two weeks before the referendum was held on 7 February 2015. FOCUS Agency collected data on a representative sample (1070 respondents) of the general Slovak population. To the best of our knowledge, this is the only representative data that was gathered in regard to the 2015 'Family' referendum.

The survey included six questions plus a basic set of sociodemographic character- istics (i.e. gender, age, education and income). The first question aimed to find out the probability that a respondent would turn out to the referendum. A set of three questions followed the exact wording of the questions used in the actual referendum and was intended to identify respondents' opinions on the referendum topics. The next question was aimed at respondents' partisanship inclinations and thus it asked respondents which party they would vote for if the legislative elections were held during the upcoming weekend. The last question asked about attitude towards religion and offered five options: (a) deeply religious, (b) religious, (c) not decided, (d) not reli- gious, (e) atheist. Since the topics dealing with the rights of sexual minorities were especially controversial within more conservative circles, this question was supposed to control for the level of religiosity among respondents and we will be referring to this characteristic as 'faith'.

Our analysis consists of two parts. The first one is focused on mobilization and examines whether voters acted consistently with the recommendation of their preferred party and attended the referendum or abstained.[1]

The second part inspects the actual voting and analyses whether voters voted consist- ently with the recommendation made by their favoured party for each of the questions. Thus, one item focused on mobilization and three items dealing with the three referen- dum topics give us a total set of four dependent variables for the analysis. Each variable is binary, with value one given to voters whose intended vote in the pre-referendum public opinion poll, when compared, corresponded to their favoured party's cue and zero if it did not.

Our main independent variable is the clarity of a partisan recommendation. For this purpose, we divided parties' recommendations into three groups according to the level of their clarity, as follows:

Clarity 1: Official statement of the party or its leadership body

Clarity 2: Official stance of the party leader, which is opposed by some party members

Clarity 3: No official statement. However, the party leader unofficially shared his/her stance with the media (without any confirmation from the internally divided party base)

We tracked the clarity of partisan cues separately for attending the referendum (or abstain- ing from such voting) and voting on the referendum questions. The data however did not allow us to distinguish clarity of partisan recommendation for each of the referendum questions but only en bloc for all three questions. The coding of clarity of partisan sugges- tion is listed in Table A1 in Online Appendix A.

Besides the independent variables, we apply a set of controls. These consist of basic sociodemographic voter characteristics that might shape their behaviour regarding the referendum in practice. First, we included gender as a binary variable with value one given to women and value zero to men. We further cover education. This variable is coded into an ordinal scale ranging from one to four, with each category given to a type of obtained education degree (e.g. elementary, lower secondary, higher secondary and university), thus the higher values indicate a person's higher education. The third control is income. This variable is also coded as categorical on a seven-point scale from one to seven with higher values indicating higher income. After that we include age (logged), and finally, the level of faith on a five-point scale ranging from one to five with higher categories indicating stronger religious status. Religious belief can be also seen as proxy for homophobia since it has been found as factor explaining homophobia in previous studies (see e.g. Adamczyk & Pitt, 2009; Besen & Zicklin, 2007; Brewer, 2003; Haider-Markel & Joslyn, 2005). We provide some further arguments for the usage of this variable in the Slovak context in Online Appendix C.

The analysis was conducted on the individual level while the focus was placed on the consistency between a respondent's reported decision and the recommendation of the party they declared they would vote for if the election were to take place the next weekend. We excluded two subsets of respondents: (1) those who declared no party preference and (2) those whose preferred party made no recommendation for mobilization or voting.[2] The first restriction respects the current research that has confirmed that party cues have an effect on its own supporters (Borges & Clarke, 2008; Zaller, 1992). Our data was collected roughly two months after the 2014 municipal election. Since individuals within an 'electoral cycle' are more inclined to state their partisan preferences shortly after the elections (Andersen, Tilley, & Heath, 2005; Arceneaux, 2005; Stevenson & Vavreck, 2000), the proximity of the last municipal election may explain the overrepresentation of people stating their party preference (which goes up to 75%). Therefore, despite a large number of respondents stating their party preference, we may still reasonably expect that by focusing on respondents who declared their party preference we can examine the effect of partisan cues on party supporters.

To analyse the consistency of voters with partisan recommendations dealing with attending or abstaining from voting on the referendum we use data from all respondents with the exception of the two groups mentioned above. However, for examining the effects of partisan cues on voting on each of the referendum questions, we restrict the dataset only to respondents who stated that they would attend the referendum. In the pre-referendum survey we use, respondents were asked to declare a percentage probability they would attend the referendum. As attendees we understand those respondents who reported a probability to attend the referendum at 70% or higher.[3]

For examining the effect of clarity of partisan cues on turnout in a referendum we use probit analysis. For this part of the analysis, we use only those respondents that declared they would attend the referendum. This group however cannot be understood as a randomly selected subset of all respondents, which can lead to biased results (Hug, 2003). Therefore, to deal with such selection bias we employ two-stage models based on probit regression analysis, also known as the Heckman correction (Heckman, 1979). Given the available data and its structure, this method is the most suitable for our analysis (c.f. Bodenstein & Kemmerling, 2011). For correcting the selection bias, we use the controls in the first stage model (i.e. turnout). Heckman correction requires at least one variable affecting the dependent variable to be included in the selection equation while being omitted in the second stage of the model. To follow this require-ment, the control covering faith is dropped from the second stage of the models. We selected this variable as we found it to be a strong predictor of the turnout to the referendum.

Context of the 2015 'Family' referendum

Slovakia represents a case with an established tradition of referendum employment. Since the country's emergence in 1993, eight referendums have been held, which makes the Slovak political system fairly familiar with the institution, even though there is only one case – EU accession – when a referendum ended up valid (Spáč, 2010). The reason for such a low number of successes is the strict institutional framework, which sets two challenging conditions that must be met for a referendum to be successful: (1) At least 50% of the registered electorate plus one voter must attend the poll and (2) a simple majority of attending voters must decide for one of the answers provided.[4] Under such conditions, the turnout in most Slovak referendums was well below the required 50%. The lowest turnout occurred in 1997, with less than 10% turnout, while the highest turnout (except for the EU accession referendum) was achieved in the 1998 referendum on banning the strategic privatization of state property, when 44.3% of voters showed up at the polling stations. It is important to note that the turnout generally increases if the referendum coincides with elections. So far, referendums were twice held on the same day as either a general or a presidential election, in 1998 and 2004, and they saw a turnout of 44.3% and 35.9%, respectively. On the other hand, the mean turnout of the other six referendums was only around 24%, and if the EU accession referendum is excluded this number decreases to under 19%. Hence, in terms of level of turnout, the timing of the referendum is of high importance.

In Slovakia, the referendums are most often initiated by political parties in the pursuit of their own interests (Nemčok & Spáč, 2018). However, the 2015 referendum represents an exception from this pattern, because it was initiated by the civic association Alliance for Family. The Alliance itself was established in 2013 with the mission to protect conservative values, especially the values related to the 'traditional' family. It operates as an umbrella structure for more than 100 mostly Christian organizations and associations dealing with social care, healthcare and other similar issues. Even though the Alliance put significant effort into presenting itself as an independent organization, its strong financial and personal ties to the Catholic church in Slovakia were undeniable (Kováč, 2015). Besides providing financial support, the Church used its dense network of churches and communities to raise awareness about the referendum and encouraged people to attend the vote (Smrek, 2015).

In the spring of 2014, the Alliance started a petition to hold a referendum about family issues and managed to collect well above the 350,000 signatures, as required by Article 95 of the Slovak Constitution. Soon after the signatures were delivered to the Slovak President, Andrej Kiska, he exercised his legal power to approach the Constitutional Court to ensure that the proposed questions did not violate constitutional law. The original petition initiated by the Alliance for Family included four questions. However, two months after being officially approached by the President, on 28 October 2014, the Constitutional Court ruled that one of the four proposed questions was unconstitutional, citing that it dealt with basic human rights and freedoms, which cannot be put to a referendum vote (Rybář & Šovčíková, 2016).[5] The elimination of only one question came as a surprise to the President, who repeatedly stated his personal doubts regarding the constitutionality of the issues, and once directly, on the occasion of the official announcement of the date of the referendum (Cuprik, 2014). Nevertheless, he honoured the Constitutional Court's ruling and called the referendum on 7 February 2015. It contained the following three questions:

(1) Do you agree that no other cohabitation of persons other than a bond between one man and one woman can be called marriage?
(2) Do you agree that same-sex couples or groups shouldn't be allowed to adopt children and subsequently raise them?
(3) Do you agree that schools cannot require children to participate in education pertaining to sexual behaviour or euthanasia if the children or their parents don't agree?

Although the Alliance proclaimed the referendum to be about the protection of family, two of the three questions dealt with same-sex marriages and a ban on the adoption of children by same-sex couples. Given that the majority of Slovak citizens declare themselves to be Catholics,[6] these topics clearly had the potential to polarize society as well as political parties.

Basically, all relevant political parties declared their position on the referendum. Moreover, they not only provided voters with a recommendation on how to vote on a particular question, but also whether to attend the popular vote (see Online Appendix A). The endorsement of a participation strategy must be perceived within a broader picture of the Slovak institutional setup. Obviously, the referendum topic was important for more conservative segments of the society. Since the majority of Slovaks recognize themselves as Catholics, it could be expected that these societal groups would attend the referendum and would vote 'yes' on the three referendum questions. Moreover, the first surveys on the referendum topic, conducted long before the referendum, revealed that a majority of the Slovak population supported the ideas promoted by the Alliance for Family. However, credible information on the estimated attendance was absent. In such a situation, the parties opposing the referendum recommended abstention from voting. Given the required turnout threshold of 50% and the expected predominance of those who attend the voting to cast a 'yes' vote, this strategy was more effective. The logic is quite straightforward, as abstaining from voting effectively reduces the turnout without any need to outnumber the mobilized 'yes' camp.

Despite an emotional campaign full of conflicts between representatives of the Church and the LGBTQ community (see Rybář & Šovčíková, 2016; Smrek, 2015), the turnout on the referendum reached only 21.4% (see Table 1), well below the required threshold. Hence, similarly to majority of referendums that have been conducted in Slovakia, the 2015 'Family' Referendum ended up invalid too.

Analysis

The general expectation of our research could be summed up as: the higher the clarity of a cue, the easier it is for a voter to 'decode' the suggestion and follow it. On the contrary, blurred and ambiguous statements should result in a divided electorate. Model 1 in Table 2 shows the results for the analysis of compliance of voters with

Table 1. Results of the 2015 'Family' referendum in Slovakia.

Question	Yes	No	Invalid/blank	Total votes	Registered voters	Turnout
1: Marriage	94.5% (892,719)	4.13% (39,088)	12,867			
2: Adoption	92.43% (873,224)	5.54% (52,389)	19,061	944,674	4,411,529	21.41%
3: Sex Education	90.32% (853,241)	7.34% (69,349)	22,084			

Table 2. Probability of referendum attendance (Probit regression).

	Model 1	
	Coef.	z
Clarity 1.	0.437***	3.10
	(0.140)	
Clarity 2.	0.090	0.69
	(0.131)	
Clarity 3.	Reference category	
Faith	0.233***	4.81
	(0.048)	
Gender	−0.179*	−1.83
	(0.098)	
Age (log)	0.096	0.70
	(0.137)	
Education	0.092*	1.75
	(0.052)	
Income	−0.005*	−1.77
	(0.003)	
Constant	−1.567***	−2.80
	(0.560)	
N	713	
Loglikelihood	−464.083	
Pseudo R^2	0.060	
Prob > chi^2	0.000	
LR chi^2 (7)	59.38	

Notes: Standard error in parentheses.
$*p < .1, **p < .05, ***p < .01$.

partisan cues regarding attending or abstaining from voting on the referendum. The coefficients show that high clarity of party recommendation (Clarity 1.) leads to higher responsiveness of voters, who follow the recommendation. Hence, when a party or its leadership issues an official statement with a clear position, it has a positive and significant effect on voters and their behaviour as compared to parties that do not make such a statement or that only unofficially present the positions of the party leaders. On the other hand, we found no such effect for cases of party leaders who proclaimed an official position towards the turnout in the referendum but who were opposed by other party members (Clarity 2.). Our model thus shows that for the mobilization issue parties have to provide clear and unambiguous messages in order to affect their supporters. Lowering the clarity due to different stances presented by various party members rather confuses the voters, as they are given contradictory suggestions as to how they should act.

For a more straightforward interpretation of the effect of clarity of partisan cues we computed their average marginal effects (see Table 3). These provide information about the effect of a unit change in the explanatory variable on the change of probability that the outcome variable takes the value one, i.e. in our case the probability that the voters acted in accordance with the suggestion of their party. For the level of clarity 2 (i.e. official position of party leader opposed by other members) there is an increase of around three percent in voters following the recommendation, however this effect is without significance. More importantly, when parties make their statements officially and without any opposing messages, the average marginal effects increase the odds by more than 16 percent that voters will take the cue, and this effect is significant. These outcomes show that recommendations

Table 3. Average marginal effects on compliance of voters with recommendation of their parties.

	Delta-method	
	Dy/dx	z
Clarity 1.	0.163***	3.17
	(0.051)	
Clarity 2.	0.033	0.69
	(0.048)	
Clarity 3.	*Reference category*	
Faith	0.086***	5.06
	(0.017)	
Gender	−0.066*	−1.84
	(0.036)	
Age (log)	0.035	0.70
	(0.051)	
Education	0.034*	1.76
	(0.019)	
Income	−0.002*	−1.78
	(0.001)	
N	713	

Note: Standard error in parentheses.
$*p < .1, **p < .05, ***p < .01$.

with a high level of clarity significantly and substantially increase the likelihood that parties will affect the behaviour of their own supporters.

As for controls, we found that only the level of faith supports the willingness of voters to follow the partisan cues. The other control variables are found not to have such effects, although gender, education and income were significant on $p = 0.1$ level. The coefficients for these three variables however show that the size of their effect is rather limited.

We now turn to the results of the effect of clarity of partisan cues when it comes to actual voting in the referendum. In order to do so we computed two-stage probit models using the Heckman correction to ensure that the selection bias does not affect our findings. Models 2–4 in Table 4 show the results. Compared to the issue of mobilization, we are faced with mixed results. For questions one and three in the Slovak referendum the clarity of partisan messages is found to be without significance. What is more, the actual effects for the highest level of clarity, i.e. clear and officially presented recommendations of parties, are found to be negative, while lower clarity – when some members oppose the official position of their leader – has a positive effect. In case of the second question in the referendum dealing with the adoption of children, both levels of clarity are significant and positive. Contrary to our expectation, however, a stronger positive effect is found for lower level clarity than for cues officially provided by parties as their only recommendation.

Among the control variables, the only one with a substantial effect is age. As the results in Models 2 and 3 in Table 4 show, older people tend to follow their party's suggestion to a greater extent, which could be interpreted in terms of their higher respect for (partisan) authorities. This effect was not, however, found in Model 5, which covers the third referendum question, and this limits our ability to generalize the role of age.

To conclude, in the case of mobilization, the partisan cues of a higher clarity increase the probability that voters will be (de)mobilized in accordance with the recommendation of the party. On the other hand, for the act of voting, no prevailing effect of clarity has

Table 4. Attendance and voting in the referendum (Probit models with Heckman selection).

	Model 2 Question 1: Marriage		Model 3 Question 2: Adoption		Model 4 Question 3: Sex education	
	Coef.	z	Coef.	z	Coef.	Z
First stage: Compliance with party						
Clarity 1.	−0.384*	−1.77	0.927***	3.59	−0.021	−0.10
	(0.216)		(0.258)		(0.206)	
Clarity 2.	0.162	0.52	1.540***	4.24	0.201	0.77
	(0.312)		(0.363)		(0.262)	
Clarity 3.	Reference category		Reference category		Reference category	
Gender	−0.096	−0.48	−0.095	−0.48	−0.149	−0.79
	(0.198)		(0.199)		(0.190)	
Age (log)	0.556**	2.17	0.703*	1.93	0.381	1.23
	(0.256)		(0.364)		(0.309)	
Education	0.013	0.13	−0.075	−0.76	−0.151	−1.62
	(0.097)		(0.099)		(0.093)	
Income	−0.005	−0.79	0.000	0.11	−0.001	−0.30
	(0.006)		(0.007)		(0.006)	
Constant	−0.310	−0.31	−2.293	−1.33	0.072	0.05
	(1.004)		(1.727)		(1.334)	
Second stage: Participation in referendum						
Faith	0.278***	5.07	0.272***	4.40	0.277***	4.55
	(0.054)		(0.061)		(0.060)	
Gender	−0.021	−0.17	−0.026	−0.20	−0.023	−0.18
	(0.129)		(0.130)		(0.130)	
Age (log)	0.357**	1.98	0.382**	2.08	0.366**	2.00
	(0.180)		(0.183)		(0.182)	
Education	0.074	1.10	0.079	1.16	0.077	1.14
	(0.067)		(0.068)		(0.068)	
Income	−0.002	−0.71	−0.002	−0.63	−0.002	−0.59
	(0.004)		(0.004)		(0.004)	
Constant	−2.566***	−3.56	−2.656***	−3.62	−2.607***	−3.56
	(0.719)		(0.734)		(0.733)	
N (uncensored N)	416 (201)		416 (201)		416 (201)	
Wald chi² (6)	10.42		22.35		6.09	
Rho	−0.998		−0.455		−0.554	
	(0.233)		(0.430)		(0.339)	
Atanh rho	−3.464		−0.492		−0.624	
	(59.737)		(0.543)		(0.490)	
Log likelihood	−339.315		−371.710		−377.747	
Prob > chi²	0.108		0.001		0.413	
LR test of indep Prob > chi²	0.024		0.366		0.198	

Note: Standard error in parentheses.
*$p < .1$, **$p < .05$, ***$p < .01$.

been found – the analyses of the referendum questions revealed different (and sometimes even opposite) trends. The data indicates that the real political struggle in the 2015 'Family' referendum in Slovakia was therefore not which side to vote for, but rather whether to attend the popular vote at all.

The most reasonable explanation seems to be the Slovak institutional setup. A referendum can become valid only when more than 50% of the electorate attend the voting. This condition leaves the 'no' camp with basically zero motivation to attend as long as the turnout does not seem like it will pass the threshold. This is the reason why the referendum turnout in 2015 fell to as low as 21.4%, which is significantly below the numbers from national parliamentary or presidential elections, however it is far from unusual for referendums in Slovakia (see Nemčok & Spáč, 2018). Voters who oppose the issue abstain from voting simply because abstention is even more effective than voting 'no', since it does not increase turnout to the level required for validity.

Therefore, the moment when a voter makes the decision to turn out for a referendum is already a moment when partisan cues play a crucial role. However, when voters within this institutional setup decide to disregard the recommendation of their party and attend a popular vote, their autonomy from the partisan cues is higher. Even though it may seem that a voter is voting in accordance with the partisan recommendation (Model 1), unlike mobilization, the clarity of the cue reveals no meaningful pattern (Models 2–4). This indicates that in a similar institutional setup, the ability of partisan cues to influence the shares of ballots cast for 'yes' or 'no' is lower, compared to their influence on turnout. This is an interesting finding, which emphasizes the fact that partisan cues should not be studied only in relation to voting but also as a strong determinant of turnout, especially in an institutional setup that sets high demands for the validity of a referendum, which is definitely the case for Slovakia.

Conclusion

In a certain institutional setup, when a high threshold is required to achieve the validity of a referendum result, the legitimate strategy of a 'no' camp is to abstain from voting. However, published studies have mostly perceived a referendum only as an act of voting either 'yes' or 'no' (Cini, 2004; Franklin, Marsh, & McLaren, 1994; Franklin, Marsh, & Wlezien, 1994; Hobolt, 2006, 2007; Hug & Sciarini, 2000; Pettersen et al., 1996; Pierce et al., 1983) and have not paid sufficient attention to the factors driving voters' decisions to attend or abstain from voting. Likewise, partisan cues have been found to be one of the main forces driving voter behaviour and their impact on mobilization has remained mostly neglected, even though its impact on a referendum's success can easily become crucial.

This study attempted to examine the impact of partisan cues on the mobilization of voters in a referendum and add a valuable extension to the body of literature dedicated to the influence of partisan cues. For this purpose, we ran a set of statistical operations on data gathered in a representative public survey conducted before the 2015 'Family' referendum in Slovakia. This referendum constitutes a great case because it kept possible intervening institutional factors constant and, additionally, the rather controversial topic related to the rights of sexual minorities caused some parties to hesitate in taking a clear stance, which allowed us to study the effects of cues on the various levels of their clarity.

Our statistical models provides compelling evidence that partisan cues related to mobilization are a force shaping voters' decisions to attend or abstain from a referendum in a similar fashion compared to recommendations of which side to vote for. Thus, the low turnout of 21.4% in the 2015 'Family' referendum cannot be perceived only as a sign of people's lack of interest. This group also includes members for whom the abstention was a legitimate political decision based on the recommendation of their preferred party, which, unlike a 'no' vote, does not help to increase turnout beyond the validity threshold.

At the same time, the clearer the (de)mobilizing recommendation is, the stronger the effect is. Therefore, if parties want to utilize the popular vote to improve their own position in the political struggles, one viable strategy is to take a clear stance. The available data however do not allow us to know whether parties expect their supporters to better accept and follow more clear recommendations, which in turn would stimulate the parties to produce statements with higher clarity. The motivations of parties to express their recommendation either in a clear or a rather blurry fashion thus remains a topic for further study.

However, higher clarity resulting in a bigger effect does not apply to how people vote. The various levels of clarity brought various (and sometimes contradictory) results. This suggests that if a voter decides to vote, despite a restrictive institutional setup similar to Slovakia's, the influence of the party's cue is lower. Therefore, and most importantly for the future studies of partisan cues, in an institutional setup that requires a high turnout threshold for validity, a party's recommendation related to mobilization becomes even more crucial for the referendum outcome than an endorsement of which side to vote for.

Further research should validate the presented results on additional cases. If the conclusions are successfully replicated, a more complex assessment of the influence of partisan cues on referendum voting will need to be developed. The sole focus on voting seems to be insufficient. The decision-making must be examined in a wider institutional framework that determines the impact of parties on voter behaviour under the institutions of direct democracy.

Notes

1. Share of party supporters in the sample and the distribution of their declared probability to attend the referendum are presented in Table B.1 included in Online Appendix B.
2. For information about coding see Online Appendix A.
3. This is due to overestimation of declaration of respondents to attend referendums and their real willingness to do so as was found in previous referendums. Although, we ran the analysis with thresholds of 50% and 60% with roughly the same results.
4. This may sound like a redundant condition, however, if the 'yes' and 'no' camps are roughly the same size and there is a substantial share of voters submitting an empty ballot, it can invalidate a referendum.
5. Full wording of the excluded question was: Do you agree that no cohabitation of persons other than those who are married should be granted the particular protections, rights and duties that the legislation as of 1 March 2014 granted only to marriages between a husband and wife; in particular, the acknowledgement, registration or recording as a lifelong partnership in front of a public authority, and the opportunity to adopt a child by the spouse of a parent?
6. Based on the data from Population Census 2011, the share is more than 62% of the population and there are more religious groups with significant representation (Statistical Office of the Slovak Republic, 2011).

Acknowledgment

Authors are deeply grateful to Martin Slosiarik from FOCUS Agency for sharing the data. In addition to that, authors would like to thank two anonymous reviewers and Sergiu Gherghina for their valuable comments.

Disclosure statement

No potential conflict of interest was reported by the authors.

Funding

This article was written at Masaryk University with the support of the Specific University Research Grant provided by the Ministry of Education, Youth and Sports of the Czech Republic.

ORCID

Miroslav Nemčok ⓘ http://orcid.org/0000-0003-3556-5557
Peter Spáč ⓘ http://orcid.org/0000-0003-4395-689X
Petr Voda ⓘ http://orcid.org/0000-0002-9383-376X

References

Adamczyk, A., & Pitt, C. (2009). Shaping attitudes about homosexuality: The role of religion and cultural context. *Social Science Research, 38*(2), 338–351. doi:10.1016/j.ssresearch.2009.01.002

Altman, D. (2011). *Direct democracy worldwide.* Cambridge: Cambridge University Press.

Andersen, R., Tilley, J., & Heath, A. F. (1999). Political knowledge and enlightened preferences: Party choice through the electoral cycle. *British Journal of Political Science, 35*(2), 285–302. doi:10.1017/S0007123405000153

Arceneaux, K. (2006). Do campaigns help voters learn? A cross-national analysis. *British Journal of Political Science, 36*(1), 159–173. doi:10.1017/S0007123406000081

Besen, Y., & Zicklin, G. (2007). Young men, religion and attitudes towards homosexuality. *Journal of Men, Masculinities and Spirituality, 1*(3), 250–266.

Bodenstein, T., & Kemmerling, A. (2011). Ripples in a rising tide: Why some EU regions receive more structural funds than others. *European Integration Online Papers, 16.* doi:10.1695/2011007

Borges, W., & Clarke, H. D. (2008). Cues in context: Analyzing the heuristics of referendum voting with an internet survey experiment. *Journal of Elections, Public Opinion and Parties, 18*(4), 433–448. doi:10.1080/17457280802305243

Brewer, P. R. (2003). The shifting foundations of public opinion about Gay rights. *The Journal of Politics, 65*(4), 1208–1220. doi:10.1111/1468-2508.t01-1-00133

Camp, B. J. (2008). Mobilizing the base and embarrassing the opposition: Defense of marriage referenda and cross-cutting electoral cleavages. *Sociological Perspectives, 51*(4), 713–733. doi:10.1525/sop.2008.51.4.713

Cini, M. (2004). Culture, institutions and campaign effects: Explaining the outcome of Malta's EU accession referendum. *West European Politics, 27*(4), 584–602. doi:10.1080/0140238042000249911

Cuprik, R. (2014, December 8). President sets date for 'family' referendum. *The Slovak spectator.* Retrieved from https://spectator.sme.sk/c/20052872/president-sets-date-for-family-referendum.html

De Vreese, C. H., & Semetko, H. A. (2004). *Political campaigning in referendums: Framing the referendum issue.* London: Routledge.

Font, J., & Rodríguez, E. (2009). Intense but useless? Public debate and voting factors in two referendums in Spain. In M. Setälä, & T. Schiller (Eds.), *Referendums and representative democracy. Responsiveness, accountability and deliberation* (pp. 341–352). London: Routledge.

Franklin, M. N., Marsh, M., & McLaren, L. (1994). Uncorking the bottle: Popular opposition to European unification in the wake of Maastricht. *JCMS: Journal of Common Market Studies, 32*(4), 455–472. doi:10.1111/j.1468-5965.1994.tb00509.x

Franklin, M. N., Marsh, M., & Wlezien, C. (1994). Attitudes toward Europe and referendum votes: A response to Siune and Svensson. *Electoral Studies, 13*(2), 117–121.

Franklin, M. N., van der Eijk, C., & Marsh, M. (1995). Referendum outcomes and trust in government: Public support for Europe in the wake of Maastricht. *West European Politics, 18*(3), 101–117. doi:10. 1080/01402389508425093

Gherghina, S. (in press). How political parties use referendums in Eastern Europe: Exploring analytical dimensions. *East European Politics and Societies.*

Gherghina, S., & Miscoiu, S. (2013). The failure of cohabitation. *East European Politics and Societies, 27* (4), 668–684.

Glaurdić, J., & Vuković, V. (2016). Proxy politics, economic protest, or traditionalist backlash: Croatia's referendum on the constitutional definition of marriage. *Europe-Asia Studies, 68*(5), 803–825. doi:10.1080/09668136.2016.1186610

Haider-Markel, D. P., & Joslyn, M. R. (2005). Attributions and the regulation of marriage: Considering the parallels between race and homosexuality. *PS: Political Science & Politics, 38*(02), 233–239. doi:10.1017/S1049096505056362

Heckman, J. J. (1979). Sample selection bias as a specification error. *Econometrica, 47*(1), 153–161.

Hobolt, S. B. (2005). When Europe matters : The impact of political information on voting behaviour in EU referendums. *Journal of Elections, Public Opinion & Parties, 15*(1), 85–109. doi:10.1080/ 13689880500064635

Hobolt, S. B. (2006). How parties affect vote choice in European integration referendums. *Party Politics, 12*(5), 623–647. doi:10.1177/1354068806066791

Hobolt, S. B. (2007). Taking cues on Europe? Voter competence and party endorsements in referendums on European integration. *European Journal of Political Research, 46*(2), 151–182. doi:10.1111/ j.1475-6765.2006.00688.x

Hug, S. (2003). Selection bias in comparative research: The case of incomplete data sets. *Political Analysis, 11*(03), 255–274. doi:10.1093/pan/mpg014

Hug, S., & Sciarini, P. (2000). Referendums on European Integration *Comparative Political Studies, 33* (1), 3–36. doi:10.1177/0010414000033001001

Jenssen, A. T., & Listhaug, O. (2001). Voters' decisions in the Nordic EU referendums of 1994: The importance of party cues. In M. Mendelsohn, & A. Parkin (Eds.), *Referendum democracy: Citizens, elites and deliberation in referendum campaigns* (pp. 169–190). Basingstoke: Palgrave Macmillan.

Kováč, P. (2015, February 10). Aliancii dala peniaze aj cirkev. Na kampaň išli desaťtisíce eur [alliance received money also from the Curch. Tens of thousands were spent on the campaing.]. Hospodárske Noviny Online. Retrieved from https://dennik.hnonline.sk/slovensko/552508-aliancii-dala-peniaze-aj-cirkev-na-kampan-isli-desattisice-eur

Kriesi, H. (2005). *Direct democratic choice: The Swiss experience*. Plymouth: Lexington Books.

LeDuc, L. (2009). Campaign tactics and outcomes in referendums: A comparative analysis. In M. Setälä & T. Schiller (Eds.), *Referendums and representative democracy: Responsiveness, accountability and deliberation* (pp. 139–161). London: Routledge.

Lupia, A., & Johnston, R. (2001). Are voters to blame? Voter competence and elite Maneuvers in referendums. In *Referendum democracy* (pp. 191–210). London: Palgrave Macmillan. doi:10.1057/ 9781403900968_10

Lupia, A., & McCubbins, M. D. (1998). *The democratic dilemma: Can citizens learn what they need to know?* Cambridge: Cambridge University Press.

McKelvey, R. D., & Ordeshook, P. C. (1986). Information, electoral equilibria, and the democratic ideal. *The Journal of Politics, 48*(4), 909–937.

McVeigh, R., & Diaz, M.-E. D. (2009). Voting to Ban same-Sex marriage: Interests, values, and communities. *American Sociological Review, 74*(6), 891–915.

Nemčok, M., & Spáč, P. (2018). Referendum as a party tool: The case of Slovakia. *East European Politics & Societies.* doi:10.1177/0888325418800551

Pettersen, P. A., Jenssen, A. T., & Listhaug, O. (1996). The 1994 EU referendum in Norway: Continuity and change. *Scandinavian Political Studies, 19*(3), 257–281. doi:10.1111/j.1467-9477.1996.tb00393.x

Pierce, R., Valen, H., & Listhaug, O. (1983). Referendum voting behavior: The Norwegian and British referenda on membership in the European community. *American Journal of Political Science, 27* (1), 43–63. doi:10.2307/2111052

Rovny, J. (2012). Who emphasizes and who blurs? Party strategies in multidimensional competition. *European Union Politics, 13*(2), 269–292. doi:10.1177/1465116511435822

Rybář, M., & Šovčíková, A. (2016). The 2015 referendum in Slovakia. *East European Quarterly, 44*(1–2), 79–88.

Sager, F., & Bühlmann, M. (2009). Checks and balances in Swiss direct democracy. In M. Setälä & T. Schiller (Eds.), *Referendums and representative democracy. Responsiveness, accountability and deliberation* (pp. 186–206). London: Routledge.

Silagadze, N., & Gherghina, S. (2017). When who and how matter: Explaining the success of referendums in Europe. *Comparative European Politics,* 1–18. doi:10.1057/s41295-017-0107-9

Smrek, M. (2015, March 4). The failed Slovak referendum on 'Family': voters' apathy and minority rights in Central Europe. *Balticworlds.Com.* Retrieved from http://balticworlds.com/the-failed-slovak-referendum-on-'family'/

Spáč, P. (2010). *Priama a zastupiteľská demokracia na slovensku: Volebné reformy a referendá po roku 1989 [direct and representative democracy in Slovakia: Electoral reforms and referendums held after 1989].* Brno: Centrum pro studium demokracie a kultury.

Statistical Office of the Slovak Republic. (2011). *Population census 2011.* Retrieved from https://census2011.statistics.sk/

Stevenson, R. T., & Vavreck, L. (2000). Does campaign length matter? Testing for cross-national effects. *British Journal of Political Science, 30*(2), 217–235. doi:10.1017/S0007123400000107

Zaller, J. (1992). *The nature and origins of mass opinion.* Cambridge: Cambridge University Press.

And yet it matters: referendum campaigns and vote decision in Eastern Europe

Sergiu Gherghina ⓘ and Nanuli Silagadze ⓘ

ABSTRACT

Referendums campaigns are important and earlier research closely analysed their general functioning, effects on turnout, and the importance of media and information for voting behaviour. However, the role of referendum campaigns as such (with all its components) in shaping voting behaviour was widely neglected. This article seeks to partially fill this gap in the literature and argues that referendum campaign is an important predictor of the voting decision as long as people perceive it as informative and follow it. We investigate this effect in the context of three referendums organized in 2015–2016 in Bulgaria, Poland and Slovakia. The results indicate that these two variables explain the decision of citizens to support referendums across different settings. Their effects are consistent and significantly stronger than alternative explanations employed in the literature such as the limited effect of campaigns, second-order elections, partisan cues or amount of information received.

Introduction

Referendum campaigns differ from election campaigns in a number of ways: run longer and thus increase the likelihood of unforeseen events, are influenced by domestic and international factors, have higher levels of electoral volatility and uncertainty among voters, lower perceived importance and involvement, and political parties may be internally divided over the policy subjected to popular vote (de Vreese & Semetko, 2004; Franklin, Marsh, & Wlezien, 1994; Hobolt, 2005; LeDuc, 2002; Silagadze and Gherghina 2018). For all these reasons, referendum campaigns are considered influential and earlier research closely analysed their general functioning, effects on turnout, and the importance of media and information for voting behaviour (Christin, Hug, & Sciarini, 2002; de Vreese, 2004; de Vreese & Semetko, 2004; Kriesi, 2006; Schuck & de Vreese, 2009; Siune & Svensson, 1993). In spite of the consensus regarding the importance of referendum campaigns, little scholarly attention has been devoted to them as explanatory variables for the way in which people vote in referendums. So far, most approaches followed either the path of policy and institutional explanations that ignored campaign or the path of intra-campaign features and developments that left out the campaign as a general process.

In this sense, a broader line of enquiry sought to explain voting behaviour along the debate issue voting versus second-order voting with empirical evidence supporting alternatively both theories (Mendez, Mendez, & Triga, 2014). Issue-voting implies that the citizens' vote is influenced by their attitudes towards the policy to be decided upon (Siune & Svensson, 1993; Siune, Svensson, & Tonsgaard, 1994). The second-order voting postulates that the attitudes towards the national political parties in general and to the incumbent government, in particular, are decisive for the vote. Referendums thus become second-order national elections where considerations about first-order national politics determine the political behaviour of citizens (Franklin et al., 1994; Franklin, 2002; Hobolt, 2007; LeDuc, 2002). In addition to these views, previous research reveals the importance of political cues communicated by elites during the referendum campaign especially for voters with little prior information (Lupia, 1994; Zaller, 1992). The lower the level of information among the electorate on an issue, the more determining the political cues for their final decision. Party endorsements serve as heuristics that help voters to arrive at competent decisions despite their lack of factual knowledge (Font & Rodriguez, 2009; Hobolt, 2007; LeDuc, 2009).

The line of enquiry focusing on intra-campaign features investigated mainly the reasons for which citizens oppose the referendum initiatives. The findings indicate that voting decision was influenced by the type and shape of messages – including here media framing – received during campaign (Hobolt, 2005; Schuck & de Vreese, 2009), the low level of information that made them oppose the status quo in the presence of a particular heuristics (Christin et al., 2002; Highley & McAllister, 2002; Kriesi, 2005) or to the risk aversion that determines voters to prefer safe and known over uncertain options (Hobolt, 2009). In the particular case of European referendums, another feature emerges, namely the challenge of a two-dimensional political space. The domestic and transnational dimensions are interlinked, both playing a role in constituting a two-dimensional political space in which the political parties operate and the campaign takes place (Shu, 2009).

The rich empirical evidence provided along these two lines of enquiry neglected the role of referendum campaign as such (with all its components) in shaping voting behaviour. To partially fill this gap in the literature, our paper argues that referendum campaign is an important predictor of the voting decision as long as people perceived it as informative and follow it. We investigate this effect in the least likely setting of supporting a referendum proposal, previous research revealed that it is easier to mobilize people against a referendum proposal. The explanatory potential of campaign is tested against the usual suspects described above in the context of three referendums organized in 2015–2016 in different East European countries (Bulgaria, Poland and Slovakia).[1] The referendums under scrutiny shared several features: each of them had three separate questions out of which at least one was not very related to the other two, none of them was valid due to low turnout, and none of them was initiated by political parties (the Bulgarian and Slovak referendums were bottom-up, while the Polish referendum was initiated by the country president). We also selected these referendums due to their diversity of topics with the aim to identify whether the explanatory power of campaign is context sensitive or holds across various topic and countries. The referendums refer to issues of a very different nature: electoral reform, political funding, same-sex marriage and adoption rights, education pertaining to sexual behaviour or euthanasia in schools, or positive interpretation of taxation. We use individual-level data from an online survey conducted in March–April 2017.

The remainder of this paper proceeds as follows. The first section presents the mechanisms through which a referendum campaign may influence voting preferences. In doing so, it uses combines findings from research on referendums with ideas inspired by findings on election campaigns. The second section presents the methodology and data used in this study, while the third one provides background information about the cases investigated in this paper. Next, we present the results of descriptive and inferential quantitative analysis with emphasis on the similarities and differences between countries. The conclusions summarize the key findings, discuss the implications of this paper and open the floor to further avenues for research.

How referendum campaigns make a difference

Referendum campaigns influence voters' preferences towards the policy through a combination of mechanisms. One of the most straightforward and arguably the most investigated is the hypodermic model that assumes an effect due to campaign features. Among these features, the information delivery is prominent due to its potential to decrease the unknown to ballot proposals (de Vreese & Semetko, 2004; Hobolt, 2005; LeDuc, 2002; Schuck & de Vreese, 2009). The information allows for a systematic processing that will be the basis of voters' calculus. Under these circumstances, citizens are more likely to make a calculus regarding their alternatives and perceived consequences based on what they learn and much less on heuristic processing based on risk propensity (Morisi, 2016). In this sense, campaigns generate large quantities of information about different aspects of the policy under consideration such as costs, benefits, implications, reasons for change or for the status quo, etc. The longer and more intense the public debates, the simpler it is for voters to make up their minds as there is a lot of available information on the issue (Font & Rodriguez, 2009). Since the issue at stake in a referendum is divisive and polarizing, most of the information is substantive with limited superficial features encountered in regular elections. Regarding the latter, media is under fire by both academics and politicians for its sensationalistic and market-based journalism that ignores the ideological components and issue-solving approaches. Nevertheless, there is empirical evidence that even under the circumstances news coverage and advertisement during campaign has a great informational value for citizens (Iyengar & Simon, 2000). Moreover, campaign has a socializing effect for the audience. Since the issue to be voted upon is intensely discussed, people become aware about its content, nuances and consequences and are likely to make an informed decision.

In addition to the campaign features, existing citizens' attitudes should be factored in to understand the complexity of campaign effects. An important strand of literature dealing with elections claims that voters make up their minds before the campaign starts based on their partisan affiliation or candidates' sociological characteristics (Berelson, Lazarsfeld, & McPhee, 1954; Campbell, Converse, Miller, & Stokes, 1960). This is also due to the fact that voters get socialized to parties, know very well the competitors and voted for some of them in the past. The studies supporting the minimal-effect hypothesis of campaign (Finkel, 1993; Gelman & King, 1993) argue that election outcomes can be predicted without accounting for the campaign. According to this perspective, voters have preferences in place before the election period and the campaign only helps to activate those latent preferences.

Some of these conclusions from election campaigns can be transferred to referendum campaigns as long as specific elements such as socialization and experience with competitors are not included. We are interested in highlighting that predispositions and information do not operate independently from each other, but rather predispositions determine what information or third-party opinion a citizen accepts, since people tend to ignore the information or opinions that do not agree with their prejudices and orientations (Marcinkowski, 2007; Zaller, 1992). Even when accounting for predispositions and previous preferences, a referendum campaign may have an effect on the vote choice. The resonance model explains how messages received during campaign reinforce voters' prevailing predispositions or preferences (Iyengar & Simon, 2000). In this case, citizens who already favour the proposal of the referendum will acquire during campaign further arguments that may give them confidence that the initial attitude was the right one; and such a belief is easily translated into a vote choice.

Two inter-related functions of referendum campaigns that transcend the two models are the agenda setting and simplification of choices. Voters do not pay attention to all the details surrounding a political issue and instead focus on a few elements that appear important at the moment. However, what is important is not a matter of objectivity or subjective choice on the side of citizens, but it is mainly a media-driven decision. Journalists decide what to cover and what to ignore and thus they model saliency within the electorate. The framing and priming of events during a campaign influences perceptions by evoking different images in the minds of particular segments in society, leading to issue interpretations (de Vreese, 2004). Such effects can be observed both in the presence of existing opinions (Domke, Shah, & Wackman, 1998) and in their absence. In particular, priming ensures that the issues considered salient by voters – saliency that can also emerge during campaign – become the criteria of evaluation in the minds of the electorate (Iyengar & Simon, 2000). To use a recent example, the discourse of the Leave camp in the Brexit referendum picked-up on the salient issue of Britain being a net contributor to the European Union. It played this card heavily during campaign and thus the assessment of people evolved around that issue set up by one of the camps. In brief, the agenda-setting, framing and priming simplify the choices for people by providing them with readily available information.

These arguments illustrate how a campaign yields a multi-faceted effect on the voting behaviour. We argue that such effects are likely to occur especially in the case of voters who support the referendum proposals. This happens for at least three reasons. First, the cognitive benefits brought by campaigns reduce the costs of uncertainty and diminish the risk propensity. Since people are more strongly motivated to avoid costs than to achieve gains (Tversky & Kahneman, 1981), those who wish to avoid costs and have a predisposition prior to the campaign, will be rather immune to the content of campaign. Perceived risk is a motivator of self-protective behaviour (Schuck & de Vreese, 2009) and thus such voters will be oriented to oppose the referendum proposals. Through its learning, persuasive and socialization processes a referendum campaign reduce uncertainty about outcomes and remove the burden from the shoulders of those seeking gains. Moreover, even those who are risk averse and under normal conditions would oppose a proposal due to its uncertain consequences (Christin et al., 2002), will face less uncertainty once exposed to campaign. Second, the efforts made by the camp supporting the referendum are on average greater than those of the opposing camp. The political elites (in case of top-down) or citizens (for bottom-up) behind the referendum are aware that quite often they start with a handicap: people have to be persuaded to support their initiative. This challenge increases when the pursued issue has low saliency in society. Consequently, the promoters of the policy subjected to referendum are likely to be more active than the opponents. The most visible result of such a visibility is a greater level of information and more persuasive ads launched to the public. Third, voters who oppose the referendum proposals may adopt a strategic behaviour and skip voting. Since many referendums require a participation quorum for validation, those who oppose the proposals have a greater say if they do not turn out. This is what could be observed in Italy where political parties opposing the referendum proposals demobilised voters and encouraged them to stay away from polls (Uleri, 2002). The existence of such a strategic behaviour indicates that those who pay attention to campaign are more likely to be open or undecided regarding a support for the referendum proposals. Following all these arguments, we hypothesize that:

H1: Citizens who perceive the campaign as informative will support the referendum proposals.

H2: Citizens who follow the campaign will support the referendum proposals.

Controls

We test the explanatory potential of the hypothesized effects against the variables highlighted in the literature as main predictors for voting behaviour: opinion before the campaign, support for government, partisan cues, access to information relative to the referendum issue and socio-demographics (education, age and gender). As previously explained, an influential body of literature posited that the beliefs formed before campaign play an important role in the final voting preference. The theory of second-order considerations claims that people often decide on their vote choice in referendums with evaluations of the incumbent government in mind. They do so either because they feel that there is not much at stake (Franklin, 2002) or because they wish to use the referendum as a punishment tool. Partisan cues were found by earlier studies as quite important determinants for voter choice. On complex issues, voters use the shortcuts received from the political parties they support (Font & Rodriguez, 2009; Kriesi, 2005; LeDuc, 2009). Party endorsements may allow citizens to imply their own position on a ballot issue without detailed information about it (Hobolt, 2007). Access to information is a variable meant to capture the amount of information to which individuals have access during campaign. Our hypothesized effect goes far beyond the amount of information in campaign and that is why we include the simple exposure to information related to the referendum (via different media environments) as a control variable. Finally, we control for socio-demographic variables since they may also have an impact on the support for the referendum proposals.

Research design

To test the hypotheses, we use individual-level data from an online survey conducted in March–April 2017 with a total number of 511 valid responses in three countries: Bulgaria (257), Poland (121) and Slovakia (133). The number of answers in the statistical analysis is lower than 511 because respondents skipped some questions or provided answers that were not included in the study (see below). We selected the most recent multiple question referendums in Eastern Europe. The variation in their topics was important because results are more robust when observing similar patterns across different types of decisions.

The survey had the same questions translated into the national language of every country. The focus of the analysis is those who voted and a probability representative sample would have been ideal to generalize findings. However, setting up such a sample was not possible because there is no official statistics regarding the features of those who turned out to vote in these referendums (socio-demographics). Instead, we use a convenience sample with a snowball distribution of the link through Facebook and e-mail addresses. While the number of answers may not look very high relative to the turnout in each of these referendums, it is less important in the context of the current analysis. Our primary goal is to understand the process through which campaigns influenced voting choice rather than making generalizable statements. We are aware that there is a self-selection bias in which those with access to Internet and skills to use devices could fill in the survey. However, all three countries have high levels of Internet access, ranging between 60 and 80% (World Bank 2017). For analysis, we use a combination of bivariate statistics and ordinal regression with a pooled and country level models.

Variable operationalization

The dependent variable of our study is the support for referendum proposals. It is measured as the answer to the following question: 'How did you vote on the referendum issues?'. Available answers were coded on a four-point ordinal scale as follows: all yes (1), two yes and one no (2), one yes and two no (3), and all no (4). A fifth option was also listed (blank vote) but since this is of no importance in the current context, it was removed from the analysis. The independent variable informative campaign (H1) is operationalized through the answers provided to the following question: 'Thinking about the referendum campaign, was it informative in providing with all necessary information about the topics?'. The available answers were coded on a four-point ordinal scale as follows: very informative (1), quite informative (2), hardly informative (3), not at all informative. The variable following campaign (H2) is measured through the ordinal answers to the question 'How much did you follow the referendum campaign?', coded as follows: very much (1), much (2), to some extent (3) and not at all (4).

The opinion before the referendum and partisan cues were operationalized as the answer to the following question: 'When voting in this referendum, to what extent did your opinion before the referendum campaign play a role in your decision?' and 'When voting in this referendum, to what extent did the position of the party for which you voted in the (year closest to referendum) parliamentary elections play a role in your decision?'. The answers were coded on a four-point ordinal scale as follows: very much (1), much (2), to some extent (3) and not at all (4). For these two items, a 'not available' answer was listed since the individual could miss the election or did not have the right to vote due to age limitations. All 'not available' answers were removed from the analysis and treated as missing data.

Government support is measured through the answers to the question 'How satisfied are you with the way the (country) government does its job?' and coded as follows: very satisfied (1), quite satisfied (2), hardly satisfied (3) and not at all satisfied (4). The amount to information during campaign is a six-point scale index cumulated after summing up the answers to the question: 'Where did you get information about the referendum topics from?'. The respondent had a multiple choice with several options and every time an option was mentioned it received a code of 1: TV, newspapers or radio, online news portals and Internet forums, Facebook, posters and leaflets, discussions with friends. The resulting index ranges from a value of 0 reflecting the situation in which a respondent did not get information from any of the five environments to a maximum of 5 in case the respondent used all the available environments.

Gender is a dichotomous variable in which male is coded 1 and female 2. Age is an ordinal variable recorded as the number of completed years at the number of survey, while education is a five-point ordinal scale ranging from primary (coded 1) to post-university degree (coded 5). The following section provides an overview of the referendums to illustrate the topics and the driving forces behind campaigns.

Background information about the referendums

The referendum experience of the three analysed countries differs. Bulgaria organised its first referendum in 2013 (bottom-up) and since then it has been very active in this field, Poland organised five referendums in its post-communist history with quite some distance between them, while Slovakia had eight referendums with only the most recent (included in our analysis) being a bottom-up procedure.

Bulgaria

The Bulgarian referendum was held on the 6th of November 2016 simultaneously with the presidential elections. The citizens were asked three major questions: the replacement of the proportional vote by a majority vote, the introduction of compulsory voting, and the reduction of the state subsidies given to the political parties – from 11 leva (5.60 €) to 1 lev (0.50 €) for each vote won. The second question was quite redundant since compulsory voting had been already introduced a few months earlier (Stoychev, 2017).

Prior to the fall of the communist regime three popular votes were held in the country – in 1922, 1946 and 1971. In modern Bulgaria, the use of the direct democratic instruments is mainly regulated by the Law on Direct Participation of Citizens in the State and Local Government. In compliance with Article 3, a national referendum can be initiated over the issues which are in the competence of the National Assembly, with the exception of constitutional arrangements, taxation and budgetary topics. The result of a referendum is mandatory if the turnout reaches the level of the turnout in the last parliamentary elections and if more than a half of votes are in favour of the proposed question. If the turnout criterion is not met but was higher than 20% and if the number of 'yes' votes exceeds 50% the National Assembly is required to discuss the issue (Milanov, 2016).

The referendum in 2016 was initiated not by a political force, but by a very well-known Bulgarian showman, Stanislav Trifonov, who has been a TV star from the beginning of the '90s (Martino, 2016). It was the first successful bottom-up initiative leading to a nationwide referendum in Bulgaria since 1989. He managed to mobilise the disenfranchised citizens. A special Facebook page was launched for subscription campaign. Not only a large number of volunteers was engaged, but also many celebrities publicly supported the

campaign. In the end, over 570,000 valid signatures instead of 400,000 required were col-
lected for six proposed questions. However, president Rosen Plevneliev referred to the
Constitutional Court questioning the legality of three questions (to halve the number of
MPs from 240 to 120, to introduce electronic voting and direct election of police chiefs).
The Court accepted the president's arguments and blocked these questions (Stoychev,
2017).

The campaign itself was criticised for lacking the substantial debate. The main political
parties were occupied by the simultaneously running presidential election campaign and
paid little attention to the referendum: 'none of the major parties registered to campaign
for the referendum at the Central Electoral Commission. Only 14 minor parties and
coalitions with less than 1% of electoral support registered, mainly because of the
money for media coverage provided by the state [about 20,000 EUR]' (Stoychev, 2017,
p. 191). In this situation, the TV show of Trifonov became the primary source of information, though one-sided, massively agitating for the 'yes' vote. This resulted in a high
degree of confusion among people over the asked questions (Cheresheva, 2016).

Those who took part in the poll overwhelmingly said 'yes' to all three questions.
However, the result was not binding, since the referendum turnout of 50.8% fell short
of the 2014 parliamentary elections turnout of 51% by a small margin of roughly 13,000
votes. Despite this fact, 'the 2016 referendum was the most successful popular initiative
in the contemporary history of Bulgaria. Although it did not produce a legally binding
result, it produced a politically legitimate demand for electoral reform' (Stoychev, 2017,
p. 192).

Poland

The Polish referendum held on 6th of September 2015 was a fifth national referendum in
the history of modern Poland. The reason behind conducting the popular vote was the
outcome of presidential elections held in May 2015. The former president Bronislaw
Komorowski, backed by the ruling centrist Civic Platform (PO) initiated the referendum
'as a panic move following his shock defeat in the first round of May's presidential election'
(Szczerbiak, 2015). Despite the prediction of all polls Komorowski came behind his main
opponent Andrzej Duda, the candidate of the right-wing Law and Justice (PiS) party.
The most surprising fact was, however, that a rock musician Pawel Kukiz won around
20% of votes with his promise to implement single-member constituencies in the Sejm
elections. A day after the elections, Komorowski declared to hold a referendum justifying
it as a reaction to the voters' wish for change – indeed he intended to win the votes of
Kukiz's supporters by this political move. In the end, Komorowski lost. The referendum,
however, will be remembered as a part of presidential campaign (Hartliński, 2015).

The legal base was the Article 125 allowing the President to call a referendum if the
Senate agrees on it. The results are binding if the turnout is more than 50%. The referendum was comprised of three questions: on introducing single-member constituencies in
elections to the Sejm, Poland's more powerful lower chamber of parliament; on maintaining the current method of financing of political parties from the national budget and introducing a presumption in favour of the taxpayer in disputes over taxation law. The first
question was the actual reason behind the initiation of the referendum and it caused
also the most of legal doubts, since its implementation contradicted the Article 96 of

the Constitution stating that the elections to the Sejm shall be inter alia proportional (Hartliński, 2015).

The whole referendum campaign was barely visible. The main axis of the campaign was the issue of single-member constituencies. The PO and Kukiz were clearly in favour of the issue, the PiS politicians claimed that they would take part in the referendum but their party did not invest much effort in mobilizing their supporters. Other parties' position was against the issue and their representatives declared not to be going to vote. This inevitably was to influence the participation rates. The second question reflected more or less the same division and the third one was not a matter of debate since every party articulated in favour of strengthening the position of citizens. The campaign itself was delegated from established parties to mainly unknown/minor societies and foundations that enjoyed the benefit of being present in the media and receiving remuneration. The parties, having in mind the approaching parliamentary elections, were not actively engaged in the debate. No true campaigning took place in comparison to the presidential or parliamentary elections (e.g. no TV commercials, no posters) (Hartliński, 2015). 'Walking around the streets of Krakow, talking to its inhabitants, watching the news and reading the national press, discussion of the issue is notable by its absence. Indeed, many Poles seem to be confused about the referendum and about the electoral system in general' (Tilles & Bill, 2015).

The lack of real campaign found its reflection in a very low level of knowledge and interest among the population and as a consequence in a miniscule turnout of only 7.8%, though all questions were approved by the voters (Hartliński, 2015). It was the first time in the Polish modern history that the result of the referendum was not binding due to the low participation. Undoubtedly the topic wasn't as important as previous ones – e.g. on the Constitution in 1997 or joining the EU in 2003 (Hartliński, 2015). One member of the Polish Electoral Commission described it as 'one of the most expensive public opinion polls in Europe' (Szczerbiak, 2015). However, the way of calling this referendum as a part of presidential rivalry and the very low-profile campaign did not contribute to winning support for more direct democracy in Poland. This popular vote was a big fiasco for the political parties (Hartliński, 2015).

Slovakia

The Slovak same-sex marriage referendum held on 7th of February 2015 was unique in many terms. The so-called Referendum on Family was the first referendum in the history of the country that was initiated not by the established political parties, but by the civil society. In record times over 400,000 signatures were collected (roughly 10% of the country's electorate) demonstrating unprecedented civil engagement with over 10,000 volunteers and more than 100 pro-life associations. Furthermore, it was also the first time in the Slovak history that the issues of sexual education, forms of modern family and adoption was subjected to public debate. The referendum campaign was highly polarizing and extremely salient (Rybar & Sovcikova, 2016).

The Alliance for Family, a civic organization established in 2013, was the main organizer of the popular initiative. Roughly one year before the referendum, in February 2014, the Slovak Parliament and the governing social-democratic Smer party passed a constitutional amendment (Art. 41) that clearly defined the marriage as a union between a man and a woman. This was not ambitious enough for the Alliance demanding not only explicit prohibition of child adoptions by same-sex couples but also the denial of legal basis for same-sex unions – the latter was proved as unconstitutional by the Court (Kużelewska, 2015; Rybar & Sovcikova, 2016). 'The referendum was meant to take a back-step and reiterate that in Slovakia a family consists of a husband (male) and wife (female) ... ' (Zordova, 2015). This would make the future attempts to change the legislation even more difficult. The argument was that the values of the traditional family are under threat since more and more countries liberalise the rules – e.g. the neighbouring Austria and the Czech Republic allow various forms of same-sex unions and child adoption by gay couples (*The Guardian*, 2015).

According to the Article 95 of the Slovak Constitution, the president of the state calls a referendum either on the basis of the National Council's resolution or if a petition receives more than 350,000 signatures. The vote is valid only if turnout exceeds 50% of all eligible voters. All referendums until this date were initiated in accordance with the first paragraph and all of them – with the exception of EU membership referendum in 2003 – failed due to insufficient turnout (Rybar & Sovcikova, 2016).

The referendum campaign was heated, debated and controversial. However, not the political parties, but the Catholic Church was one of the main players in the campaign, supporting the Alliance both morally and financially: for instance, petition sheets were available in the local churches and priests openly encouraged their parishioners to support the petition, providing theological backing (Rybar & Sovcikova, 2016; Smrek, 2015). Shortly before the referendum date, Pope Francis addressed the Slovak people: 'I greet the pilgrims from Slovakia and, through them, I wish to express my appreciation to the entire Slovak church, encouraging everyone to continue their efforts in defence of the family, the vital cell of society' (Harris, 2015). In contrast, the leading figures from the political elite refused to give a position on a referendum topic, thus, 'the overriding silence of high officials and political parties on the issue' was one of the main peculiarities of this popular vote (Kral, 2015).

The advocates framed the campaign in a quite positive manner, stressing the desire to preserve the status quo in regard to 'marriage' definition and to give parents more rights to decide about the content of their children's education. The slogan of the Alliance was 'Three Yeses For Children' which defined the confrontational tone of the campaign, depicting the homosexuals 'as perpetrators who seek to challenge the status quo' (Smrek, 2015). Thus, the public debate, concentrated along two lines, namely the attitudes towards homosexuals and the role of the Catholic Church in public life (Rybar & Sovcikova, 2016). The opponents – mainly the LGBT minority represented by the non-governmental organisation Iniciatíva Inakosť campaigned for not taking part in the referendum (Valkovičová, 2017).

In the end, the vote was invalid due to the low turnout of 21.4%, below the average compared to other referendums. However, over 90% of voters said 'yes' to all the three questions: whether marriage can only be a union of a man and a woman, whether same-sex couples should be banned from adoptions, and whether children can skip classes involving education on sex and euthanasia.

Analysis and results

This section starts with a bivariate correlation between the variables to observe the statistical relationships on a one to one basis. It continues with ordinal regression models ran for several variables. Figure 1 explores the ways in which people voted at aggregate level and in each of the three countries, to illustrate the degree of variation on the

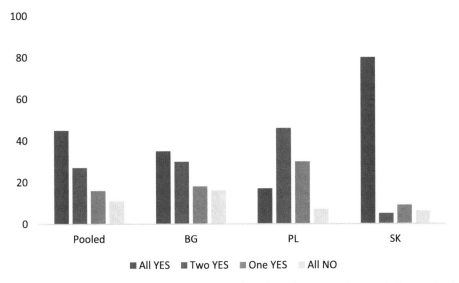

Figure 1. Voter distribution according to the support for referendum topics (*N* = 511). (Source: Statistical Office of the Slovak Republic).

Notes: The wording of referendum questions differed across the examined cases. Bulgaria: (a) Do you support the national representatives to be elected by majoritarian electoral system with absolute majority in two rounds? (b) Do you support the introduction of compulsory voting in elections and referendums? (c) Do you support the annual subsidy for financing the political parties and coalitions to be 1 BGN for every valid vote at the last parliamentary elections? (Source: Central Electoral Commission). Poland: (a) Are you in favor of the introduction of single-mandate electoral districts in the elections to the Sejm of the Republic of Poland? (b)Are you in favor of maintaining the current method of financing political parties from the state budget? (c) Are you in favor of introducing the general rule of doubts about the interpretation of tax law in favor of the taxpayer? (Source: National Electoral Commission). Slovakia: (a) Do you agree that the concept of marriage denotes solely the legal bond between one man and one woman, but it must not denote any other cohabitation between persons? (b) Do you agree that it should not be allowed to couples or groups of persons of the same sex to adopt and subsequently raise children? (c) Do you agree that schools should not require participation of children in the field of sexual education or euthanasia if their parents or the children themselves do not agree with the content of such education?

dependent variable. The graph illustrates that the highest percentage among the total number of respondents (45% in all three countries) supported all three referendum questions. This trend is observable in Bulgaria and Slovakia, the exception to the rule being Poland where the highest percentage of respondents (46%) voted yes to two questions as opposed to 17% who supported all three questions. One explanation for the massive vote in this direction is that two out of three questions were for change, while the third was to maintain the status quo. The latter referred to public party funding and the referendum results indicated that almost 83% of those who turned out to vote answered negatively to this question. in Slovakia the large percentage of votes in favour of all three proposals is due to the quite radical measures proposed in this referendum against same sex marriage, adoption and non-compulsory sexual and euthanasia education in schools. Since the three topics are related, the likelihood to support all of them is high. This is an issue reflected also in the official results when more than 90% of those who went to the polls casted a positive vote for each of them.

Table 1 includes the bivariate correlation coefficients between the support for referendum proposals and all other variables. The consistent observation across the pooled and country level data is that informative campaign is the variable that correlates the highest with support for the referendum proposals. The relationship goes in the

Table 1. Bivariate correlation with support for the referendum proposals.

Variable	Pooled	Bulgaria	Poland	Slovakia
Informative campaign	0.42***	0.51***	0.24**	0.16*
Follow campaign	0.14***	−0.01	0.01	0.16*
Pre-campaign opinion	0.10**	−0.03	−0.05	0.11
Satisfaction with government	−0.03	−0.06	0.21**	−0.04
Party cues	0.01	0.21***	0.12	−0.10
Access to information	−0.07	0.11	−0.04	−0.19**
Gender	−0.02	0.01	0.16	−0.15
Age	0.01	0.01	0.11	−0.10
Education	−0.09	−0.02	0.07	−0.11

Notes: Correlation coefficients are Spearman's rank.
N varies between 396 (party cues) and 473 (informative campaign).
***$p < .01$; **$p < .05$; *$p < .1$.

hypothesized relationship (H1) with respondents who find the campaign informative supporting all the proposals. The weakest relationship is in Slovakia, mostly due to the low variation on the dependent variable. In that particular case, irrespective of how respondent found the campaign, many of them cast a positive vote to all three questions. This result is not surprising if we keep in mind that some voters in Bulgaria and Poland were confused about the topics of the referendums (see the previous section). Those are the cases in which the referendum campaign can have an important effect by clarifying issues, educating the public and helping voters decide whether they support the proposal.

The bivariate correlations provide empirical support for H2 only in the pooled and Slovak model with respondents who closely follow the campaign being more inclined to favour the referendum proposals. In the other two cases, there is statistical independence with no relationship between these two variables. In the pooled model the variables corresponding to the main effects correlate the strongest (at the highest level of statistical significance) with the dependent variable. The variable informative campaign correlates in all but the Slovak model the highest with the support for referendums and that indicates robust empirical support for the first hypothesis.

Among the controls, only the pre-campaign opinion, access to information and education correlate with support for referendum proposals. People who cast a vote according to their attitude before the campaign have a slight tendency to support the proposals as opposed to those who do not have one. This relationship goes in the same direction only in Slovakia at country level, in Bulgaria and Poland it is reversed with people who do not hold pre-campaign opinions being more likely to support all referendum proposals. People with less access to information are slightly re likely to support the referendum proposals (−0.07 in the pooled model), a relationship that is quite strong in Slovakia (it is the highest correlation coefficient, statistically significant at the 0.05 level). Less educated people are more likely to support referendum proposals, a relationship that holds also in Slovakia but it is reversed in Poland – where mode educated people support the proposals – and displays statistical independence in Bulgaria.

Other controls with relevant correlation at country level are satisfaction with government, party cues and gender. In Poland, citizens who are satisfied with the activity of the government are more likely to support the referendum proposals (0.21, statistically significant at the 0.01 level). This observation is quite intuitive since it is the only referendum among the three investigated that had been initiated top-down, by political elites. In Bulgaria, those respondents who followed the opinion of the party for which they voted in the most recent legislative elections prior to the referendum are more likely to support the three proposals (coefficient 0.21, statistically significant at the 0.01 level). In Poland, the direction of relationship is similar, while in Slovakia it goes in the opposite direction with people who ignore their parties being slightly more likely to support the referendum. The latter can be explained through the ambiguity of party positioning on the referendum topics. The messages of political parties were not obvious, cues were unclear and thus we cannot observe a relationship between these and the voting decision. Finally, in Poland male are more likely to support the referendum proposals, while in Slovakia more female are among the supporters.

These bivariate correlations are an initial estimation of the relationship between variables. We will now turn to a regression analysis that seeks to assess causality. We run two types of ordinal regression models (due to the nature of the dependent variable): without control variables and with control variables. In the models with controls we exclude the socio-demographics for the following reasons: (1) the bivariate analysis showed the existence of poor relationships with the support for referendum proposals, (2) we ran regression analysis with them and the results confirm the existence of a very weak effect and (3) the interpretation of results is more parsimonious with fewer controls. In brief, by not reporting them there is not much substantive information lost.

Table 2 includes the odd-ratios for the two main effects. The reference category for all the variables are the absence of those features, e.g. for informative campaign, it is the category of people who voted against all three proposals. At pooled level, the citizens who consider the referendum campaign as very informative are more than three times more likely to support the referendum proposals (OR = 3.02, statistically significant at the 0.01 level) as opposed to those who do not find the campaign informative at all. Voters who followed very much the campaign are 1.24 times (statistically significant at the 0.1 level) more likely to support the proposals as opposed to those who did not follow at all. At country level, the effect hypothesized in H1 finds empirical evidence in all countries, with strength varying from 1.94 time more likely in Slovakia to 3.66 (statistically significant at the 0.01 level) in Bulgaria. The empirical support for H2 is mixed at country level where only Slovakia goes in the hypothesized direction: voters who follow campaign very much are two times (OR = 2.01) more likely to vote for referendum proposals as opposed to those who did not follow at all. In Bulgaria and Poland, people who follow the campaign are less likely (OR = 0.83 and OR = 0.90) to support the referendum proposals compared to those respondents who did not follow at all the campaign.

Table 2. Ordinal regression with support for the referendum proposals as DV (no controls).

Variable	Pooled	Bulgaria	Poland	Slovakia
Informative campaign	3.02*** (0.38)	3.66*** (0.62)	2.23*** (0.66)	1.94 (0.87)
Follow campaign	1.24* (0.16)	0.83 (0.15)	0.90 (0.26)	2.01 (0.90)
Pseudo R^2	0.08	0.11	0.03	0.06
Log likelihood	−543.03	−287.17	−128.49	−44.58
N	472	242	109	121

Notes: Reported coefficients are odds-ratios, standard errors in brackets.
***$p < .01$; **$p < .05$; *$p < 0.1$.

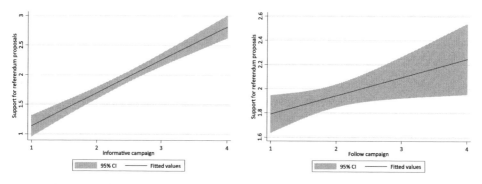

Figure 2. The marginal effect of informative campaigns and follow campaigns (pooled model).

The differences in the size of effect between H1 and H2 can be better visualized when comparing the two marginal effects in Figure 2, modelled at the pooled level. The left side of the graph depicts the marginal effect of Informative campaigns on the support for referendum questions. It shows a strong effect where the perception of high or very high informative campaign makes a substantive difference in the way in which voters support the referendum proposals. The rights side of the graph depicts the marginal effect of following the campaign and it is much weaker. The interval on which it has an effect on the dependent variable (vertical axis) is considerably smaller compared to the effect of informative campaigns.

Table 3 includes the ordinal regression models with control variables. Informative campaign remains a very strong predictor in the pooled model where people who perceive the campaigns as very informative are almost three times more likely (OR = 2.94, statistically significant at the 0.01 level) to support all three proposals. The effect of following campaigns (H2) is also positive but considerably weaker than H1. Pre-campaign opinion has a positive effect on support for proposals, while satisfaction with the government and party cues have a negative effect. Access to information has no effect on the voting behaviour. This observation is relevant because it indicates that campaign means much more than simply information. The empirical evidence in our cases illustrates that there is no effect of pure information, while the campaign overall – as long as people consider it informative and follow it – has a consistent positive effect on people's behaviour.

Table 3. Ordinal regression with support for the referendum proposals as DV (with controls).

Variable	Pooled	Bulgaria	Poland	Slovakia
Informative campaign	2.94*** (0.43)	3.28*** (0.65)	1.80* (0.63)	2.31* (1.11)
Follow campaign	1.13 (0.17)	0.68* (0.15)	1.29 (0.50)	1.38 (0.72)
Pre-campaign opinion	1.15 (0.11)	0.88 (0.13)	0.94 (0.28)	1.36 (0.41)
Satisfaction with government	0.89 (0.12)	0.82 (0.17)	1.57* (0.38)	1.11 (0.66)
Party cues	0.87 (0.10)	1.57** (0.52)	1.11 (0.23)	0.54 (0.22)
Access to information	0.97 (0.10)	1.17 (0.17)	1.14 (0.29)	0.72 (0.27)
Pseudo R^2	0.08	0.11	0.04	0.12
Log likelihood	−433.12	−212.79	−107.65	−40.93
N	379	180	93	112

Notes: Reported coefficients are odds-ratios, standard errors in brackets.
***$p < .01$; **$p < .05$; *$p < .1$.

The country level models indicate a strong and consistent empirical support for the first main effect (H1). The second main effect (H2) is also quite consistent and with the exception of Bulgaria in the other countries goes in the hypothesized direction. The rest of variables have only isolated effect in some countries, e.g. satisfaction with government in Poland or party cues in Bulgaria. The major conclusion of the statistical analysis is that the two main variables (H1 and H2) are the only ones with a consistent effect across the three investigated referendums; this observation is revealed both by the bivariate and multivariate statistical analysis.

Conclusions

This paper argued and tested the importance of referendum campaign as a predictor for voting decision by looking at its perceived informative character and the degree to which people follow it. It analysed this effect in the least likely setting of supporting referendum proposals on different topics in Bulgaria, Poland and Slovakia. The study relied on individual-level analysis coming from a web survey conducted in the spring of 2017. The results indicate that the two variables explain the decision of citizens to support referendums across different settings. Their effects are consistent and significantly stronger than alternative explanations employed in the literature such as the limited effect of campaigns, second-order elections, partisan cues or amount of information received.

The implications of these findings go beyond the comparative study of the three East European countries and they could have an impact on the broader study of voting behaviour during referendums. At theoretical level, our study reveals the importance as campaign as a valuable explanatory variable for the decisions taken by citizens in referendums. So far, research focused mainly on components of campaigns (information or media priming/framing) or campaign actors (parties or initiators) but has paid little attention to the campaign per se. Our results show that campaign is much more than information and it may yield much stronger relevance than the actor involved. Consequently, it is a determinant that could be included in further frameworks for analysis. At empirical level, the perception of campaign and degree to which people follow it appears to have consistent effect across different types of referendums. These are the only variables (especially the perceived informative feature of campaign) with such features among the ones considered. They are not context sensitive and are useful explanations for the way in which people vote.

One limitation of this study is the convenience sample on a fairly limited number of voters used to observe these behavioural patterns. Further research could address this issue by conducting a study on a large sample that could also pursue representativeness as long as data regarding the profile of voters will become accessible. Another avenue for further research is a more qualitative approach that involves interviews to explain the underlying mechanism. For example, we showed that the perception of informative campaign matters but we cannot know what is behind that perception. Focus groups or extended semi-structured interviews with voters could clarify the meaning and substantiate our findings.

Notes

1. The generic term of Eastern Europe is used to define the broader region to which the three countries belong. There are several definitions of the region and various ways to label these

countries, e.g. two of these countries can be considered Central Europe, while the third lies in South-Eastern Europe. Since identification issues lie beyond the goal of this article, we follow the definition used by the United Nations (https://unstats.un.org/unsd/methodology/m49/#geo-regions) that sees all these three countries as belonging to Eastern Europe.

Acknowledgements

The authors are very grateful for the constructive comments and suggestions received on earlier drafts of this paper from the participants at the International Workshop Democratic Innovations in Eastern Europe (Södertörn University Stockholm, 2017), the Seminar Series of the Åbo Akademi University Finland and at the graduate research seminar at the Autonomous University of Madrid.

Disclosure statement

No potential conflict of interest was reported by the authors.

ORCID

Sergiu Gherghina ⓘ http://orcid.org/0000-0002-6627-5598
Nanuli Silagadze ⓘ http://orcid.org/0000-0001-6251-7011

References

Berelson, B. R., Lazarsfeld, P. F., & McPhee, W. N. (1954). *Voting: A study of public opinion formation in a presidential campaign*. Chicago: University of Chicago Press.
Campbell, A., Converse, P., Miller, W., & Stokes, D. (1960). *The American voter*. New York, NY: Wiley.
Cheresheva, M. (2016). *Referendum on political system confuses Bulgarians, Balkan Insight*. Retrieved from http://www.balkaninsight.com/en/article/upcoming-referendum-raises-concern-in-bulgaria-11-01-2016
Christin, T., Hug, S., & Sciarini, P. (2002). Interests and information in referendum voting: An analysis of Swiss voters. *European Journal of Political Research, 41*(6), 759–776.
de Vreese, C. H. (2004). Primed by the euro: The impact of a referendum campaign on public opinion and evaluations of government and political leaders. *Scandinavian Political Studies, 27*(1), 45–64.
de Vreese, C. H., & Semetko, H. A. (2004). *Political campaigning in referendums: Framing the referendum issue*. London: Routledge.
Domke, D., Shah, D. V., & Wackman, D. B. (1998). "Moral referendums": values, News media, and the process of candidate choice. *Political Communication, 15*(3), 301–321.
Finkel, S. E. (1993). Reexamining the "minimal effects" model in recent presidential campaigns. *The Journal of Politics, 55*(1), 1–21.
Font, J., & Rodriguez, E. (2009). Intense but useless? Public debate and voting factors in two referendums in Spain. In M. Setala & T. Schiller (Eds.), *Referendums and representative democracy: Responsiveness, accountability and deliberation* (pp. 162–185). London: Routledge.

Franklin, M., Marsh, M., & Wlezien, C. (1994). Attitudes toward Europe and referendum votes: A response to Siune and Svensson. *Electoral Studies, 13*(2), 117–121.

Franklin, M. N. (2002). Learning from the Danish case: A comment on Palle Svensson's critique of the franklin thesis. *European Journal of Political Research, 41*(6), 751–757.

Gelman, A., & King, G. (1993). Why are American presidential election campaign polls so variable when votes are so predictable?. *British Journal of Political Science, 23*(4), 409–451.

Harris, E. (2015). *Pope Francis backs traditional marriage as Slovakia vote looms, Catholic News Agency.* Retrieved from https://www.catholicnewsagency.com/news/pope-francis-backs-traditional-marriage-as-slovakia-vote-looms-37102.

Hartliński, M. (2015). The 2015 referendum in Poland: Direct democracy notes. *East European Quarterly, 43*(2–3), 235–242.

Highley, J., & McAllister, I. (2002). Elite division and voter confusion: Australia's republic referendum in 1999. *European Journal of Political Research, 41*(4), 845–861.

Hobolt, S. B. (2005). When Europe matters: The impact of political information on voting behaviour in EU referendums. *Journal of Elections, Public Opinion and Parties, 15*(1), 85–109.

Hobolt, S. B. (2007). Taking cues on Europe? Voter competence and party endorsements in referendums on European integration. *European Journal of Political Research, 46*(2), 151–182.

Hobolt, S. B. (2009). *Europe in question: Referendums on European integration.* Oxford: Oxford University Press.

Iyengar, S., & Simon, A. F. (2000). New perspectives and evidence on political communication and campaign effects. *Annual Review of Psychology, 51*(1), 149–169.

Kral, D. (2015). *Despite a controversial referendum on same-sex marriage, democracy remains alive and well in Slovakia, LSE European Politics and Policy (EUROPP) Blog.* Retrieved from http://bit.ly/1vh9yEe

Kriesi, H. (2005). *Direct democratic choice: The Swiss experience.* Plymouth: Lexington Books.

Kriesi, H. (2006). Role of the political elite in Swiss direct-democratic votes. *Party Politics, 12*(5), 599–622.

Kużelewska, E. (2015). How far can citizens influence the decision-making process? Analysis of the effectiveness of referenda in the Czech Republic, Slovakia and Hungary in 1989–2015. *Baltic Journal of European Studies, 5*(2), 171–196.

LeDuc, L. (2002). Referendums and elections: How do campaigns differ? In D. M. Farrell & R. Schmitt-Beck (Eds.), *Do political campaigns matter? Campaign effects in elections and referendums* (pp. 145–162). London: Routledge.

LeDuc, L. (2009). Campaign tactics and outcomes in referendum. In M. Setala & T. Schiller (Eds.), *Referendums and representative democracy* (pp. 139–161). London: Routledge.

Lupia, A. (1994). Shortcuts versus encyclopedias: Information and voting behavior in California insurance reform elections. *American Political Science Review, 88*(1), 63–76.

Marcinkowski, F. (2007). Beyond information and opinion. The importance of public communication in the referendum process. In Z. T. Pallinger, B. Kaufmann, W. Marxer, & T. Schiller (Eds.), *Direct democracy in Europe: Developments and prospects* (pp. 94–107). Wiesbaden: VS Verlag für Sozialwissenschaften.

Martino, F. (2016). *Bulgaria, amid presidential elections and the referendum, OBC Transeuropa.* Retrieved from www.balcanicaucaso.org/eng/Areas/Bulgaria/Bulgaria-amid-presidential-elections-and-the-referendum-175104.

Mendez, F., Mendez, M., & Triga, V. (2014). *Referendums and the European union: A comparative inquiry.* Cambridge: Cambridge University Press.

Milanov, V. (2016). 'Direct Democracy in Bulgaria', Pázmány Law Working Papers, pp. 1–18. Retrieved from http://www.plwp.jak.ppke.hu/

Morisi, D. (2016). Voting under uncertainty: The effect of information in the Scottish independence referendum. *Journal of Elections, Public Opinion and Parties, 26*(3), 354–372.

National Referendum 2015. (2015). *National Electoral Commission.* Retrieved from http://referendum2015.pkw.gov.pl/341_Polska

National Referendum 2016. (2016). *Central Electoral Commission.* Retrieved from http://results.cik.bg/pvrnr2016/tur1/referendum/index.html

Referendum 2015 – General information. (2015). *Statistical Office of the Slovak Republic*. Retrieved from http://volby.statistics.sk/ref/ref2015/en/info.html

Rybar, M., & Sovcikova, A. (2016). The 2015 referendum in Slovakia: Direct democracy notes. *East European Quarterly, 44*(1–2), 79–88.

Schuck, A. R. T., & de Vreese, C. H. (2009). Reversed mobilization in referendum campaigns: How positive news framing can mobilize the skeptics. *The International Journal of Press/Politics, 14*(1), 40–66.

Shu, M. (2009). Coping with a two-dimensional political space: Party mobilisation in referendums on European integration. *European Journal of Political Research, 48*(3), 397–431.

Siune, K., & Svensson, P. (1993). The Danes and the Maastricht treaty: The Danish EC referendum of June 1992. *Electoral Studies, 12*(2), 99–111.

Siune, K., Svensson, P., & Tonsgaard, O. (1994). The European Union: The Danes said 'no' in 1992 but 'yes' in 1995: How and why? *Electoral Studies, 13*(2), 107–116.

Silagadze, N., & Gherghina, S. (2018). When who and how matter: explaining the success of referendums in Europe. *Comparative European Politics, 16*(5), 905–922.

Slovak conservatives fail to cement gay marriage ban in referendum. (2015). *The Guardian*. Retrieved from https://www.theguardian.com/world/2015/feb/08/slovak-conservatives-fail-gay-marriage-ban

Smrek, M. (2015). *The Failed Slovak Referendum on "Family": Voters' Apathy and Minority Rights in Central Europe, Baltic Worlds*. Retrieved from http://balticworlds.com/the-failed-slovak-referendum-on-"family"/

Stoychev, S. P. (2017). The 2016 referendum in Bulgaria. *East European Quarterly, 45*(3–4), 187–194.

Szczerbiak, A. (2015). *Who won Poland's 'referendum war' and how will it affect the October election? LSE European Politics and Policy (EUROPP) Blog*. Retrieved from https://polishpoliticsblog.wordpress.com/2015/09/11/who-won-polands-referendum-war-and-how-will-it-affect-the-october-election/

Tilles, D., & Bill, S. (2015). *Poland's referendum and election: The big issues no one's talking about, notes from Poland*. Retrieved from https://notesfrompolandcom/2015/09/04/polands-referendum-and-election-the-big-issues-no-ones-talking-about/

Tversky, A., & Kahneman, D. (1981). The framing of decisions and the psychology of choice. *Science, 211*(4481), 453–458.

Uleri, P. V. (2002). On referendum voting in Italy: YES, NO or non-vote? How Italian parties learned to control referendums. *European Journal of Political Research, 41*(6), 863–883.

Valkovičová, V. (2017). "Regrettably, it seems that breaking one border causes others to tumble": nationalism and homonegativity in the 2015 Slovak referendum. *POLITIQUE EUROPÉENNE, 55*, 86–115.

World Bank. (2017). *Individuals using the Internet (% of the population)*. Retrieved from https://data.worldbank.org/indicator/it.net.user.zs

Zaller, J. R. (1992). *The nature and origins of mass opinion*. Cambridge: Cambridge University Press.

Zordova, D. (2015). A Take on Slovakia's Same-Sex Referendum, The Central European Journal of International and Security Studies. *eContribution*. Retrieved from http://www.cejiss.org/econtribution/a-take-on-slovakia-s-same-sex-referendum

'Never just a local war': explaining the failure of a mayor's recall referendum

Sergiu Mişcoiu

ABSTRACT

The November 2017 referendum for the recall of Dorin Chirtoacă, Mayor of Chişinău (Moldova), largely failed because of the citizens' low turnout. Why do recall referendums fail and, in particular, why was this boycott strategy successful? My assumption is that the referendum was perceived not only as a tool to eliminate a major political competitor and thus weaken the anti-presidential opposition, but also as a wider attempt to gain extensive political control. I will use secondary data and data obtained from a focus-group research in order to show that the following factors determined the outcome of the boycott: the popular mistrust of institutions and parties, the perceived decisive importance of the Capital's control nationwide, the citizens' will to prevent the concentration of power, and the perception of the broader geopolitical stakes of the recall.

Introduction

An extensive literature refers to citizen-initiated local referendums, generally considered to be an indicator of the development of direct democracy at the local level (Kriesi, 2005; Qvortrup, 2014; Schiller, 2011; Schmitter, 2000, p. 19). However, referendums for the recall of mayors have rarely been approached by scholars mainly because this practice is not widespread within the legislation: in numerous systems, the recall of mayors takes place either automatically or not at all during their terms in office. Moreover, the procedures and the local contexts are too specific for consistent, relevant and comparable data to be assembled and analysed (Kersting & Vetter, 2003; Rallings, Thrasher, & Cowling, 2002, p. 67).

Nevertheless, such referendums play a key-role for several reasons. First, in some political systems, they are the only solution available to citizens for the removal of a mayor who has not only discontented them but has also abused their confidence and, generally, is accused of illegal actions during his/her term in office (Böhme, 2004; Garret, 2004). Then, referendums for the recall of mayors could affect the distribution of power at all levels, including the national one, by reshaping the pre-existing alliances of parties and lobby groups in relation with their respective stances concerning the opportunity and the validity of those removals from office. This could take place especially when the respective mayor is perceived to be a prominent political leader, as it happened in 2014, in Colombia, with the clashes over the referendum for the recall of Gustavo Petro, the opposition's

Mayor of Bogota, by the Dos Santos government (Welp & Rey, 2015, pp. 79–81). Finally, such referendums could have wider effects on the perception of the degree of responsiveness and accountability of the elected politicians and, more generally, on the degree of legitimacy of the political system itself (Gherghina, 2017, pp. 613–615). They could either strengthen the bond between citizens and decision-makers, in the cases where a successful recall matches the publicly perceived need to remove somebody who acted against the common interest. On the other hand, it could aggravate the rejection of the 'system' as a whole by the public, who may experience discontentment if they perceive the recall referendum as a tool to get rid of popularly elected officials who could challenge the establishment (Setälä, 1999).

In the rather modest amount of literature that discusses the issue of mayors' removal from office via popular suffrage, recall referendums have been analysed from several perspectives (Cronin, 1989; Qvortrup, 2011). The assessment of the recall processes' degree of legitimacy has provided one of the most relevant angles of analysis, as it allows for understanding not only the stakes and the results of the vote, but also the more complex (institutional, sociological and ideological) mechanisms that explain the evolution of the relationships between the citizens and their political representatives. Other perspectives include an approach to the administrative and political inter-institutional processes leading to the decision to hold recall referendums or the study of the effects of such referendums over the power-relations within the micro or macro levels of the political systems where they take place (Jimenez, 2001). All in all, most researches reveal the increasing sensitivity of the citizens invited to approve the deposal of their mayors about aspects related to the legality, the opportunity and the rightfulness of the recall procedure, as well as a more salient penchant for mobilizing and protesting either in favour or (more commonly) against the recall motions (Welp, 2013, pp. 13–16).

In the following pages, I will analyse the literature and select four main factors that generally contribute to the failure of recall referendums. Then, I will present the methodology used for the organization and analysis of the focus groups. Finally, before trying to analyse the factors that can explain the failure of the 2017 referendum for recalling the Mayor of Chişinău via the results of a focus-group research, I will first present the context of the recall referendum and underline the specific conditions that led to the transformation of a corruption affair into a crucial issue with geopolitical implications.

Reasons for the failure of recall referendums

Within the rather narrow range of contributions that approach recall referendums, the issue of the general causes behind the occasional failure of such public consultations has rarely been discussed in a systematic way (Serdült, 2015). The main reason for this is the low number of recall referenda and the overwhelming importance of the particular respective contexts on their dynamics and outcomes. Nevertheless, several reasons for the failure of referendums have been invoked.

Firstly, the general lack of trust in political systems (institutions, parties, politicians etc.) has been pointed out as being a key-factor that determines the negative outcome of referendums, in general, and of recall referendums, in particular (Hug & Tsebelis, 2002). People are more likely to be disinterested in any political action, including in referendums, if they do not trust their representatives (Smith, 1976). Moreover, as they understand that recall referendum are generally valid if there is a minimum threshold of participation, citizens may strategically boycott public consultations to show their disapproval of their political leadership. In this research, I expect this factor to have influenced the outcome of the recall referendum. Mistrust of public institutions and parties is likely to produce an intentional demobilization of the voters, who, by boycotting the consultation, convey a message of resentment and warning against the political establishment. Moreover, such recall referendums, whose validation requires a certain proportion of attendance, are the best opportunity citizens have for refusing to do what they are asked to by a political leadership they do not trust (Mendelsohn & Parkin, 2001, p. 19).

Secondly, recall referendums fail because citizens may be convinced of the critical importance that control over their city has for the local, regional or even national political actors (Welp & Rey, 2015). They may either boycott the referendum, which thus becomes invalid, or vote for keeping their mayor by rejecting the recall motion, according to what they perceive to be the strategy most likely to succeed. Citizens generally tend to overrate the importance of their city and consequently they are likely to believe that gaining control over it is an objective of the entire political establishment. Thus, they will act in order to block the attempt at removing the mayor and to maintain control over the city. The people's perception about the high importance of the political disputes over their city's control should indeed influence their behaviour with respect to the referendum. Previous experience shows that the citizens' tendency to inflate the role of their city and, implicitly, that of their mayors' recall referendums has been constant (LeDuc, 2003). The importance people attach to their cities, especially when the removal of their first public managers appears on the agenda, is likely to determine their solidarization around the incumbent mayors.

Then, the difference between the political orientation of the mayor and that of the national or the regional/state/provincial government is likely to contribute to the failure of the referendum (Uleri, 2002, pp. 863–865). Citizens will rather boycott the consultation if they perceive it as being related to their mayor's different political views, to his/her opposition to the central or regional government's policy or to his/her potential to become a national leader. One mayor's different political stance in relation to those of the national or regional majorities is generally seen as a marker of that city's particular orientation and distinct individuality. Citizens may mobilize even more in order to support their elected mayor if they consider that the mayor 'stands alone' against some other regionally or nationally dominant parties or groups of interest.

Finally, recall referendums fail when citizens are convinced that there is a wider national or even international stake of the recall initiative. This factor is more salient in major cities, such as country capitals, whose mayors are generally important national political leaders, or in divided societies, where issues such as the national political strategy or the country's geopolitical position are regarded as contentious (Welp, 2013). Thus, citizens are likely to reject a government's attempt to recall a mayor who supports one of the country's major geopolitical orientations against that government's will to impose the opposite direction in foreign policy.

Research design

Given the low number of recall referenda, the selection of our case study was made by eliminating all the other possibilities. Few cities in Central and Eastern Europe have organized recall referenda and the sizes of those cities are generally rather small – to a large extent, rural communities or, at best, medium-sized towns. Admittedly, for the political establishment, the relevance of holding or getting political control over such local communities is lower and, consequently, citizens are mobilized by other, essentially local factors. In fact, Chişinău was the only major city of the region – and more precisely, a capital – where such a recall referendum could be convoked after 1989.

As far as methodology is concerned, in order to check if the above-mentioned factors were relevant in our case of the recall referendum, I organized a field qualitative research consisting of three focus groups, as follows: the first with former voters of Mayor Dorin Chirtoacă in the 2015 elections, who boycotted the recall referendum (FG1, 8 participants); the second with former voters of other candidates or citizens who did not vote in 2015 and who boycotted the recall referendum (FG2, 7 participants); the third with citizens who participated in the recall referendum regardless of their voting behaviour in 2015 (FG3, 8 participants). The main characteristics of the FG participants are synthetized in Appendix.

A two-part scenario was used: the first part was common to all the three FGs, while the second was specific to each of the three different FGs, targeting relevant issues, such as particular motivations of thought and action. For the FG results analysis, I used an adapted version of the methodology proposed by John M. Creswell (Creswell, 2014). I resorted to a two-layered analysis – that of the individual options and motivations, on one hand; and that of the groups' dynamics and its influence on the individuals' opinions, on the other hand. The research focused on issues such as the strength of individual beliefs, the reasons for correlations between beliefs and behaviours, the articulation mechanisms of different political topics or events and the propensity for changing or reinforcing the participants' views on the main topic of the research. The adaptation I made consisted in a stronger insistence on the individual level, which is more relevant for depicting the reasons behind a recent civic and electoral behaviour, and less on the groups' dynamics, except for those situations in which the participants had no clear view on a particular issue and the FG experiment made them form some opinions, following their interactions with the others.

The 2017 referendum in the Moldovan political context

The Republic of Moldova is one of the ex-Soviet countries that has been facing numerous challenges related to the very definition of its collective identity, as it is divided between a Romanian (Moldovan)-speaking majority, a Russian-speaking large minority and several other ethno-linguistic minorities (mainly Ukrainian and Gagauz), not to mention the more general transition-related difficulties (Henry & Mişcoiu, 2016, pp. 209–214). After the break-up of the USSR, the Republic of Moldova reached its independence but had to immediately pay the price of a short yet traumatic war with the secessionist region of Transnistria, later on transformed into a frozen conflict and a permanent *casus belli* with Russia (Secrieru, 2011, pp. 241–243). After a first period of relative dominance of the largely anti-Soviet pro-Romanian majority (1991–1996), Moldova passed successively from a more consensual but still pro-Western government (1996–1999) to a decade in which the Communist Party (PCRM) maintained its hegemony. This party installed a regime that was generally characterized as a semi-consolidated authoritarian one (with a President elected by the Parliament, who could, in fact, control thus both the parliamentarian majority and the Government) and that reoriented Moldova geopolitically towards the Russian Federation, while preaching 'Moldovenism' as a particular ideology of Moldo-va's own way (March, 2007, pp. 599–601; Quinlan, 2004). The PCRM's control of the whole institutional framework and of the Moldovan society became increasingly salient under the semi-consolidated authoritarian rule of President Vladimir Voronin (Way, 2003).

In this context, the victory of the 29-year-old Liberal Party's Vice-President, Dorin Chir-toacă, in the second round of the Chişinău municipal elections of 2007, with the support of all the opposition parties, was perceived as a major setback for the PCRM and an indication of a possible general majority change. Like most Eastern European capitals, Chişinău was more developed and more westernized than the national average, and it rapidly became a bulwark against the hegemony of the Communists and a stronghold of pro-European pol-itical forces. It also became a predilect target of choice for the PCRM, especially as Mayor Chirtoacă was vocally supporting the campaign of his party president, Vasile Ghimpu, a more radical pro-Romanian popular politician and a bitter opponent of Voronin's regime (Hale, 2014, pp. 392–397).

In April 2009, the contestation of the parliamentary election results led to a series of riots, sit-ins and other popular pressures that the incumbent communist government repressed in a violent way. Wider and more persistent demonstrations consequently occurred, while the new Parliament was unable to acquire the necessary majority to elect a new President. This forced the authorities to organize new elections (in September), which finally ended with the victory of the pro-Western opposition's coalition (made up of the pro-Western Liberals/PL and Liberal-Democrats/PLDM and of the Democrats/PD, the latter having recently seceded from the PCRM). While the April-July 2009 movement was considered a revolutionary upheaval (the 'Moldovan Spring'), the new majority faced numerous difficulties – the first being the election of a new president, an operation that required a qualified majority, which they lacked (Kennedy, 2010, pp. 62–77). Finally, after the dissent of a more consistent group of Communist MPs, the second dissolution of the Parliament and another set of elections organized in 2010, a relatively wider pro-European majority was installed and the former Head of the Constitutional Court, Vasile Timofti, was elected as President, in 2012. Moldova officially re-embarked on its pro-Western course. In spite of its heterogeneity, the governmental coalition resisted and seemed to be able to succeed in implementing a programme of liberal reforms inspired and supported by the European Union, while Moldova became the first post-Soviet repub-lic (except for the Baltic states) to be invited to sign the EU pre-accession agreement, in November 2013 (Mişcoiu, 2014, pp. 431–446).

In 2014–2015, a series of major corruption scandals, culminating with the literal vanish-ing of one billion USD from three majors banks (whose accounts were actually refilled by the Moldovan State Treasury in order to prevent their collapse) and with the indictment of the former reformist Prime Minister Vlad Filat (PLDM, 2009–2013), profoundly ravished the people's confidence in the pro-Western coalition (Tudoroiu, 2015). While this did not prevent the consecutive re-election of Chirtoacă as Mayor of Chişinău, in 2011 and in 2015 (albeit with smaller margins), it destabilized the incumbent coalition and facilitated the emergence of two key-players: within the opposition, the Socialist Party (PSRM), a dis-sident group of the PCRM, led by the populist leader Igor Dodon; within the majority, the Democratic Party (PDM), led by the businessman and media tycoon Vladimir Plahotniuc, who unofficially started to gain control over the pro-European coalition's parties and over an increasing number of state institutions.

The November 2015 parliamentary elections resulted in an almost hung assembly, where the PSRM dominated the PCRM. Within the pro-Western coalition, the PDM distanced itself from the PLDM and the PL. The new governmental coalition, consisting of the same three parties, faced numerous difficulties in reaching consensus: no less than three different Prime-Ministers and two other caretaker Prime-Ministers held office from December 2015 to December 2017. In November 2016, the first on-term presidential elections were organized after the constitutional reform that introduced the direct popular election of the President of the Republic. The clash took place between the candidate of the new pro-European Party for Action and Solidarity/PAS, Maia Sandu (endorsed by the remaining members of the incumbent pro-European coalition), and the Socialist candidate, Igor Dodon (endorsed by the remaining members of the PCRM, most of whose MPs had joined the PSRM). Although officially endorsing Maia Sandu, Vlad Plahotniuc and his wide networks of influence left numerous channels of communication open with Igor Dodon, while Sandu was much more bitterly criticized than Dodon in the media owned by the Democrat leader during the campaign (Goşu, 2016). As expected, Dodon finally won with a 6% margin, but lost by a narrow difference in the city of Chişinău, confirming the well-entrenched political dissonance between the capital and the rest of the country.

The cohabitation between the Socialist President and the Democrat-led majority oscillated between phases of apparent inter-institutional conflict (the President being several times suspended by the Constitutional Court for refusing to appoint some ministerial nominees designated by the PD Prime Minister Pavel Filip) and phases of appeasement and consensus (as it was the case with the electoral system's reform bill). These periods of rapprochement were heavily criticized by the (pro-Romanian) unionists and by the pro-Europeans (of the Party for Action and Solidarity, led by Maia Sandu, and of the emerging Dignity and Truth Platform of Andrei Năstase), as well as by some of the PL members, who accused Vlad Plahotniuc of being the 'puppet master' behind all these oscillatory moves (Necşuţu, 2017).

In this context, in early 2017, an important corruption scandal erupted in relation to a contract for granting the management of Chişinău's pay parking system to a private company. The granting procedure was contested by the communist and socialist groups within the City Council and by some civil activists as being unlawful and opaque, while the beneficiary of the contract was denounced as a 'ghost company'. While the parking contract's saga started as early as in 2015, it was only in 2017 that the corruption implications hit the headlines and that judicial institutions started to act. In April 2017, Vice-Mayor Nistor Grozavu, who had signed the contract that was never approved by the City Council, was arrested alongside other public officials and businessmen. In spite of denying any knowledge about this contract, Mayor Chirtoacă was also indicted in May 2017 (he was arrested and then placed under judicial control, which means that he is obliged not to leave the Capital and to be available at any time if convoked by the investigators). In July, the Court suspended the mayor from office pending the investigation.

Since Chirtoacă repeatedly refused to resign and denied all accusations throughout that summer, in September the PSRM gathered 70,000 signatures for organizing a local referendum aimed at recalling the suspended mayor. According to the Electoral Code, the mayor was to be recalled if more voters than the ones who had voted in his favour at the previous elections voted for his recall and, simultaneously, if they represented at least half of the total number of voters who had participated in the elections. This meant about 33% of the total number of registered voters. Because of that, the strategies of the two camps were different: the pro-recall camp wanted to mobilize the voters by showing them the need to replace the mayor, while the anti-recall coalition campaigned in favour of boycotting the referendum. On 19 November 2017, only 17.5% voted in the recall referendum (87% of them were in favour of the recall). Consequently, the referendum was invalidated.

Explaining the failure of the referendum

In order to understand the success of the boycott campaign, presented in the contextual analysis above, I will try to see, via the FG research, if the factors discussed in the theoretical section were relevant. I will first discuss these factors in the Moldovan context, in order to make my line of reasoning fully comprehensible.

The popular mistrust of institutions and parties

Moldova is among the countries with one of the lowest levels of confidence in public institutions and political parties, which suffer not only because the dominant public perception is that they are unable to properly fulfil their tasks, but also because of their high degree of instability and inconsistence (IPP, 2015). As a wide range of literature shows, the view according to which institutions are unstable and weak generally feeds the citizens' lack of appetite for participating in elections and referenda (Catterberg & Moreno, 2006; Gilley, 2006; Kalu, 2006). In Moldova, the dominant opinion is that both institutions and parties are extensively manipulated by interest groups which unofficially control them and that those interest groups are connected with some foreign lobbying networks, especially with those belonging to the pro-Kremlin Russian oligarchs (IRI, 2017). My assumption was that this generalized mistrust of institutions and parties prevented the citizens' involvement in political activities, as well as their electoral participation, and that it consequently determined a lower turnout at this recall referendum.

The perceived decisive importance of the capital's control nationwide

The overwhelming importance that citizens invest in the political control exerted over their national capitals is often considered to be an explanatory factor of their voting behaviour (Qvortrup, 2011). One of Moldova's particularities is the overwhelming importance of its capital, Chişinău, where almost one quarter of this country's total population lives. The other major cities are far from being challengers of the capital: their conquest by the PSRM or the PDM from the Communists, the Liberal-Democrats or the Liberals is certainly strategically important but it far from provides them with access to sizable resources, as control over Chişinău would offer. Moreover, recent research has shown that mayors are considered to be stronger and more credible than the other political actors (LKP, 2017). Thus, my assumption was the following: because they believed that the dispute over the control of the capital was critically important and that the recall referendum was largely supposed to exchange the present control over Chişinău with that of the initiative's promoters, the voters boycotted the recall referendum in order to thwart this attempt at 'dispossession'.

The citizens' will to prevent the concentration of power

The Moldovans wanted to avoid that power falled into the hands of the two main political competitors – the Socialists and the Democrats. As several studies suggest, the overconcentration of power into the hands of a limited number of political actors is often perceived by the public as being dangerous in that it limits the democratic diversity and prevents genuine alternations in power (Dresden & Howard, 2016). All the major Moldovan cities except for the capital are under the control of some well-entrenched politicians, described by the press as 'potent local barons', who have been members or close supporters of the Communist Party and who are nowadays split between the Socialists and, to a lesser but increasingly considerable extent, the Democrats (Călugăreanu, 2017). While the Liberal Party has almost entirely lost its influence, it has nevertheless remained entrenched in Chișinău, even if, since the 2015 elections, the majority in the City Council has apparently switched in favour of Vladimir Plahotniuc's own nebulous and trans-partisan networks (Timpul, 2016). After Dodon's election in November 2016, Chirtoacă remained the only major politician who was associated neither with the President's Socialists or with Plahotniuc's Democrats. What I wanted to find out is whether the boycotters of the recall referendum actually intended to maintain the *status quo* by not allowing the two major parties and their related interest groups – the PSRM and the PDM – to remain the sole political competitors via a definitive elimination of PL's mayor, Dorin Chirtoacă.

The perception of the geopolitical stake of the referendum

The Moldovan citizens credited with a huge geopolitical importance the possible replacement of the pro-Western mayor with a pro-Russian one. The outbreak of this corruption affair, which led to the indictment of Dorin Chirtoacă, to his suspension and, ultimately, to the recall referendum, was initially reflected by the media and perceived by the public opinion as yet another indication of the endemic corruption that permeated the Moldovan institutions. However, it rapidly switched to being presented as affair settling of scores between different political factions (the President's Socialists, Plahotniuc's Democrats, and the remainder of the Liberal Party, opportunistically allied with Maia Sandu's new opposition) and between different institutions (the Chișinău City Hall, the Anti-Corruption Centre (CNA), the Presidency and the Government). As the recall campaign advanced, it was even rebranded as a critical choice between the West (boycotting the referendum) and the East (voting for Chirtoacă's recall). It is a widely held public belief that Dorin Chirtoacă resisted throughout time not mainly because of his administrative skills but rather because of his undisputable pro-Western and pro-Romanian commitment (LKP, 2017). Hence, the 'geopolitical factor' was to work like this: the recall referendum boycotters internalized the geopolitical-stake argument and the recall referendum participants were rather indifferent to it.

The focus group results

The popular mistrust of institutions and parties

The FG research revealed that this mistrust factor was indeed relevant. The motivations of the first two FG members for having boycotted the referendum were almost similar. Most

FG2 participants explained that they had boycotted the 2017 recall referendum precisely because, as one of them put it, it was another 'useless and fake political show' (*V.I., housewife, former absentee in 2015*). Among the Chirtoacă's former voters of FG1, the resentment against institutions, parties and politics in general was slightly lower but still very present, with the variation that it naturally concerned the pro-Russian politicians much more than the pro-Western ones:

> There is no wrongdoing in Moldova that is not due to the Bolsheviks. Most parties and institutions are controlled by them and this is why Moldova has never properly distanced itself from the former Moldovan SSR. [*Soviet Socialist Republic – m.c.*] (*D.C., manager, former Chirtoacă voter in 2015*)

At the same time, the FG1 and FG2 participants tended to despise the whole political and institutional system, the latter also being convinced that the country's current organization was meant to

> [...] alienate the Moldovans, to push the most skilled ones to leave forever, and to allow whoever is left to remain in power. Who are they? All, literally all of them, from the Liberals to the Communists and from the so-called Democrats to the Socialists. (*A.N., unemployed, former absentee in 2015*)

By contrast, among the FG3 members, trust in institutions and especially in the 'cohesive patriotic action of the Church, of the Army and of the Head of State' (*A.K., schoolteacher, Socialist voter in 2015*) was significantly higher. The members of FG3 did not only have a general better opinion about leaders and institutions (and, to a lesser extent, about parties), but they distinguished between 'strong, traditional and necessary' institutions and 'artificial ones, imposed by NATO and the EU' (*S.O., public officer, Socialist voter in 2015*). They also pointed out that Chirtoacă's alleged corruption deeds reflected a plan of the West to 'steal the national assets' and to 'weaken the legitimate state institutions' (*T.T., worker, Communist voter in 2015*). All in all, the boycotters had a lower opinion about the political and the institutional framework and actors, while the participants in the recall referendum believed that such initiatives could be a remedy against the institutional system's shortcomings and a bulwark against the destructive interferences 'of the West'.

The perceived decisive importance of the capital's control nationwide

Within the FGs, the questions concerning the essential importance of the capital city and the need of the key-players to control it were answered affirmatively by all of the FG1 participants and by most of the FG2 ones. The FG discussions emphasized the preoccupation of Chirtoacă's voters to protect 'their mayor':

> - If *they* take over Chișinău, they could easily take over Moldova as a whole. (*P.V., student, former Chirtoacă voter in 2015*)

> - We won't allow this, that's for sure, we will keep our mayor, that's the best thing we have and this says a lot about what Moldova unfortunately is. (*O.N., consultant, former Chirtoacă voter in 2015*)

The FG debates also highlighted the acknowledgement by most of the FG2 members of the fact that control over the capital was the 'real stake of the recall referendum and not frauds or corruption' (*A.I., dentist, former absentee in 2015*). As one of the FG2 participants pointed out,

> Nobody is so dumb to believe that it is precisely now that they have discovered the parking affair and that they have not all been involved in it, as well as in other similar schemes. What they wanted was the City, for themselves and only for themselves. (*L.I., driver, former Liberal-Democrat voter in 2015*)

However, unexpectedly, the FG3 participants were not significantly less inclined to attribute such a great importance to control over the Chişinău mayoralty. In fact, they claimed to have mobilized themselves precisely to 'get rid of an obscenely corrupt mayor' (*E.B., retired, former Socialist voter in 2015*). Moreover, some FG3 members pointed out the political advantage that President Dodon would bring if he were to be elected mayor of the capital city 'for the first time since Independence' (*L.P., nurse, former Socialist voter in 2015*). For them, the emergence of a 'serious mayoral candidate, who would make a difference by comparison with Chirtoacă's vicious clique' would be the only chance the city had in order 'to survive and to become again a respected capital' (*A.K., schoolteacher, Socialist voter in 2015*). Consequently, this factor (b) acted in both ways and did not determine the differentiation between the boycotters and the voters: both those who boycotted the referendum and those who participated had mobilized themselves because they believed that the matter of political control over Chişinău was critically important.

The citizens' will to prevent the concentration of power

The FG-based research allowed me to check the validity of the assumption that the citizens' intention to prevent the dominance of only one or of some political forces had contributed to the referendum's failure. This intention was naturally more obvious in the case of the first FG members, who had voted for Chirtoacă before and who wanted to keep him in office since they believed that 'we should prevent the spread of the *Red Evil*' (*D.G, writer, former Chirtoacă voter in 2015*). Still, it also proved to be the dominant opinion of the FG2 participants. As one of them put it in a suggestive and metaphoric way,

> I didn't vote in 2015 because I don't think either Chirtoacă or Dodon [who was his opponent in the second round – *my comment*] was fit to lead our Capital. But this time, for the recall referendum, I certainly wanted to avoid Plahotniuc and Dodon, who are in fact allies and not at all enemies, remaining the only wolves to gut the Moldovan lamb. [*G.R., electrician, former absentee in 2015*]

The fear that the overall governance of Moldova was to be seized by those who were perceived to be a couple of true-false opponents – President Dodon and PD's leader Plahotniuc – was widely spread also among most FG participants, including the less open and talkative ones, and, paradoxically, even among some members of the third FG. Two of the seven FG3 participants in the referendum who had voted against the recall of the mayor – one of them by wrongfully believing that this was actually the strategy of the anti-recall opposition, the other because of the fact that she 'has never missed a single election since 1991' (*N.O., musician, former Our Party voter in 2015*). Beside these two particular cases, other two FG3 participants – both belonging to the Russian speaking minority and having voted in favour of the deposition of the Mayor – expressed their concerns about the overwhelming power of Vladimir Plahotniuc, while being also sceptical about the authenticity of the rivalry between the latter and President Dodon:

> Dodon's liability is his lack of courage in dealing with Plahotniuc. He should put an end to this connivance and crush this dangerous tycoon. But, at the same time, he should teach Maia [Sandu – m.c.], Ghimpu and Chirtoacă a lesson, for their corruption and anti-Moldovan sentiments are notorious. [*A.U., engineer, former Socialist voter in 2015*]

Thus, for themselves and for other FG3 participants (four out of seven), the need to 'put an end to the Chirtoacă-Ghimpu mafia-like regime in Chişinău' (*O.B., retired, former Socialist voter in 2015*) was more important than any other political consideration, including the risk of its replacement by another group of influence.

The perception of the geopolitical stake of the referendum

Most participants in the first FG were convinced that 'what was at stake in the referendum was the very future of Moldova – either with Russia or with Romania and Europe' (*A.C., bartender, former Chirtoacă voter in 2015*). Moreover, the FG1 members described the 'putsch attempt against the elected mayor' as 'an extension of Russia's new war against Eastern Europe' (*R.R., designer, former Chirtoacă voter in 2015*). In the same vein, some of the FG2 participants argued about the 'artificiality of the anti-corruption campaign' against Chirtoacă (seen as the scapegoat of 'an entirely corrupt system') and about the fact that it was crucially important to 'show *them* that they are not allowed to play with the Moldovans like they play with kindergarten kids and that the country is not for sale to Moscow' (*L.I., driver, former Liberal-Democrat voter in 2015*).

The FG3 participants were more inclined to de-dramatize the consequences of the vote and to defend the idea that the entire transformation of this corruption affair into a historically decisive turning point was meant to deflect attention from the real issue, namely the 'theft of Moldova by the so-called pro-European parties, starting with the PL' (*student, too young to vote in 2015*). For the recall referendum participants, the fact that Chirtoacă was a pro-Romanian leader and had close relations with the former Romanian President Traian Basescu, who supported the Moldovan unionists, was definitely not a factor that the citizens of Chişinău had to take into consideration when they cast their vote in the public consultation of November 2017. Rather, 'they had to remove a corrupt mayor, it was as simple as that' (*N.O., musician, former Our Party voter in 2015*). Therefore, this factor's influence proved to be real: as fantasist as it may have appeared to some of the participants in the recall referendum, the argument according to which the vote was to decide not just the removal from office of an allegedly corrupt politician, but the historic fate of the Republic of Moldova persuaded the boycotters against going to the polling stations.

Conclusions

The complexity of Moldova's political landscape and the alleged implications of what a successful recall referendum might have generated over-inflated the different actors' need to transform the public consultation into a political war about the country's future. How did the citizens perceive the nature of the recall referendum and their role within it? Out of the four factors I tested in my research, three proved to be relevant, while the fourth proved to have no bearing over the voters' reasons to participate in or to boycott the recall referendum. Indeed, the popular mistrust of institutions and parties reinforced the citizens' strategy to boycott the public consultation rather than to participate in it and vote against the recall of the mayor. Moreover, the citizens of Chişinău who boycotted the referendum feared the concentration of power into the hands of the two main political competitors – the Socialists and the Democrats – and wanted to prevent this by keeping the Liberal Dorin Chirtoacă in office. More importantly, they perceived the referendum as an effort to replace a pro-Western mayor with a pro-Russian one, and, by doing so, to crush the sole non-cooperative opponent to President Dodon's plan to completely place Moldova within the orbit of Moscow's influence. By contrast, the focus groups revealed that the perception of the decisive importance of the Capital's control was not a factor of differentiation between the boycotters and the participants, as both groups believed that holding Chişinău was a particularly valuable asset for any political competitor[1].

More generally, we may conclude that the 2017 referendum for the recall of the Mayor of Chişinău was a widely relevant political process because of several reasons. First, it emphasized the difficulties of applying one of the most useful tools available to citizens in dealing with their representatives. Theoretically, the citizens' empowerment through their right to recall their mayors should boost their civic interest and participation (Serdült & Welp, 2017). However, as the case presented above shows, the conditions related to the participation quorum turned the recall campaign from a debate about the mayor's actions into one about voters' mobilization and demobilization strategies. Given the recurrence of the participation threshold criteria needed to validate recall referendums in different political systems worldwide, my present case study suggests the need for a more comprehensive future comparative research, with multiple theoretical and empirical implications.

Then, because it highlights the voters' penchant for countering what they perceive as the establishment's interference in their local affairs. Referendums fail if their promoters appear to be 'aliens' who intrude, by initiating the recall procedure, into the well-established relations between a mayor and his or her constituents. Citizens react by building a wall around their mayors and reject the intrusion by developing various forms of local patriotism, as recent research also shows (Serdült, 2015; Welp, 2016). The failure is more severe if the recall referendum is thought to be initiated by and to benefit of groups who have little to do with the politics of that city.

This research also emphasizes the particular development of the citizens' views on the significance of the recall referendum. As theory and other empirical research imply (Qvortrup, 2011), citizens are less inclined to have an opinion during the first indirect institutional stages of the recall procedures and, consequently, they are rather willing to act in a conformist way (which, in this case, means accepting the recall procedure or being indifferent to it). Initially, those who are undecided seem to be numerous and more interested in the concrete issues for which the recall may have been convoked. Eventually, however, throughout the debates organized during the recall campaign, they become increasingly interested in the wider (real or imaginary) implications of that recall referendum and, because of the new magnitude attributed to the issue, they will exert much greater cautiousness in considering the possibility of deposing their mayor. Thus, an element to follow in future research will be the conditions that foster the extension of the meaning of recall referendums and the impact of that extension on their final results.

Finally, this research opens the way for a more exhaustive reinterpretation of the theses related to the nature of such consultations: to a greater extent than other public consultations, local recall referendums are rarely only about recalling an elected official. Instead, both political players and citizens perceive them as occasions to settle a series of other political accounts. Political actors use the opportunity to gain various comparative advantages in relation with their competitors and allies, while citizens see them as a chance to deliver messages of support or, more frequently, of discontent. Further research could use the findings of this study in order to contribute to the understanding of the broader and intertwined implications of recall referendums. In this respect, the issue of whether the meaning of a participation threshold can certify the existence of the people's will to recall an official or to enforce a transparent mechanism in order to politically sanction an elected politician appears to be considerably relevant.

Note

1. Several months after the conclusion of this research, in February 2018, Dorin Chirtoacă resigned from his office in order to provoke the organization of early municipal elections, which were expected to be more favourable to the pro-Western parties than the on-term elections scheduled for 2019. Andrei Năstase, the leader of the Truth and Justice Platform, succeeded in defeating the PSRM candidate in a tight but clear second round vote, but the elections were annulled by the court in June 2018 for alleged violations of the electoral law. This was denounced by the European Parliament and the Western embassies as a judicially-orchestrated anti-democratic coup. These developments stress once again the importance that the major power-players grant to control over the Capital of Moldova.

Disclosure statement

No potential conflict of interest was reported by the author.

References

Böhme, D. (2004). *Die Abwahl von Bürgermeistern – Institution und Praxis*. [The Election of Mayors – Institution and Practice]. Bamberg: Universität Bamberg.

Călugăreanu, V. (2017, July 26). What's Next for Moldova? *Deutsche Welle*. Retrieved from www.deutschewelle.org

Catterberg, G., & Moreno, A. (2006). The individual bases of political trust: Trends in new and established democracies. *International Journal of Public Opinion Research*, *18*(1), 31–48.

Creswell, J. W. (2014). *A concise introduction to mixed methods research*. London: Sage.

Cronin, T. E. (1989). *Direct democracy. The politics of referendum, initiative and recall.* Cambridge, MA: Harvard University Press.

Dresden, J. R., & Howard, M. M. (2016). Authoritarian backsliding and the concentration of political power. *Democratization, 23*(7), 1122–1143.

Garret, E. (2004). Democracy in the wake of the California recall. *University of Pennsylvania Law Review, 153,* 239–284.

Gherghina, S. (2017). Direct democracy and subjective regime legitimacy in Europe. *Democratization, 24*(4), 613–631.

Gilley, B. (2006). The determinants of state legitimacy: Results for 72 countries. *International Political Science Review, 27*(1), 47–71.

Goşu, A. (2016). Republica Moldova: ce urmează? *Revista 22, 95,* 1932.

Hale, H. E. (2014). *Patronal politics: Eurasian regime dynamics in comparative perspective.* Cambridge: Cambridge University Press.

Henry, V., & Mişcoiu, S. (2016). Le discours politique et la quête identitaire en République de Moldavie [political discourse and identity search in the Republic of Moldova]. In S. Mişcoiu, & N. Păun (Eds.), *Intégration et désintégration en Europe Centrale et Orientale. Cahiers FARE no. 9* (pp. 221–254). Paris: l'Harmattan.

Hug, S., & Tsebelis, G. (2002). Veto-Players and referendums around the world. *Journal for Theoretical Politics, 14*(4), 465–515.

Ipp. (2015). *Barometrul de Opinie* [Barmometer of Public Opinion]. Institutul de Politici Publice. [web page]. Retrieved from www.ipp.md

Iri. (2017, February-March). *Opinion Survey on the Trust in Institutions.* [web page]. International Republican Institute – Magenta. Retrieved from www.iri.org/country/moldova

Jimenez, W. (2001). Revocatoria del mandato: Experiencias, dificultades, ajustes necesarios. *Territorios, 5,* 35–48.

Kalu, K. N. (2006). Citizenship, administrative responsbility, and participation in governance: One more look. In N. Kakabadse, & A. Kakabadse (Eds.), *Governance, strategy and policy: Seven critical essays* (pp. 73–94). New York: Palgrave.

Kennedy, R. (2010). Moldova. In D. Beachain, & A. Polese (Eds.), *The colour revolutions in the former soviet republics* (pp. 221–245). London: Routledge.

Kersting, N., & Vetter, A. (2003). *Local government modernization in Europe. The closing the gap between democracy and efficiency.* Opladen: Leske and Budrich.

Kriesi, H. (2005). *Direct democracy choice. The Swiss experience.* Lanham: Lexington Books.

LeDuc, L. (2003). *The politics of direct democracy.* Toronto: Broadview Press.

Lkp. (2017, May). *Extensive Research on the Public Support for Institutions.* [web page]. Lake Research Partners. Retrieved from www.lkpsec.com

March, L. (2007). From moldovanism to Europeanization? Moldova's communists and nation building. *Nationalities Papers, 35*(4), 601–626.

Mendelsohn, M., & Parkin, A. (eds.). (2001). *Referendum democracy: Citizens, elites, and deliberation referendum campaigns.* Basingstoke: Palgrave Macmillan.

Mişcoiu, S. (2014). Moldova. In S. Habdank-Kołaczkowska (Ed.), *Nations in transit. Democratization from Central Europe to Eurasia* (pp. 431–446). London: Rowman and Littlefield.

Necşuţu, M. (2017, December 18). Vlad Plahotniuc, Moldova's Unloved 'Puppet Master', *Balkan Insight.* Retrieved from www.balkaninsight.com

Quinlan, P. (2004). Back to the future: An overview of Moldova under Voronin. *Demokratizatsiya, 12* (4), 485–504.

Qvortrup, M. (2011). Hasta La Vista: A comparative institutionalist analysis of the recall. *Representation, 47*(2), 61–70.

Qvortrup, M. (2014). *Referendums around the world: The continued growth of direct democracy.* Basingstoke: Palgrave MacMillan.

Rallings, C., Thrasher, M., & Cowling, D. (2002). Mayoral referendums and elections. *Local Government Studies, 28*(4), 67–90.

Schiller, T. (ed.). (2011). *Local democracy in Europe.* Wiesbaden: VS Verlag für Sozialwissehschaften.

Schmitter, P. (2000). *How to democratize the Euro-polity and Why bother*. New York: Rowman and Littlefield.

Secrieru, S. (2011). The transnistrian conflict – new opportunities and old obstacles for trust building (2009–2010). *Southeast European and Black Sea Region Studies*, *11*(3), 241–263.

Serdült, U. (2015). A dormant institution - history, legal norms and practice of the recall in Switzerland. *Representation – Journal of Representative Democracy*, *51*(2), 161–172.

Serdült, U., & Welp, Y. (2017). The levelling up of a political institution. Perspectives on the recall referendum. In S. P. Ruth, Y. Welp, & L. Whitehead (Eds.), *Let the people rule? Direct democracy in the twenty-first century* (pp. 137–154). Colchester: ECPR Press.

Setälä, M. (1999). Referendums in Western Europe – A wave of direct democracy. *Scandinavian Political Studies*, *22*(4), 327–341.

Smith, G. (1976). The functional properties of the referendum. *Journal of Political Research*, *4*(1), 1–23.

Timpul. (2016, December 21). Ce se intampla cu Chișinăul? [What Happened with Chisinau?] [web page]. Retrieved from www.timpul.md

Tudoroiu, T. (2015). Democracy and state capture in Moldova. *Democratization*, *22*(4), 655–678.

Uleri, P. V. (2002). On referendum voting in Italy: Yes, no, or non-vote? How Italian parties learned to control referendums. *European Journal of Political Research*, *41*(6), 863–883.

Way, L. (2003). Weak states and pluralism: The case of Moldova. *East European Politics and Societies*, *17*(3), 454–482.

Welp, Y. (2013). ¿Por qué Perú? Análisis de la revocatoria del mandato en perspectiva comparada [Why Peru? An analysis of recall in comparative perspective]. *Elecciones*, *12*(13), 13–51.

Welp, Y. (2016). Recall referendums in Peruvian municipalities: A political weapon for bad losers or an instrument of accountability? *Democratization*, *23*(7), 1162–1179.

Welp, Y., & Rey, J. (2015). Recall referendum and direct democracy. An analysis of the recent experiences in Bogota and Lima. *Anuario Lationoamericano. Ciencias Politicas y Relaciones Internacionales*, *2*, 71–84.

Appendix

Characteristics of the FG participants.

FG no.	Initials	Age	Sex	Profession	Attitude in the 2015 municipal elections
FG1	D.C.	37	M	manager	Chirtoacă voter
FG1	P.V.	24	F	student	Chirtoacă voter
FG1	O.N.	45	M	Consultant	Chirtoacă voter
FG1	D.G.	52	M	writer	Chirtoacă voter
FG1	A.C.	28	F	bartender	Chirtoacă voter
FG1	E.N.	37	F	Secretary	Chirtoacă voter
FG1	P.F.	41	M	Unemployed	Chirtoacă voter
FG1	R.R.	25	M	Designer	Chirtoacă voter
FG2	V.I.	48	F	housewife	absentee
FG2	A.N.	54	F	unemployed	absentee
FG2	A.I.	36	M	dentist	absentee
FG2	L.I.	51	M	driver	PLDM
FG2	E.B.	68	F	Retired	PSRM
FG2	G.R.	51	M	Electrician	absentee
FG2	U.N.	24	F	Saleswoman	PLDM
FG3	A.K.	47	F	schoolteacher	PSRM
FG3	S.O.	53	M	public officer	PSRM
FG3	T.T.	61	M	worker	PCRM
FG3	L.P.	46	F	nurse	PCRM
FG3	N.O.	58	F	Musician	Our Party
FG3	A.U.	51	M	Engineer	PSRM
FG3	O.B.	72	M	Retired	PSRM
FG3	U.I.	20	F	Student	too young to vote

Direct democracy in an increasingly illiberal setting: the case of the Hungarian national referendum

Zoltán Tibor Pállinger

ABSTRACT

Since 1989 seven nation-wide referendums have been held in Hungary. However, the function of direct democracy remained unclear. It is by no means insignificant, but its use is confronted with two major challenges: Hungary's political system is extremely majoritarian and predominantly representative. The conceptional and practical flaws limit the interaction between the representative and direct-democratic system, thereby restricting the development of more deliberative forms of politics. The paper will give an overview on the practice of direct democracy and will show how the ruling elites use direct-democratic instruments to gain political dominance. It also wants to contribute to the clarification of the role of direct democracy within a representative political system on a theoretical level and to help to better understand functional changes of direct democracy in the process of hybridisation. In terms of methodology, this paper represents a theory-led cross-section through Hungary's democratic history.

Introduction

There is an ongoing debate whether democracy is in crisis, but the notion of 'crisis' can be questioned. Whereas the different challenges in different spheres of democracy, do not add up the deconsolidation of established democracies (Merkel, 2014), the situation in Central Eastern Europe appears to be more nuanced. Coman and Tomini (2014) bluntly state that democracy in the region is in a crisis, which generally can be characterised by abuses of power, attempts to break the constraints of checks and balances and to centralise executive power. This tendency goes hand in hand with the intensification of nationalist and populist politics (Ágh, 2015). Within this trend Hungary seems to represent a special case:

> The case of Hungary remains the most puzzling. While it was set as a model of democratic consolidation in the EU's post-communist space, it also experienced the most severe challenges to democratic institutions that have taken place in the region since the end of communism. (Herman, 2016, 258)

These trends are also reflected in several democracy rankings like Freedom House (https://freedomhouse.org/) or Bertelsmann Transformation Index (https://www.bti-project.org/en/home/). Summing up, the 'chaotic democracy', which existed in Hungary until 2010, degraded into a Potemkin façade democracy and went even further down to an electoral autocracy after the elections of 2014 (Ágh, 2015). However, the democratic backsliding took place, whilst Hungary maintained its membership in the EU. This fact is influencing the system's unique characteristics in two ways: on the one hand, EU membership constrains to a certain degree the Hungarian government's marge de manoeuvre; on the other hand, it provides legitimation and material resources as well, thereby contributing to the stabilisation of the system. Bozóki and Hegedűs (2018) coined the term 'externally constrained hybrid regime' to describe the state of the precarious equilibrium between democratic and non-democratic components, which is characteristic of the current Hungarian political system.

The democratic system established after 1989 was influenced by the negotiated transition. Fearing that the state party could prevail in free elections, the opposition insisted on institutional guarantees for securing democratic transition. Therefore, strong power-sharing elements like a mixed-member electoral system, a strong Constitutional Court (CC), the requirement of a 2/3 majority for constitutional changes and for important acts were included in the new constitutional system. However, the party system evolved in the direction of a two-party system and the competition between the two main party blocks became more intense and divisive, thereby weakening the institutions of consensus democracy, like the parliament, the CC, the independent National Bank and interest groups (Bozóki, 2012). In 2010 the Fidesz Party (Fidesz – Magyar Polgári Szövetség; Fidesz – Hungarian Civic Alliance) and its ally the Christian Democratic People's Party (Kereszteny Demokrata Néppárt – KDNP) won a landslide victory in the elections, giving them a 2/3 majority in the parliament. Because of the near collapse of the former ruling parties, the former two-party system became a dominant-party system. The majority enabled the Fidesz-led government to adopt a new constitution (Fundamental Law, FL), without being dependent on the support of any opposition party. The FL was criticised for undermining the rule of law, the separation of powers, and thereby also democracy itself (Scheppele, 2013), however Victor Orbán, leader of the Fidesz Party and Prime Minister, argued that the electoral victory of 2010 gave his government a mandate to complete the transition and to lay the foundations of a consolidated democratic system. He describes this new system with the term 'illiberal democracy' (Orbán, 2014). In the wake of the financial crisis of 2008, the Fidesz-led government seized the opportunity to re-centralise power and strengthen the central government vis-à-vis local governments even more by invoking the necessity to concentrate power in order to be capable of effective crisis management. This line of reasoning fit perfectly into the government's conception of politics: on the institutional level, the majoritarian elements of the system have been reinforced against the consensual ones. Checks and balances have been weakened, independent institutions like the CC, the National Bank were filled with loyal party supporters, the position of the executive and especially that of the Prime Minister were strengthened, and also the electoral law became more majoritarian and more disproportionate. Furthermore, the government is increasingly targeting critical NGOs, thereby curtailing the room for manoeuvre of oppositional civic groups. The Fidesz-led government is very conscious of its power and willing to utilise it without compromising in order to reform the society according to its own vision. Shortly after it came to power, the new government claimed to have created a new political community, the so-called System of National Cooperation (Nemzeti Együtmüködés Rendszere), which should ensure that the country develops along a stable path which is defined by popular will, which in turn is embodied by the ruling parties. This provides an ideological justification of exclusionist politics (Pap, 2018). According to Antal current Hungarian politics can be characterised by strong populist tendencies: 'Before 2010 the populist forces were opposition parties and the post-2010 period is the era of governing populism in Hungary' (2017, 5). While the populist forces tend to monopolise political representation by excluding certain groups from politics, this variety of populism leads to repoliticisation of all the segments of Hungarian society (Antal, 2017).

In such a situation the room for manoeuvre of the opposition is limited. The parliamentary way for pursuing its agenda is barred. Because the governing parties are also dominant in the media, the opposition has to turn to alternatives: under such circumstances the use of referendums could be an appropriate tool. One would assume that the frequency of use of referendums has accelerated since 2010, but quite the contrary is true. Between 2010 and 2017 only one referendum was held which moreover was initiated by the government. It is therefore the aim of this paper to explain the use of referendums in Hungary on the national level[1] and why the opposition was not able to resort to this instrument more often. Furthermore, it also wants to contribute to the clarification of the role of direct democracy within a representative political system on a theoretical level and help to better understand functional changes of direct democracy in the process of hybridisation. In terms of methodology, this paper represents a theory-led cross-section through Hungary's democratic history.

Direct and representative democracy

Direct democracy can be defined as an institutional arrangement by which citizens have the right to decide factual issues themselves, meaning that they are allowed to raise issues on the political agenda or decide some factual issues by vote, without the mediation of the parliament. Thereby, three types of direct-democratic instruments can be discerned. Instruments triggered by government authorities, mandatory referendums and citizens' initiatives (Schiller, 2016). The use of direct-democratic instruments has quadrupled during the twentieth century. This increase can be attributed to the third wave of democratisation, the process of European integration and to growing discontent with the functioning of representative democracy (Marxer & Pállinger, 2007). Therefore, direct democracy is often seen as appropriate tool to counter the 'democratic malaise' (Newton, 2012, 3). However, the increasing use of direct-democratic instruments has not supplanted representative democracy anywhere, but only complemented it (Altman, 2011). Contrary to the assumption that direct democracy weakens party rule per se, Hornig has demonstrated that political parties have generally adjusted their strategies, using direct democracy as a tool in the political competition. Thus, direct democracy is on the average not an instrument of breaking the dominance of the political parties, but rather tends to reproduce their relative strength (Hornig, 2011).

The functions and effects of direct-democratic instruments cannot be determined a priori, as they depend on their design and their attunement to the representative system: on the one hand they have to be formally compatible with the representative process and the legal system, but on the other hand they also have to conform to the functional logic of the political system (Marxer & Pállinger, 2007). The possibility of the use of direct-democratic instruments can enhance the regime's legitimacy (Ghergina, 2017). By refining the possibilities of preference articulation, by furthering accountability and elite control, and by enhancing participation, which in turn strengthens citizens' capabilities and knowledge, direct democracy can contribute to the improvement of democracy's quality (Newton, 2012).

Direct democracy can display contradictory effects. Smith proposes a typology which differentiates direct-democratic instruments according to the degree of control exercised by political authorities upon the whole procedure and their effects on the position of the government. According to Smith, there is a continuum between the poles from 'controlled' to 'uncontrolled'. The outcome of the referendum may be supportive or detrimental to government's positions (pro- or anti-hegemonic) (Smith, 1976).

Direct-democratic instruments may be further differentiated regarding the competence to trigger the procedure, the competence to define the subject of the referendum question, the character of decision (decisive or approving), and the procedural rules (counting rules, existence of quorums, etc.) (Jung, 2001). Instruments that are triggered by a political majority and decided by a simple majority of votes tend to have majoritarian effects, whereas instruments triggered by a political minority and decided by qualified majorities tend to display consensual effects.

Governments initiate referendums to strengthen their position, to solve intra-party or intra-coalition disputes, to push through legislative projects against resistance, in order to pre-empt topics from being used in the election campaign and for the legitimisation of important political questions (Morel, 2007). Opposition parties on the other side initiate referendums to push through legislative projects against the resistance of the majority, to enhance their chances in the forthcoming elections, to delay unwanted government initiatives and to take on an issue (Vospernik, 2014). In this context, one also has to mention that governing as well as opposition parties can use referendums for the mobilisation of their supporters. Based on these findings Vospernik takes the analysis a step further linking direct democracy to the consensus – majoritarian typology of Lijphart (Vospernik, 2014). For him the main differentiating factor regarding direct-democratic instruments is the authorship and their effectiveness. Taking only decisive referendums into account, he distinguishes between governmental, oppositional and obligatory processes of direct democracy which can be effective or not. Thus, the impact of the direct-democratic instrument is dependent on the interrelation of authorship and effectiveness (Vospernik, 2014). Government-initiated referendums are consensus-oriented, when ineffective, i.e. when the government loses. They are majoritarian, when they are effective, i.e. when the government wins.

Opposition-initiated referendums are consensus-oriented, when effective, which means that the opposition wins the referendum or the following election. They are majoritarian if they are ineffective, which means that opposition parties permanently lose referendums. Finally, obligatory referendums display consensual effects, when opposition parties are included in the decision-making process or if the government decides single-handedly and is defeated. However, if the government wins a referendum that it has triggered without including the opposition the obligatory referendum displays majoritarian effects (Vospernik, 2014). Based on these arguments, Vospernik postulates that on the one hand governmental direct democracy has an affinity for majoritarian democracy and that an intense oppositional direct democracy is not compatible with majoritarian democracy, therefore direct-democratic instruments are only used rarely in majoritarian democracies. On the other hand, oppositional direct democracy has an affinity for consensus democracy. But in the case of one-party cabinets the use of direct democracy tends to be strongly oppositional (Vospernik, 2014). Furthermore, one has to consider that the impact of direct democracy also depends on the frequency of its use, having the most profound effects in countries in which these instruments are applied as a routine procedure and form an integral part of the political system (Marxer & Pállinger, 2009).

Modern polities exhibit a fundamentally representative foundation of political power, direct democracy thus can be seen as a complementary institutional device, which performs specific functions for the (representative) system. In such an understanding direct democracy is a dependent variable of the type of democracy. When the latter changes, the functions and usage of direct democracy will change correspondingly. According to Vospernik's thesis the Hungarian political system – being predominantly representative and majoritarian – should not make intense use of direct-democratic procedures, therefore also their impact should be limited. Taking into account the reinforcement of the majoritarian traits of the Hungarian political system during the last few years, a further weakening of direct-democratic decision-making should be observable.

The legislation on direct democracy in Hungary

Direct-democratic instruments, introduced during the democratic transition in 1989, were alien to Hungarian political traditions and caused since their introduction a problem regarding their adjustment to the predominant representative system. Therefore, in a first phase, the CC grew into the position of a major actor in shaping direct democracy by clarifying procedural ambiguities. Its fundamental decisions became guiding principles for the parliamentary law-making.

In 1997 the parliament amended the constitution (Act 1997/XCVIII) and the act on referendum and popular initiative (Act 1998/III), thereby lowering the approval threshold from 50% to 25% and clarifying some procedural questions. In 2011 the parliament adopted the new FL, which restored the 50% participation threshold, abolished the agenda initiative and the parliament's competence to initiate a nation-wide referendum. Finally, the parliament adopted a new act on referendum and popular initiative (Act CCXXXVIII/2013), which implemented the new basic law's provisions and brought further procedural clarification.

The Hungarian FL (Art. B, Sect. 2 FL) states that direct democracy should be restricted to exceptional cases; the representative mode of exercising power should be the norm. Being the supreme organ of popular representation (Art. 1, Sect. 1 FL), the parliament possesses the legislative monopoly and budgetary sovereignty (Art. 1, Sect. 2, Lit. a-c FL). However, if a citizens' initiative leads to a successful referendum, the direct exercise of power supersedes the representative. In this case, the parliament has to execute the 'popular will' by legislating corresponding measures (Ruling 52/1997 (XI. 14) of the CC). This conception has two problematic aspects: firstly, there seems to be a contradiction between the principles of the parliament's legislative monopoly and the binding character of a successful referendum. This tension is somewhat relaxed in practical terms: popular votes can only decide factual questions, whereas it is the parliament's duty to enact the corresponding bills. It is a political obligation which can't be enforced legally. Secondly, the process of popular law-making and the process of parliamentary/representative law-making are completely separated. The whole procedure – in the case of a successful referendum – 'is under the influence of the interested citizens' (Ruling 52/1997 (XI. 14,) of the CC). The strict procedural separation prevents a dialogue between the representatives and the civil sphere. The parliament only takes a formal decision on conducting the ballot and providing the necessary funding. However, a substantive discussion on the referendum question doesn't take place. Furthermore, the parliament is permitted neither a recommendation for the attention of the citizens, nor is it allowed to make a counter-proposal.

Instruments

As Article 8, Section 2 FL states: 'National referendums may be held about any matter falling within the functions and powers of the National Assembly.' The constitution provides for three types of referendums (Art. 8, Sect. 1 FL). The constitutional changes of 2011 did not basically alter the instruments of direct democracy. The three kinds of referendums were typologically unchanged. However, the old 'proper' agenda initiative, which existed in the old constitutional setting, was abolished.

Popular initiative (Art. 8, Sect. 1 FL): 200,000 eligible voters can initiate a so-called national referendum, which aims at deciding a political question or expressing an opinion. The result of a successfully held referendum is binding on the parliament (Art. 8, Sect. 4 FL). Now, there is a 50% + 1 participation threshold, whereas between 1997 and 2012 there was a 25% + 1 approval quorum. The new provisions represent a return to the original rules, which were in force between 1989 and 1997 (Komáromi, 2014). The triggering of this instrument is not controlled and its effects can be either pro- or anti-hegemonic. Typically, this instrument would be used by oppositional parties either to push their agenda through against the will of the government or to veto governmental propositions.

Popular agenda initiative (Art. 8, Sect. 1 FL): based on its own consideration, the parliament can schedule a 'national referendum' upon the initiative by 100,000 eligible voters. This kind of referendum aims at deciding a political question or expressing an opinion. If the referendum is successful, the results are binding for the parliament (Art. 8, Sect. 4 FL). The abovementioned participation threshold is also applied to this instrument. Because the triggering depends on the parliament's discretion this instrument can be classified as controlled. It is very unlikely that the governing majority would call for a referendum if the proposition is put forward by opposition groups. However, it is conceivable that the governing majority might call for a referendum which is initiated by its supporters but was not able to gather the necessary 200,000 signatures for the full-scale initiative. This provision opens up a possibility for the governing elite of arena switching in order to mobilise their supporters. However, there is risk by applying this instrument, because its effects cannot be controlled in advance and they may be either pro- or anti-hegemonic.

Plebiscite (Art. 8, Sect. 1, FL): based on its own consideration, the parliament can schedule a 'national referendum' upon the initiative of the president or the government, which aims at deciding a political question or expressing an opinion. If it is successful, the results are binding on the parliament (Art. 8, Sect. 4 FL). Under the old constitutional regulations, one-third of the members of parliament were also entitled to initiate a plebiscite (Act 1949/CC, Sect. 28/C [4]). According to the majoritarian logic of Hungarian parliamentarianism, this instrument is government-controlled, however, there is also a risk, because it is not possible to control its effects in advance, which may either be pro- or anti-hegemonic.

At first glance, the subject matter of the initiatives seems to be quite comprehensive. However, in the next section, the FL constricts the scope of possible subjects (Art. 8, Sect. 3 FL). The FL and act on referendum and popular initiative have, to some extent, contributed to the clarification of some open questions. Most importantly the ban on constitutional initiatives, which was not regulated in the former constitution, has been made explicit and absolute.

Procedures

The current procedures have evolved through an interplay of legislative acts and rulings of the CC. The first major steps were the constitutional changes of 1997 and the ensuing Act on Referendum and Popular Initiative. These steps helped to properly establish the role of the National Election Commission (NEC) and redesigned the procedures regarding citizens' initiatives.

The present act on referendum and popular initiative is an attempt to reduce the number of 'unserious' initiatives by introducing the requirement that at least 20 citizens have to support with their signature the initiative proposal and giving the president of the National Electoral Office (NEO) the right to examine preliminarily the proposal's compliance with the legal prerequisites and to reject it within five days. There is no appeal against this decision, but the unaltered proposal may be submitted again and must be put on the agenda of the NEC. Furthermore, the treatment of concurring initiatives has been clarified: in case of initiatives dealing with the same subject, priority is given to the one which was submitted first. The process has been made unambiguous, avoiding contradicting legislative demands on the parliament. Seemingly logical in theory, these provisions became very problematical in practice (see below). The time limits were also modified and the initiators have the right to withdraw the proposal before the submission of the signatures. Finally, also the system of legal remedy has been reformed. Appeals against decisions of the NEC have to be addressed to the Kúria (administrative court) instead of the CC. Also new is that the Kúria may alter the NEC's decision in its stead. Before, the only possibility was to order the NEC to re-decide the question, which in the past could lead to continuous iterations. There is still in some exceptional cases the possibility of appeal to the CC (Komáromi, 2014).

The popular initiative process starts with the initiators submitting a specimen of the signature sheet to the NEC for validation, which denies validation if the question does not meet the legal requirements. After the validation, the proponents have 120 days to collect the necessary signatures. Afterwards, the NEC has to validate the collected signatures. If the proposition meets the legal requirements the parliament has to put the question on the agenda within 30 days. In the case of the popular agenda initiative or the plebiscite, the parliament must take a formal decision on conducting the ballot. If 200,000 or more valid signatures are collected, the parliament must schedule the referendum and provide the necessary funds. After the parliament's decision, the President has 15 days to call to call for the national ballot. The referendum is valid if more than 50% of the voters have participated and more than half of them are in favour of the proposition. In case of a successful referendum, the parliament has to pass a bill which implements the content of the popular decision. The current procedures are not very 'user-friendly', they are very detailed and offer numerous points for legal, administrative and political interventions, thereby rendering the process non-transparent.

The practice of direct democracy

Transition-related referendums in 1989/1990

The first two nation-wide referendums ever held were related to the democratic transition. The Hungarian Socialist Party's (Magyar Szocialista Párt – MSZP) reached an agreement with the opposition in September 1989, which laid the foundations for the new democracy and had to be implemented by the parliament. Two opposition parties, the Alliance of Free Democrats (Szabad Demokraták Szövetsége – SZDSZ) and Fidesz, wished for more radical changes. They aimed at dismantling the instruments of power of the MSZP and also wanted the state party to render an account of its belongings. They also asked to postpone the presidential elections until after the general elections. After a successful collection of signatures, the parliament was obliged to call a referendum. The MSZP was ready to discuss some of the questions, and, in fact, the parliament implemented some of the requested measures, rendering two of the initiatives unnecessary. But there were no legal means to withdraw the obsolete proposals. The presidential elections and the disclosure of the MSZP's accounts, however, remained a stumbling block. The referendum campaign helped the radical opposition to raise its popularity. In the referendum on 29 November 1989, the MSZP was defeated on all four questions. This frustrated its attempts at retaining at least some of its power (Babus, 1990).

After the general elections in 1990, the former opposition came into power and the MSZP was marginalised. It tried in turn to strengthen its position and initiated a referendum on the question of whether the president should be elected directly by the citizens. It succeeded in gathering the necessary signatures and the parliament had to schedule the ballot. The referendum, which was held on 29 July 1990, failed, because of the low turnout. With these two ballots, the immediate phase of transition was concluded.

European integration

The referendum on NATO accession in 1997 was initiated by the parliament and the referendum on EU accession in 2003 was prescribed by the constitution. Both referendums were government-led and effective. These foreign-policy-related referendums were highly symbolic and served the purpose of legitimising Hungary's western integration. However, considering the traditionally low level of political participation in Hungary (Tardos, 2009), the parliament even had to change the 'rules of the game' for the 1997 referendum by lowering the participation threshold in order to guarantee a positive outcome. It also had to change the constitution in 2002 (Act 2002/LXI) in order to make a popular vote on EU accession possible.

Referendums in a consolidated democracy

The 2004 ballots were triggered by popular initiatives; they were searching to achieve narrowly defined, concrete goals. The extra-parliamentary MP (Munkáspárt – Worker's Party) began the successful collection of signatures in the autumn 2003, aiming at the cancellation of the privatisation in health care. In December 2003 the CC declared the concerned law, which provided for the privatisation in health care, unconstitutional, but the popular vote had to be held nevertheless. However, due to the legal struggles, it only could be scheduled for 5 December 2004. Due to this and the saliency of the other referendum on the dual citizenship (see below), the campaign was not very disruptive. Opinion surveys show that the citizens' decisions were motivated by individual attitudes and assessments rather than by party-based ideological positions. Meanwhile, in the spring of 2004, the World Federation of Hungarians started a successful collection of signatures for a referendum which aimed at granting Hungarian citizenship to ethnic Hungarians living abroad. The referendum was also scheduled for 5 December 2004. In general, the conservative parties have a more supportive stance on these issues than the liberal and left-wing parties. Knowing the symbolic value of this question, the governing MSZP kept a relatively low profile, whereas the conservative Fidesz Party was supportive of the proposition. This campaign was more ideologically charged and intense than the other. Nevertheless, as in the other question, voters' decisions were more influenced by individual attitudes and assessments than by ideological, party positions. Both referendums were invalid due to low voter turnout (Karácsony, 2009).

Deconsolidation and the struggle for power

Hungarian politics has become increasingly polarised during the second half of the last decade. The MSZP was able to win the general elections of 2002 and 2006. After the election of 2006, it became clear that the country's financial situation was worse than expected. The government was forced to cut back state spending. National health care and tertiary education stood, among others, at the top of the government's reform agenda. The measures that were announced from June 2006 onwards, rapidly eroded the government's popularity. During the campaign for the regional elections in autumn of 2006, a non-public speech given by Prime Minister Gyurcsány in May to the members of the socialist parliamentary group was leaked to the media and became publicly known in September. The Prime Minister admitted that his government had lied to the public about the state of the country (Szoboszlai, 2009). The conservatives and the extreme right started protests and riots at Parliament's Square. On 2 October 2006, Gyurcsány announced that he would ask for a vote of confidence against himself. Opposition leader Orbán dismissed this proposal and issued an ultimatum to the MSZP to dismiss Gyurcsány and to start negotiations with the opposition about the instalment of an expert cabinet. If these demands were not met, he threatened, the opposition would call for mass demonstrations. On 6 October, the parliament expressed its confidence in the prime minister, which led to new protests.

Recognising the futility of its endeavours, the opposition nevertheless sought to retain its momentum and came up with the idea to overthrow the government by referendum. Opposition leader Orbán declared on 23 October 2006 that a referendum against the government's austerity measures would be 'the last remaining democratic instrument' to oust the government (Bartafai, Fischer, & Schindler, 2009). With recourse to referendum Fidesz aimed at directing the protests into constitutional channels and at sustaining the pressure on the government.

On 24 October 2006, the conservative opposition deposited seven referendum proposals at the NEC for validation, which were carefully chosen and covered a wide range of interest groups that were affected by the government's austerity measures. After a lengthy legal struggle, at which core lay a conflict between the CC and the NEC on how to interpret the list of excluded issues in the constitution, the NEC approved on 25 June 2007 three questions (Szoboszlai, 2009).

The austerity measures were very unpopular, therefore, the opposition had no problems collecting the necessary signatures and the parliament had to schedule a referendum for 9 March 2008. The opposition successfully turned the referendum into a judgement on the government's policies (Karácsony, 2009). After the opposition's triumph at the ballot box, all the three fees were abolished. But there were also indirect consequences: the governing coalition fell apart, and the MSZP had to form a minority government. Thus, the referendum helped the opposition to retain momentum until the next general elections in 2010, in which they gained a landslide victory.

The colonialisation of direct democracy

The referendum struggles between 2006 and 2008 encouraged other groups to launch referendums. Only two of these initiatives met all the formal criteria. They were scheduled for ballot, but the ballot was finally prevented by the elite's manoeuvres. The first referendum, initiated by two private citizens, aimed at preserving the unitary health insurance system and preventing private investment in the healthcare sector. The parliament decided on 9 June 2008 to call a referendum although it had already cancelled the reforms in May. Therefore, it was not obliged to call for referendum, because the subject matter of the referendum had ceased to exist. It did not, however, want to take the blame for an action that would have potentially contradicted the people's will. Some private persons appealed to the CC which annulled the parliament's decision and instructed it to re-decide the case. Therefore, the parliament had to cancel the referendum on 19 November.

In the context of the abolition of fees referendum campaign, a private citizen made an initiative, according to which MP's expenses would only be refunded if accompanied by an official invoice. This initiative was very popular. On 17 April 2009, the parliament had to call for referendum. It was clear that such a proposal would have a direct influence on the MPs' financial situation. Therefore, the parliament decided on 29 June to modify the law on the MPs' expenses. These modifications went formally in the same direction as the initiative but were merely semantic with regard to the substance. Most of the expenses were transformed into regular wage elements and the amount of payments stayed roughly the same. Some private persons appealed to the CC against the parliament's decision to call a referendum. The CC annulled the parliament's decision and instructed it to cancel the referendum.

The next example of a prevented referendum concerns the question of shop opening hours. In autumn 2014 the government decided to impose a ban on Sunday sales. This measure was very unpopular and incited different civic groups and opposition parties to formulate popular initiatives to lift the ban. These proposals could have served as common platform. Ultimately, these attempts proved unsuccessful, but it also became clear that the question of the ban on Sunday sales had a great potential. In the following months, a strange race between supporters and opponents of the ban took place. The supporters of the ban took advantage of the ban on concurring initiatives: during the Kúria's proceedings, it was not possible to submit a new question for validation during 90 days. They started to submit apparently inadmissible proposals, thereby blocking the opponent's initiative. Due to the formalistic practice of the NEC, this approach proved very successful.

The possibility of submission of the proposal began at the moment the Kúria's decision was released online. From this moment on, it was possible to submit new proposals personally at the NEO's office, and their chronological order was determined by a time clock. Supporters of the ban were successful in pre-empting opponents, sometimes by seconds. Supposedly, there was also foul play going on. This 'game' went on from spring 2015 until 23 February 2016, when MP István Nyakó was prevented by some strongmen, which were standing and shuffling around him, from submitting his proposal. Instead, the strongmen helped an old lady (the wife of a former Fidesz deputy mayor) to submit her proposal first. These tumultuous scenes were made public and stirred a storm of indignation. These strongmen, who were working as subcontractors for a private security company owned by one of the vice presidents of Fidesz, were supposedly acting out of political motivation to intimidate the opposition. The concerned vice president of Fidesz, of course, denied any involvement on the nation-wide television news channel Hír TV (https://hirtv.hu/). Nevertheless, the NEC validated initial proposal and saw no problem in the fact that Mr Nyakó was impeded by force. Furthermore, it validated the question, although it should have been dismissed on formal grounds. This was widely seen as a political decision by the NEC. The Kúria annulled the NEC's decision to validate the question of the old lady on April 6 because she was only able to submit first through the help of the strongmen. Thus, István Nyakó's question had to be considered as having been correctly submitted and therefore valid. This decision opened the possibility for signature collection on a topic that was very popular. The government reacted quickly and revoked the ban on Sunday sales on 12 April 2016, thereby preventing a potentially successful and therefore threatening campaign by the opposition. Another result was that the act on referendum and popular initiative was later modified, reforming the impracticable prescriptions on concurring proposals.

There was also a final case of a prevented referendum in the autumn of 2017. A soon as the NEC validated a question of the oppositional MP Gábor Vágo for prolonging the statute of limitation for corruption to 12 years, the parliament adopted – as the oppositional newspaper Magyar Nemzet reported – the corresponding amendment of the penal code, thereby pre-empting another possibly popular topic for the opposition (https://www.mno.hu/). Between 2009 and 2016 no referendum was held. From 2010 on the governing parties had a two-thirds majority in parliament, which allowed them to enact a new constitution and profoundly alter the political system. The opposition was not able to halt the governing parties. In such a situation, initiatives could have been an instrument to influence the government's policy, but no successful initiative was launched. However, between 2012 and 5 June 2016, 328 questions were submitted to the NEC for validation. Only 15 were validated; 313 were rejected. Most of the questions were rejected on grounds of ambiguity (62%), formal errors (48%), bona fides/proper use (16%) and competence of the parliament (12%) (Farkas, 2016, p. 111).[2] 79% of these proposals were submitted by private persons, 16% by political parties and only 5% by civic organisations and NGOs (Farkas, 2016, p. 36).

Thus, it can be stated that the NEC's (and also the CC's) reasoning is very formalistic and has a negative attitude towards popular participation. The no-ambiguity-rule is interpreted in an especially narrow sense. Since the implementation of the new FL the judicial branch has been weakened and has become more supportive of the government's policies (Szente & Gárdos-Orosz, 2018). Although the opposition is disunited and was not able to organise effective anti-government campaigns between 2010 and 2016, all but one of the 10 successful citizens' initiatives which led to a referendum to date, were initiated by opposition parties. This shows that a successful initiative needs considerable organisational capacities, which only parties can provide. The (parliamentary) parties are acting successfully as cartel parties in order to prevent access of new actors to the political arena via popular initiatives.

By campaigning permanently since 2010, the governing parties are seeking to mobilise support in their favour. In 2010 they created a new instrument the so-called National Consultation (Csink & Kovács, 2015). This instrument is informal and has no legal basis. Citizens are invited to express their opinion via a questionnaire on a topic chosen by the government. The answers are evaluated by the administration and made public. To date there have been seven National Consultations on (1) questions regarding pensions, in which only retired persons were consulted (2010), (2) guiding principles of the new constitution (2011), (3) social questions, (4) economic questions (2012), (5) questions regarding 'immigration and terrorism' (2015), (6) seeking the citizen's support regarding controversial questions with the EU 'Stop Brussels' (2017) and (7) mobilising support against an European migrant quota (the so-called Soros Plan). These consultations are highly controversial: the questions are manipulative and it is not clear, how the questionnaires are analysed. Furthermore, the costs of the National Consultations have to be paid for by the taxpayers. Whereas the governing parties stress their will to take into account people's opinions, the opposition criticises the National Consultation as populist measures of propaganda.

Against the background of the growing numbers of migrants, the question of migration got at the top of the Hungarian political agenda even before the migrant crisis reached its peak in August 2015. Reacting to the European Commission's idea on migrant relocation, Jobbik (Jobbik Magyarországért Mozgalom – Jobbik, the Movement for a Better Hungary) requested in May 2015 a referendum against the migrant quota in case that idea should be adopted by the EU and announced in a press conference that it started to collect signatures (https://www.jobbik.hu). This attempt must be seen as a political action, which aimed at mobilising the party's supporters, because the referendum proposal was never submitted. In any case, it would have fallen under the forbidden topics clause of the FL, because it aimed at the modification of international treaties. Consequently, Jobbik proposed a bill for changing the FL allowing referendums on international obligations if they affect Hungary's immigration policy, which was not put on the parliament's agenda.

Meanwhile, the governing parties started signature a collection of their own for a petition against the quota in November. On 24 February 2016 the prime minister announced that the government would submit a referendum proposal whether to accept mandatory EU quotas for relocating migrants with the concrete question 'Do you want the European Union to be entitled to prescribe the mandatory settlement of non-Hungarian citizens in Hungary without the consent of the National Assembly?'[3] The NEC validated this proposal on 29 February 2016, but the decision was legally challenged. However, the Kúria confirmed on 3 May the decision of the NEC. According to the Kúria the proposed referendum did neither aim at changing the accession treaty nor at applying additional conditions at the implementation of decisions of EU organs by Hungary. This decision was severely criticised by civic organisations like the Hungarian Helsinki Committee (Magyar Helsinki Bizottság), which claimed that the referendum question did not meet the constitutional standards, because it did not fall within the functions and powers of the parliament and was moreover not unambiguous (https://www.helsinki.hu/). The parliament decided on 10 May to order a referendum. Both the decision of the Kúria and that of the parliament were challenged at CC, but the court dismissed the appeals and the president scheduled a nation-wide referendum for 2 October 2016.

In Hungary, three outcomes are possible for referendums. Either the 'yes' or 'no' votes win or the referendum is invalid. These framework conditions determine the possible campaign strategies for the political actors. Because of the wording of the referendum question the government – and also Jobbik – had to campaign in favour of a 'no' vote. For the government, the optimal outcome would be a majority of 'no' votes and a participation rate of more than 50% of all eligible voters. Since it was clear from the onset that a vast majority of the voters opposed the relocation quota, the opponents of the referendum were in a difficult situation, because – as the opinion research institute Ipsos pointed out – also their supporters were not in favour of the quota (https://www.ipsos.com/hu-hu). Therefore, they theoretically should support the government's proposal, but considering the polarisation of Hungarian politics, this was not a viable option. That's why, the optimal outcome for them would be an invalid referendum. Therefore, they either had to call for a boycott of the referendum or for casting invalid votes. This logic determined the course of the campaign and the arguments which the actors put forward.

In spite of the long and intense campaign only 41.32% of the voters cast a valid vote, therefore, the referendum was not valid.[4] All parties assessed the result according to their previous position. Would the referendum have been conclusive and valid, there would have been no possibility to change the constitution, but under these circumstances, the government seized the chance to initiate a constitutional amendment. Not disposing of a two-thirds majority, the government tried – ultimately unsuccessfully – to reach an agreement with opposition parties. Afterwards, the governing parties were using their defeat to denounce the opposition as being unpatriotic and jeopardising Hungary's security. However, the governing parties came finally out as winners of this struggle, because they were able after their repeated electoral victory in 2018 to implement the provisions of the referendum – with the support of Jobbik – through a new amendment of the FL on 20 June 2018 (http://www.parlament.hu/).

Conclusions

In accordance with the theoretical expectations, the scope of direct democracy in Hungary has been limited since the beginning. The application of the new instruments was gradually fine-tuned through an interplay between judiciary and legislative actions. During the first and second decade of the existence of direct democracy in each period, six referendums were held. Successful referendums were held in order to legitimise the country's Western integration and occurred also during political crises. Since 2009 only one government-initiated referendum has been held, but numerous referendum proposals were fended off by the NEC and prevented/pre-empted by the governing majority.

Because of the prevalence of the representative system, direct democracy is continuously pushed back. Political parties adapted the use of the direct-democratic instruments to the system's logic. Nowadays, direct democracy is primarily used (and controlled) by the political elite as a tool to mobilise their supporters. In this sense, direct democracy is 'colonialised' by the representative system and the political elite. Initiative proposals from outside the political elite have practically no chance of succeeding. Therefore, the control function of direct democracy is virtually non-existent.

However, as van Eeden (2018) rightly points out not all political parties were equally successful in appropriating the direct-democratic instruments: it was Fidesz which recognised its potential after the referendums of 2004 and went on to instrumentalise it for its own purposes during its struggle for power. After its landslide victory and the installation of an illiberal democracy, Fidesz is even trying to monopolise the use of direct democracy.

The reinforcement of the majoritarian traits since 2010 has also altered the quality of the system. This seems to support Antal's thesis on the role of elite populism and illiberal democracy (2017, 6). The governing elite tends to depict all its proposals as being the sole embodiment of the national interest, thereby excluding alternate proposals. Therefore, the alleged recourse to popular will is not genuine, because the governing elite tries to define the national interest exclusively and to monopolise political representation. Authentic direct democracy is replaced by pseudo instruments like the National Consultations which are completely controlled by the government, giving no room for genuine dialogue.

The separation of the citizens' and the parliamentarian law-making, impedes political learning through deliberation. Referendums occur too rarely to foster accountability. The curtailing of direct democracy through the constitutional changes, the establishment of a strong system of gate-keeping and the centralisation of political power has limited its potential for enhancing participation and further refining interest articulation. However, with the possibility of uncontrolled and anti-hegemonic decisions an element of uncertainty still exists within the political system, which may open a window of opportunity for exerting a stronger control on the governing elite. Thus, direct democracy can – in exceptional cases – function as a safety valve, but under 'normal' circumstances it is rigorously controlled by the political elite.

Since 2010 Hungary has receded into a 'diffusely defective Democracy', which combines democratic and authoritarian modes of functioning (Bogaards, 2018). In this context, the present study contributes to elucidating the process of democratic decline and shedding light on the role of direct democracy in hybrid regimes between liberal democracy and authoritarianism (Qvortrup, 2017).

Notes

1. Although the Hungarian CC provides for referendums on the local level the main focus of this paper is on the national level. Being a strongly centralised country, local authorities are dependent on the central government and represent no independent power centres. Because these tendencies have been reinforced since the accession to power of the Fidesz-led government in 2010, the importance of the local level has diminished even more and the central and most important arena of Hungarian politics lies at the national level.
2. Most questions were rejected with more than one justification, which is why the sum totals more than 100%.
3. The initial signature collection was, however, continued even after the government announced the referendum in order to mobilise the government's supporters.
4. 98.36% of the participating voters voted against the quota. Numbers retrieved from the NEO (http://www.valasztas.hu).

Disclosure statement

No potential conflict of interest was reported by the author.

References

Ágh, A. (2015). De-Europeanization and de-democratization trends in ECE: From Potemkin democracy to the elected autocracy in Hungary. *Journal of Comparative Politics, 8*(2), 4–26.
Altman, D. (2011). *Direct democracy worldwide.* Cambridge: Cambridge University Press.
Antal, A. (2017). The political theories, preconditions and dangers of the governing populism in Hungary. *Politologicky Casopis, 24*(1), 5–20.
Babus, E. (1990). Népszavazás – 1989 [Referendum – 1989]. In S. Kurtán, P. Sándor, & L. Vass (Eds.), *Magyarország Politikai Évkönyve 1989-röl* (pp. 209–215). Budapest: AULA Kiadó.
Bartafai, I. L., Fischer, M., & Schindler, P. V. (2009). Tizenkét honap krónikája [The chronicle of twelve months]. In P. Sándor & L. Vass (Eds.), *Magyarország Politikai Évkönyve 2008-ról* [Supplementary DVD]. Budapest: DKMKA.
Bogaards, M. (2018). De-democratization in Hungary: Diffusely defective democracy. *Democratization, 25*(8), 1481–1499.
Bozóki, A. (2012–2013). The transition from liberal democracy: The political crisis in Hungary. *Meditations, 26*(1), 1–23.
Bozóki, A., & Hegedűs, D. (2018). An externally constrained hybrid regime: Hungary in the European Union. *Democratization, 25*(7), 1173–1189.
Coman, R., & Tomini, L. (2014). A comparative perspective on the state of democracy in Central and Eastern Europe. *Europe-Asia Studies, 66*(6), 853–858.
Csink, L., & Kovacs, J. T. (2015). *National Consultation in a constitutional aspect: Direct democracy or political marketing?* Unpublished manuscript, The Research Group on Participatory Democracy of the Faculty of Law and Political Sciences of the Pázmány Péter Catholic University and the Centre for Democracy Studies at the Danube Institute of the Andrássy University Budapest, Budapest.
van Eeden, P. (2018). *Discover, instrumentalize, monopolize: Fidesz' three-stepped blueprint for a populist takeover of referendums.* Manuscript submitted for publication.
Farkas, B. (2016). *Direkte Demokratie in Ungarn: Warum scheitern Volksinitiativen?* [Direct democracy in Hungary: Why do popular Initiatives fail?] (Unpublished master's thesis). Andrássy University Budapest, Budapest.
Ghergina, S. (2017). Direct democracy and subjective regime legitimacy in Europe. *Democratization, 24*(4), 613–631.
Herman, L. E. (2016). Re-evaluating the post-communist success story: Party elite loyalty, citizen mobilization and the erosion of Hungarian democracy. *European Political Science Review, 8*(2), 251–284.
Hornig, E.-C. (2011). *Die Parteidominanz direkter Demokratie in Westeuropa* [Direct democracy's party dominance in Western Europe]. Baden-Baden: Nomos.
Jung, S. (2001). *Die Logik direkter Demokratie* [The logic of direct democracy]. Wiesbaden: Westdeutscher Verlag.
Karácsony, G. (2009). A népszavazási döntések motivációi Magyarországon [The motives of the referendum decisions in Hungary]. In Z. Enyedi (Ed.), *A Népakarat dilemmai. Népszavazások Magyarországon* (pp. 197–225). Budapest: Századvég Kiadó.
Komáromi, L. (2014). *A népszavazásra vonatkozó szabályozás változásai az Alaptörvényben és az új népszavazási törvényben* [The changes of the regulations regarding the referendum in the Basic

Law and the new act on the referendum] (MTA Law Working Papers, Working Paper 35/2014). Budapest: MTA Társadalomtudományi Kutatóközpont, Jogtudományi Intézet.

Marxer, W., & Pállinger, Z. T. (2007). System contexts and system effects of direct democracy – direct democracy in Liechtenstein and Switzerland compared. In Z. T. Pállinger, B. Kaufmann, W. Marxer, & T. Schiller (Eds.), *Direct democracy in Europe. Developments and prospects* (pp. 12–29). Wiesbaden: VS Verlag.

Marxer, W., & Pállinger, Z. T. (2009). Stabilising or destabilising? Direct-democratic instruments in different political systems. In M. Setälä & T. Schiller (Eds.), *Referendums and representative democracy. Responsiveness, accountability and deliberation* (pp. 34–55). London: Routledge.

Merkel, W. (2014). Is there a crisis of democracy? *Democratic Theory, 1*(2), 11–25.

Morel, L. (2007). The rise of 'politically obligatory' referendums: The 2005 French referendum in comparative perspective. *West European Politics, 30*(5), 1041–1067.

Newton, K. (2012). Curing the democratic malaise with democratic innovations. In B. Geissel & K. Newton (Eds.), *Evaluating democratic innovations. Curing the Democratic Malaise?* (pp. 3–20). London: Routledge.

Orbán, V. (2014, July 29). Full text of Viktor Orbán's speech at Băile Tuşnad (Tusnádfürdő) of 26 July 2014. Retrieved from http://budapestbeacon.com/public-policy/full-text-of-viktor-orbans-speech-at-baile-tusnad-tusnadfurdo-of-26-july-2014/10592

Pap, A. L. (2018). *Democratic decline in Hungary: Law and society in an illiberal democracy*. London: Routledge.

Qvortrup, M. (2017). The rise of referendums: Demystifying direct democracy. *Journal of Democracy, 28*(3), 131–152.

Scheppele, K. L. (2013). The rule of law and the Frankenstate: Why governance checklists do not work. *Governance, 26*(4), 559–562.

Schiller, T. (2016). Direkte Demokratie in der vergleichenden Politikwissenschaft [Direct democracy in comparative politics]. In H.-J. Lauth, M. Kneuer, & G. Pickel (Eds.), *Handbuch vergleichende Politikwissenschaft* (pp. 441–452). Wiesbaden: VS Springer.

Smith, G. (1976). The functional properties of referendum. *European Journal of Political Research, 4*(1), 1–23.

Szente, Z., & Gárdos-Orosz, F. (2018). Judicial deference or political loyalty? The Hungarian Constitutional Court's role in tackling crisis situations. In Z. Szente & F. Gárdos-Orosz (Eds.), *New challenges to constitutional adjudication in Europe. A comparative perspective* (pp. 89–110). London: Routledge.

Szoboszlai, G. (2009). Országos népszavazás 2008-ban. Elözmények, következmények, szabályozások és értelmezések. Szavazzunk-e arra, hogy többet fizessünk? [National referendum in 2008. Antecedents, consequences, rules and interpretations. Should we vote on paying more?]. In P. Sándor & L. Vass (Eds.), *Magyarország Politikai Évkönyve 2008-ról* (pp. 244–272). Budapest: DKMKA.

Tardos, R. (2009). Ötven: ötven: Részvétel és távolmaradás a 2008-as népszavazáson [Fifty-fifty: participation and abstention in the referendum of 2008]. In Z. Enyedi (Ed.), *A népakarat dilemmái. Népszavazások Magyarországon és a nagyvilágban* (pp. 133–195). Budapest: Századvég Kiadó.

Vospernik, S. (2014). *Modelle der direkten Demokratie. Volksabstimmungen im Spannungsfeld von Mehrheits- und Konsensusdemokratie – Ein Vergleich von 15 Mitgliedstaaten der Europäischen Union. Mit einem Vorwort von Arend Lijphart* [Models of direct democracy. Referendums in field of tension between majoritarian and consensus democracy – a comparison of 15 member states of the European Union. With a Preface by Aredn Lijphart]. Baden-Baden: Nomos.

Deliberative democracy and trust in political institutions at the local level: evidence from participatory budgeting experiment in Ukraine

Dmytro Volodin

ABSTRACT

Deliberative democracy assumes that management decisions based on open voluntary and fair procedures are rational and just. This article presents arguments that deliberative democracy can bolster trust in democratic institutions. Moreover, deliberative practices can increase citizens' level of political trust not only in stable democracies but also in hybrid regimes. This is demonstrated through an examination of participatory budgeting in Ukraine, with the use of data from a field experiment in 2015–2016 (with 740 participants).

Introduction

Democratic theory has suggested that for democracy to be effective it needs citizens who trust in the governing institutions (see Norris, 2011; Rothstein & Stolle, 2008; Sztompka, 1999). Nevertheless, the current long-term trend of decline in trust for national governments and other political institutions shows that 'trust is in short supply' (Asen, 2013) in almost all advanced democracies. Moreover, some scholars connect this decline in trust (Armingeon & Ceka, 2013) with other negative tendencies, such as the drastic drop in voter turnout (Siaroff, 2009) and political involvement. Bearing in mind these tendencies, a lot of scholars argue that contemporary democracies are experiencing a 'crisis', 'the end of representative politics' (Tormey, 2015), a kind of 'deficit' (Meny, 2003; Moravcsik, 2002; Norris, 2011) and even 'death' (Keane, 2009).

It seems that current representative democracy, through its mechanism of the election, is unable to provide effective opportunities for citizens to participate and influence the decision-making process (Gherghina, 2017). Moreover, if people believe and see the decision-making process in their country to be ineffective, the level of trust in institutions responsible for this process will be eroded. Therefore, currently, we can observe that public skepticism towards politicians and government officials is spreading to almost all of the advanced industrial democracies (Kumlin, 2013). These aspects are supported by a number of empirical researchers (see Amnå & Ekman, 2013; Hooghe & Kern, 2017; Van Biezen, Mair, & Poguntke, 2012) and data from various surveys, including the World Value Survey and the European Social Survey.

The contemporary theory of democracy (for instance Hetherington, 2005; Newton, 2018; Uslaner, 2002) proposes a number of solutions on how trust could be improved, and one of the approaches here is the theory of deliberative democracy.

This article uses the theory of deliberative democracy as a basic concept for several reasons. First of all, some studies show that participation in deliberation creates a psychological effect which gives citizens more confidence in politics (Morrell, 2005). Moreover, current literature on deliberative democracy (see Festenstein, 2005; Hauser & Benoit-Barne, 2002) identifies deliberation as a potential source of trust; however it concentrates mostly on interpersonal trust, lacking proper explanation of how deliberation is connected with political trust.

In this paper, I take up a question hitherto underexplored in the deliberative democracy literature: how does deliberation influence the level of political trust in deliberative settings?

As deliberation leads to more inclusive and wider participation, to improved democratic skills and knowledge about political processes among ordinary citizens, I argue that deliberation can bolster trust in political institutions and such an outcome is also confirmed by several case studies which will be described later in the text.

Furthermore, I believe that particularly in the case of 'hybrid' regime,[1] implementations of deliberative practices are more important than for stable democracies. In hybrid regime, a low level of trust can erode immature democratic institutions and therefore, the process of transition could be postponed. Additionally, population and elites could question the efficiency of a democratic form of government as they see negative tendencies in countries which for years were promoted as successful democracies, and as a consequence ask for non-democratic solutions.

These arguments are tested in the context of Ukrainian hybrid democracy, using data on people's political trust before and after participation in participatory budgeting in Chernivtsi, a regional centre in southwestern Ukraine, with the use of data from a field experiment in 2015–2016.

My reasons in this paper develop over three main sections. In the first section, I distinguish the potential impact of deliberation on the decision-making process in general and the level of trust in particular. This is followed by a discussion about the relationships between deliberation, deliberative democracy and political trust. The second section presents the research design, in which I explain the case selection and research methods used. In the last section, I present and interpret the empirical results of the deliberative experiment at the local level in Ukraine.

Theoretical underpinning

I understand deliberation as a process of reasoned exchange of arguments, the use of which enables a group of people to express their opinions about the defined problem and to try to reach a collective decision through prepared communication. At the same time, deliberative democracy can be described as a form of democracy in which a systematical deliberation is a core approach to improving the collective decision-making process. It involves citizens who can produce collective consequential decisions by offering reasons to one another in the best interests of consensus, or supposedly to avoid conflicts (Fung, 2005; Parkinson, 2006).

The existing literature has a number of different examples and cases which describe the potential and main advantages of deliberation in particular and deliberative democracy in general.

First, deliberative democracy assumes that management decisions based on open voluntary and fair procedures are rational and just. In addition, deliberative democracy produces more responsibility for decision-making and provides social cohesion between individuals from different backgrounds (Fishkin, 2011); therefore, the outcome of deliberative events will be accepted as politically legitimate. Current research shows that deliberation was a crucial element in legitimizing decisions achieved during constitutional reforms in Ireland (Farrell, O'Malley, & Suiter, 2013), Iceland (Landemore, 2015) and Romania (Gherghina & Miscoiu, 2016).

Second, the authorized citizens will have a real influence on decision-making processes through the knowledge that their participation in the activities of deliberative democracy will have a valuable impact on society (Ross, 2011). Deliberation helps to clarify controversies among citizens and justify their decisions. It creates much more empathy, develops one's civic position and improves the quality of opinions.

Third, the process of deliberation has a significant, positive educational effect. Participation in deliberation increases knowledge on the topic of deliberation (Fishkin & Luskin, 2005) and produces 'civic virtue', which can be understood as the 'creation of more active, informed and cooperative citizens with more developed democratic capabilities' (Worthington, Rask, & Minna, 2013, p. 51).

Scholars have offered some explanations of how deliberative democracy could bolster trust in democratic institutions. However, before presenting their ideas, I should devote more attention to the concept of trust itself.

Social science proposes a number of approaches to how various aspects of trust, including political trust, can be defined, classified and measured (see Almond & Verba, 1963; Giddens, 1990; Sztompka, 1999; Uslaner, 2002). This article focuses on political trust in institutions as an indirect measurement of citizens' belief in the institutions which govern them (Newton, 2018; Zmerli & Hooghe, 2013). These beliefs are transformed into citizen support for such institutions and they frequently assess these institutions from the perspective of the benefit which they could or should provide. Therefore, political trust is based on the pursuance of citizens' expectations by political institutions (Chiru & Gherghina, 2012).

Political trust has direct effects on both the long-term stability of the regime and its effective functioning. If in a particular country there is a high level of political trust, it means that a long-lasting confident relationship between the government and the citizens has been achieved. Therefore, even if government decisions are unpopular in the short run, people will believe that long-term benefits will be provided. Also, according to various scholars (Norris for example[2]), political trust can enhance the public's acceptance of democratic values and ideals. Therefore, it is crucial for hybrid regimes to improve the level of political trust, as this could help the citizenry to accept democratic values and norms. However, this is a twofold approach – declining political trust could bring dissatisfaction among citizens in democratic principles and norms.

In the case when political trust is very low for a long time, the situation will erode the legitimacy of a regime, which is the main pillar of the democratic system. On the other hand, a high level of political trust among citizens in political institutions in the democratic system creates public space which can motivate political actors to implement more innovative political decisions.

How deliberative democracy can enhance trust in democratic institutions? For example, Hauser and Benoit-Barne (2002, p. 271) argue that deliberation has a significant potential to build trust among citizens by building a 'civic community based on relations of collaboration'. Additionally, as outlined by Festenstein (2005, p. 143): 'Deliberation … can enhance fidelity among participants and promote respect for diverse viewpoints … therefore deliberation can build trust'.

From the practical perspective, Font and Blanco (2007) proved that citizen juries in Spain, in situations when they have procedural legitimacy, make an essentially positive contribution to the building of political trust (relating to a sense of citizenship and engagement in public affairs; citizens' influence in decision-making; and their capacity to produce outputs that more closely mirror their preferences).

In analyzing political trust and deliberation, more attention should be paid at the local level – the level of local bodies and communities. It is the first stage in which citizens face the authorities and, particularly here, people could learn how to participate in the decision-making process and explore practical results of deliberation. If political trust was improved at this level (local), it could create a basis for enhancing the level of trust on a national scale (this is a logical chain: participation in deliberative events at the local level together with other potential outcomes could increase the level of political trust – citizens who see practical results of deliberation will trust the deliberative approach more – deliberative experience will be transferred from the local level to national level – citizens that participate in a variety of deliberative practices at national level will trust institutions that initiate and support such deliberative practice).

Although the number of instruments associated with deliberative democracy is huge, this article considers that the implementation of participatory budgeting will have a more visible impact on political trust at the local level. Despite the fact that some scholars (Cabannes, 2004) argue that participatory budgeting should be classified as instruments of participatory democracy, I strongly support an idea, that if the process of participatory budgeting includes deliberation than this process should be classified as deliberative. It is not a form of collective advise as the final decision on the projects is done by voters (and about project priorities and project ideas by authors and participants of the participatory budgeting process) and the allocation of money is approved by the city officials before the start of the whole participatory budgeting process (allocation for participatory budgeting is approved together with the whole city budget). Unlike many other deliberative instruments, which concentrate mostly on one aspect in the decision-making process, participatory budgeting covers all of the stages: from setting up priorities in a deliberative process (through deliberation between involved parties) to decision-making and on to co-implementation, accompanied by monitoring and control (Khutkyy, 2017). It can work at different levels of governance: town districts, city level, or even states. As participatory budgeting involves citizens and local officials, who are responsible for financial aspects, the following logic is visible: the citizens' trust in officials increases when they (citizens) see that officials use fair processes that focus on equality, respect, honesty and lack of favoritism (Van Ryzin, 2011, p. 745). Moreover, one of the most recent results from a participatory experiment in New York shows that citizens' trust in local government was expanded by participating in participatory budgeting (Swaner, 2017).

Bearing in mind arguments which have been presented before, my idea is to find out whether in other political realities (hybrid space) the same result (an increase of trust) could be achieved. Therefore, following hypothesis has been formulated and tested in the empirical section of this paper:

> H: Implementation of deliberative practice in the decision-making process is expected to increase the level of citizens' political trust at the local level.

Research design

Overview

Attempting to verify the hypothesis that implementation of the PB model could increase the level of political trust at the local level, together with the local NGO[3] a field experiment was organized in the city of Chernivtsi, a regional city centre in southwestern Ukraine, where the PB model was launched in 2016.

Current empirical efforts and progress consist of the consultation of variety of documentation, several participants interviews that have been carried out, as well as field observation of a deliberation. To ensure data reliability, a triangulation of data sources was attempted through seeking information not only through secondary written resources but also participant interviews and a field observation of a deliberative event in Chernivtsi.

The research itself was conducted in three phases: (1) The preparatory survey: the main goal of the first round was to evaluate the level of initial political trust in Chernivtsi and to select the next target group for analysis – people who declare their wish to participate in the further deliberative event. As a result of this stage, initial data on citizens' political trust in local institutions was obtained. This stage was based on inclusive participation that was insured by random selection of the participants; (2) the analysis of a particular participatory budgeting event and its deliberative component and (3) the post-survey related to a measure of the citizen's level of political trust after participation in deliberation. The main goal of this stage was to evaluate the potential change in the level of political trust within the selected city.

The following sections would offer some brief discussion on local context and specificities of the first participatory budgeting examples in Ukraine, the case selection as well as the actual methods utilized together with some considerations and challenges encountered.

Local context

Despite years of transition and two 'Maidans' (The Orange Revolution in 2004 and Euromaidan in 2014), Ukraine is still classified as a hybrid regime. The situation is made worse by the fact that the level of trust in political institutions in Ukrainian realities is very low.

All available research shows that Ukrainians have little trust in institutions. Based on the data of the World Social Survey Wave 6, this situation could be illustrated in the following way: among state and society institutions, Ukrainian citizens have the greatest confidence in the Church (66.2% of respondents) and the Ukrainian Armed Forces (60.9%) (Table 1).

Table 1. The level of political trust among Ukrainian citizens (2005–2015), %.

	Ukraine		
How much you trust:	2005–2009	2010–2014	2015
The church	64.4	75.2	66.2
The armed forces	51.4	58.7	60.9
The legal system	29.3	25.2	13.4
The police	31.6	31.6	24.6
The national parliament	17.5	20.4	27.2
Political parties	15.1	22.0	12.7
The national government	23.6	25.4	28.7

Source: WWS and study of the Sociological Service of the Razumkov Centre from 2015.

Deliberation in the decision-making process is almost completely absent in the Ukrainian practice. Unfortunately, to this day its experience has been limited to several projects where deliberation at the local level (particularly 'mini-public forms') was used.

At the national level, despite the fact that the central authorities have an obligation to organize permanent advisory structures, only about 50% of them regularly organize public council meetings involving representatives of civil society. Also, it should be noted that the legislation about advisory bodies currently in place does not contain specific procedures for their activities; therefore, many public councils exist only on paper.

The first case which could be defined as 'deliberative' began in 2015 when, thanks to international donors support (USAID, Polish-Ukrainian cooperation initiative (PAUSI)), the participatory budgeting process was launched in Ukrainian cities such as Chernihiv, Cherkassy, Lutsk, Chernivtsi and Poltava (preparations began in 2015 but participatory budgeting itself started in 2016).

Case and sample selection

During the initial analysis of the documentation related to participatory budgeting in Ukraine (in 2016), only the city programme of participatory budgeting in Chernivtsi from the outset included information that meetings with potential authors and discussions of project proposals should be a mandatory part of the whole process. Therefore, I have selected this particular participatory budgeting process as it had more 'deliberation' than others.

From the perspective of political trust, since the level of citizens' trust in political institutions is significantly low in the whole country (according to recent sociological research), it makes no significant difference which city in Ukraine is chosen for my empirical analysis, thus Chernivtsi is a reasonable selection.

The initial group from which the sample was selected was residents of Chernivtsi city (266,005 people). On the one hand, taking the whole population into consideration, we have all residents of the city who potentially interested in active participation in the decision-making process. However, on the other hand, it is a very heterogeneous age group and not everybody would be able to participate in deliberative events and the decision-making process. Therefore, I narrowed my analysis to the group which includes people older than 18 years (the number of potential voters). According to data from the last parliamentary election, there are 189540 residents with the right to vote in Chernivtsi.

As it was expected that the sample would be small (less than 5% of the entire population), a correction factor was applied. Therefore, with confidence interval 97%;

normalized deviation 1.96 and allowable margin of error 4%, the representative sample size for the analysis was calculated – 740 people. Selection of respondents was carried out using the quota method for regional distribution (for conventional urban districts of the city). For more objectivity, the method of random selection was applied. For that purpose, the numbers of the houses (in the case of single-family houses) or apartments (in the case of tower blocks) from districts were randomly selected using a random number generator. Data was received from local building-utilities administrator offices (known as ZhEKs).

Variable operationalization

The dependent variable of this paper is political trust. This was operationalized through the answers provided by respondents to the following question: 'What is your level of trust in the following political institutions?' Subsequently, the following regional institutions were mentioned: the mayor; the city council; the regional council; the regional state administration. Respondents could rate those items on a 4-point scale, including 'do not trust at all' (E); 'rather do not trust' (D); 'hard to answer/no answer' (C); 'rather trust' (B) and 'completely trust' (A). I am not presenting in detail the level of political trust in such institutions as the 'regional council' and 'regional state administration' as they were not involved in the participatory budgeting at the city level.

Independent variable: deliberation (participation in deliberative events related to the participatory budgeting process in Chernivtsi).

Control variables: gender (male, female), age (in years), socio-economic status.

Deliberative activities and citizens' political trust: empirical verification at the local level

The first stage of the experiment: preparatory survey

The preparatory survey among the sample took place during in August 2015 covering all of the selected districts. The survey was conducted on different days of the week and at different times of day in order to reach different population groups. The biggest problem during the survey was that people (especially the 18–60 group of males) were afraid that under the guise of an opinion poll, they would receive military subpoenas and therefore withdrew from participation in the survey. During the first attempt to organize a door-to-door survey (10–15 August), 59% of people did not even open the door. Therefore, the survey was repeated in a slightly different way: a door-to-door survey and phone survey were organized in which respondents were randomly selected from the conditional urban districts (based on telephone directories). It was decided that the sample fraction for the phone survey should be bigger than for the door-to-door survey (65% and 35% of the sample, respectively). Moreover, for the phone survey, a random interval was applied – the random number was generated and used as an interval for phone number selection. The second attempt to receive answers from local was organized on 25–30 of August. It should be underlined that a number of initially selected respondents (about 102) refused to take part in the survey. Therefore, they were replaced by local residents from the same conventional urban districts; thus, the number of the sample was secured. The respondents represented almost all age groups (excluding young people under 18 years of age), levels of education, gender, financial status. Nevertheless, due to the space limit, I present main results of the survey related to issues of trust. The findings from the preparatory survey related to the level of trust are presented in Table 2 below.

The results received almost exactly correspond with data from the World Values Survey Wave 6 for Ukraine and illustrate the situation in which the level of political trust low. Based on these results, we can state that only 42% of respondents can be described as 'trusting citizens' (answers A 'completely trust' + B 'rather trust') in 'the mayor' and 35% in 'the city council'. On the other hand, 47% ('the mayor') and 52% ('the city council') of respondents can be classified as 'distrustful citizens' (answers E 'do not trust at all' + D 'Rather do not trust').

The next section of questions in the preparatory survey was dedicated to the problem of participation in the decision-making process at a local level. Intentionally, the questions did not mention 'deliberative democracy' itself as it was quite obvious that local residents had no idea about this concept or understood it rather a different way.

This group consisted of four questions:

1) Can you say that you are actively involved in civic activity?
2) In recent years, several civic councils, including representatives of non-governmental organizations and the media, were created in the city. Have you heard anything about their work?
3) Is there a need to improve civic engagement in Chernivtsi through residents' involvement in city management and the decision-making process?
4) Are you prepared to take part in civic activities to enhance the role of local residents in the process of decision-making which will be organized by the NGO?

Based on the answers to the survey question (4), 284 persons were selected for further participation in deliberative activities. Moreover, these respondents were divided into two target groups. First, 227 local residents who had no previous experience in active civic participation (Group 1) and a second group consisting of 57 persons (Group 2) who did have such experience.

According to the survey data, the level of trust in political institutions at the local level among representatives of Group 1 was slightly smaller than among Group 2. More detailed results are presented in Table 3.

Table 2. Level of trust among respondents to political institutions. Results of the preparatory survey in Chernivtsi, %.

	Do not trust at all	Rather do not trust	Rather trust	Completely trust	Hard to answer/no answer
The mayor	20	27	34	8	11
The city council	22	30	31	4	13
The regional council	21	28	26	3	22
The regional state administration	22	26	25	2	25

Source: own calculations.

Table 3. Level of political trust at local level within G1 and G2 groups (before participation in the deliberation), %.

Question: What is your level of trust for the following political institutions:	G1			G2		
	Trusting	Distrusting	Hard to answer/ no answer	Trusting	Distrusting	Hard to answer/ no answer
The mayor	31.86	57.84	10.30	28.78	61.53	9.69
The city council	33.82	56.86	9.32	44.23	53.78	1.99

Source: own calculations.

Taking these results into consideration, it is clear that residents who have any experience trust the city council more (33.82%) and this value is less than the level of trust for the same institution in the general sample (35%). The trust in 'the mayor' is, in turn, far less than for the general sample (31.86% versus 42%).

In its turn, locals with some experience in civic activity at the local level trust the city council more (44.23%), which is less than the level of trust for the same institution in the general sample; at the same time, the level of trust for the mayor is only 28.78%, much less than 42% for the general sample.

The second stage of the experiment: participatory budgeting process

Background

The general political context for implementation of such deliberative activity was rather encouraging, as the young, new mayor of the city was open to the possibility of working with the civil sector; therefore, the idea of implementing participatory budgeting on a rolling basis received support from the city council.

The draft resolution related to the participatory budgeting was approved on 31 March 2016 and on 12 May the implementation programme was accepted by the city council. All of this gave the necessary legal mandate to the whole process. The whole process was organized in the following way: from 1 July to 5 September 2016 – submission of the project proposals. All interested citizens had an opportunity to submit a special form with the project idea described.

In accordance with the decision of the city council, the total budget of the first participatory budgeting process was determined up to 1% of the city general fund revenues (without transfers). In 2016 this amount was around 13 MIO UAH (approx. 546,000 EUR). It was proposed that according to the scope and the budget, all projects be divided into two groups: the big projects with a budget of 300,000 UAH – 1 MIO UAH and the small projects with a budget up to 300,000 UAH. Moreover, it was agreed that each big project idea should be supported as a minimum by 50 local residents and the small ones by 25. This was done to involve as many local residents as possible. This process of project proposal submission was accompanied by information and education campaign provided by the city council and interested NGOs.

Deliberation

During the participatory budgeting process, the city council organized several meetings with local residents related mostly to the technical aspects of the participatory budgeting process – how to write a project, how to submit the project, necessary supporting documents, etc. In its turn, BARD organized a number of seminars and training sessions dedicated to deliberation itself and citizen enlightenment. The main goal of these meeting was to ensure that the whole participatory budgeting procedure is in line with deliberative practice (comply with deliberative criteria[4] and general model of the participatory budgeting). Each meeting was moderated by a BARD representative. Moreover, outside experts in the field of urban management (representing both governmental and private institutions) participated in the discussions. In total, BARD organized four meetings.

In general, 210 local residents participated in these discussions (this includes 143 people from the target group and 67 additional participants who came to the meetings. In additional, more than 760 people participated in discussions related to the composition of projects through social media). These meetings had several blocks: informational, educational and discussion. The informational and educational blocks (first meeting) were dedicated to presenting the general idea of deliberative democracy as an approach to involve citizens in the decision-making process in general and participatory budgeting in particular. The first meeting lasted three hours (with a 15-minute refreshment break) and started with a presentation of the idea of the participatory budgeting approach and its successful realization in other cities around the world. Special attention was paid to describing the Polish experience of participatory budgeting. For this purpose a large amount of informational and promotional materials related to the Polish participatory budgeting procedures (especially from Warsaw) were translated into Ukrainian languages and distributed among the participants. Moreover, as it has previously been observed, the audience lacked general knowledge about city finances, so special presentations about financial literacy, urban budgeting and finance were designed and demonstrated.

The following meetings (the second and the third) were dedicated to small-group deliberation, in which citizens connected the expert information to their personal experience of the city's problems and their ideas for projects. One of the crucial prerequisites for the emergence of deliberation is the organization of discussion. The second meeting was dedicated to discussing particular problems of the city and how the local residents could solve them with the help of the participatory budgeting process. The meeting began with an overview of general urban management principles, a presentation of the general plan of Chernivtsi and the main problems of the city according to the experts. The general discussion was dedicated to the issue of whether the distribution of public funds within participatory budgeting could be effective in the everyday realities of Chernivtsi. There were many different opinions, some of which highlighted completely opposite viewpoints. For example, one of the participants stated that ' ... participatory budgeting is a harmful initiative because lay citizens are not able effectively to manage the city budget. Moreover, in a time of war additional financial resources should be directed to helping soldiers from Chernivtsi fighting in eastern Ukraine'. Another contributor underlined that 'Participatory budgeting is a decision to put aside the "viewer ticket" and, for total satisfaction, start to change "the scenery" independently ... this is the decision of own responsibility for a common result ... ' However, according to the post-meeting survey, the vast majority of participants stated their support for the participatory budgeting process. During the third meeting (4 h with a 30-minute refreshment break), participants were randomly divided into three smaller groups. Each group worked with a facilitator, focusing on the next question:

(1) 'What are the main problems of the city? What should be done on a first-priority basis?' (members of the group had to select the top 3 ideas);
(2) 'How could the projects within participatory budgeting procedures address the general and particular problems of the city?';

At the end of the meeting, all of the results were presented. Participants underlined that the main problems of the city related to such spheres as the public road system and the quality of the communal facilities and health service. During the meeting, opinions changed slightly. The view prevailed that public roads and other complicated issues such as communal and health services require extremely large investments which could not be allocated within the budget of the participatory budgeting. Therefore, it would be more efficient to allocate funding to the sports and cultural projects. The last meeting was related to the discussion of the project ideas. Each initiative group working on a project idea had an opportunity to present their idea to other members of the discussion (including experts) and to receive comments and additional pointers on how to develop their ideas.

Deliberation was also present at the level of the expert committee meetings.[5] For example, members of the expert committee covered all of the topics of the process, ranging from the key principles to more technical and organizational aspects. Discussions were based on reasons and it was visible that participants were trying to consider all possible options before taking a position.[6] Therefore, the council can be treated as a genuine deliberative body.

Almost all participants tried to deliberate on issues that were put on the agenda. Not only did they ask questions and make comments, they provided reasons for their positions. However, the communicative dimension was seriously lacking. Although its composition was designed to provide a variety of perspectives, in practice this was rarely the case, which created delays and slowed the process of deliberation.

Analyzing deliberation during the public meetings, it should be underlined that the meeting organized by the city council almost entirely lacked the deliberative dimension. First of all, the meetings during the information campaign were dedicated only to the issue of explaining some of the technical aspects of the participatory budgeting process: templates for project ideas, criteria of eligibility, financial and administrative aspects, and so on. There were few meetings between members of the expert committee and the authors of the proposals.

Throughout the process, several online tools were used to enhance the deliberative process. These included: webpage bard.cv.ua, tools for online polling (SurveyMonkey), social media (Facebook, Vk.com) and the general platform https://gb.city.cv.ua/about. For example, citizens had an opportunity to read about the participatory budgeting process and its implementation around the world, with access to necessary forms and documents. Moreover, all the projects submitted were displayed on the platform. However, this platform did not provide the possibility for the discussion itself; therefore, this was supposed to take place during the meetings.

Results of the participatory budgeting process

In total, 58 projects (18 big and 40 small) worth 23,483513 UAH were submitted to the expert commission. Nevertheless, 21 projects were not approved by the expert commission. The main reasons for lack of approval were the following: 5 projects were not in compliance with Ukrainian legislation; 5 projects proposed an increase in the number of staff in budget institutions, financed from the local budget; 3 projects were outside of the jurisdiction of the local administration; 2 projects were of unaccomplished character.

During the voting process (was organized between 17 October and 1 November 2016), foresaw two approaches: traditional vote – the voter should fill in a paper form in administrative service centres in every district of the city (4705 votes were received through this method) and electronic vote – through the special internet platform https://gb.city.cv.ua/ (7096 votes were received through this method).

In total, 11801 votes were received; however, this corresponded to 8094 unique voters (some votes were disregarded) representing about 4.5% of the total population of Chernivtsi. After the process of voting was complete, the expert commission had three weeks to calculate all votes and draw up the list of winning projects. The local residents selected 31 projects among 37 proposed (6 big and 25 small, with a total budget of 10,045,434 UAH. Voting pattern is presented in the graph. Figure 1 here).

Evaluation of change in trust level

In the first survey, 284 local residents agreed to take part in a further deliberative activity (G1 – 227 local residents that had no previous experience in active civic participation and G2 – 57 persons who had such experience). All of them took part in participatory budgeting but in a different form. The number of people declined to attend meetings just before the start; however, all of them took part in the voting procedures.

Therefore, finally, meetings were attended by 143 persons from the target group (105 persons from Group 1 and 38 from Group 2). Moreover, participants of these meetings submitted 5 big and 11 small projects to the commission of experts for further evaluation. It should be noted that among the winners were 4 projects developed and submitted by

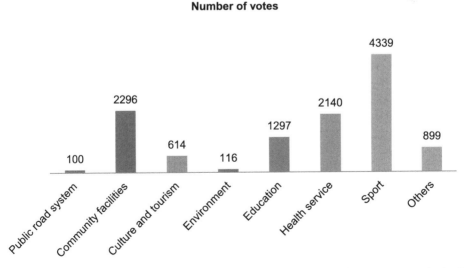

Figure 1. Number of votes (in a paper form and electronic votes) during the participatory budgeting process in Chernivtsi. Source: Own analysis.

Table 4. Level of political trust at local level within G1 and G2 groups (after participation in the deliberative event).

Question: What is your level of trust for the following political institutions:	G1			G2		
	Trusting	Distrusting	Hard to answer/ no answer	Trusting	Distrusting	Hard to answer/ no answer
The mayor	46.04	45.05	8.91	40.81	44.90	14.29
The city council	53.46	36.87	9.67	46.00	42.00	12.00

Source: own calculations.

the representatives of target group. After voting and approval, the list of winning projects, the last part of the survey among participants, was organized.

Therefore, local residents that had no previous experience in active civic participation trust expressed more trust in the mayor than the city council after the process of participatory budgeting. Similarly, locals who had previous experience in active civic participation trust the mayor more; however, their trust in the city council is significantly lower (Table 4).

Drawing a comparison between the level of trust among respondents from two different groups before the deliberative event and after, the following changes were observed: the level of trust in the city council is up 19.64%, while the level of trust in the mayor of the city has risen by about 14.18%. Among participants of group G2, the level of trust in the city council is up almost 2%, while the level of trust in the mayor of the city has risen to about 12%.

Conclusions

The theory of deliberative democracy has a long and rich history. Developed as a theory of political communication, and later as a theory of legitimacy, it currently represents an essential line of research in democratic theory.

Implementation of the deliberative procedures has many practical outcomes: from enhancing participation in decision-making processes and improving political literacy among citizens to increasing the level of political trust.

This article has presented an empirical examination of deliberation's impact on political trust at the local level. The main findings indicate that the participatory budgeting in Chernivtsi had an immediate and significant impact which has implications for how residents of Chernivtsi will engage in civic conversations about public planning in the future. This event created the expectation that residents of the city should be included in a constructive civic dialogue with their public officials about how to design the public realm. In addition, the whole process captured the imagination of the public and created the opportunity for additional meetings on other significant planning issues.

The results of the experiment provide evidence to support the hypothesis that participatory budgeting, as an element of deliberative democracy procedure, can change the level of political trust.

At the same time, I have to admit that this research has several significant limitations. First of all, focusing only on one locality in Ukraine may not yield high generalisability. Secondly, time factor should be taken into consideration. In participatory budgeting political trust emerges after implementation of projects in the end of the whole cycle, not just in the decision-making cycle.[7] Therefore, from evidence-based perspective it is more valuable to measure the change in the trust level when all investment proposals selected by the residents will be implemented. Additionally, factors which could diminish the connection between the deliberation and trust should be defined and analysed.

Nevertheless, the perspectives gleaned from the research endeavour are arguably valuable in the context of deliberative democracy model implementation in Ukrainian reality.

A lot more defintely remains on the avenues for future research. Firstly, the theoretical foundation has to be further strengthened and refined. In considering the effectiveness of deliberative practices and its impact on political trust, there is also the need to further validate theoretical postulations with attempts to strengthen the findings. Furthermore, what would be interesting, it is uncover potential unintended consequences of deliberation, by focusing not only on the level of political trust but whether there is an educative and empowerment effects on the citizens who had experiences deliberation and how attitude changes and what extend does hint at a potential democratic education.

Notes

1. Such regime combines democratic characters with autocratic ones. For example, frequent and direct elections may be accompanied by political repression or controlled mass media (Morlino, 2009).
2. See Norris 2000.
3. Bucovinian Agency for Regional Development (BARD). BARD is a regional think tank specializing in various civil projects and opinion surveys. When in 2015 my research has received specific grant from Open Society Foundation (grant number IN2014-15554), I involved this organization into my project. BARD was responsible for survey procedure, analysis of observations, organization of deliberative events, cooperation with local authorities.
4. Minimal requirements for the process based on Habermas' approach. For more details see Habermas, 1994, (Strandberg and Gronlund in Geissel & Joas, 2013, p. 145).
5. This commission consists of representatives of the city council, local NGOs and community leaders. The main function of the commission is to review submitted projects for compliance with technical and financial criteria. Only approved projects can be admitted to further voting.
6. BARD representative was a member of this committee; therefore, I have used her observations.
7. I thank anonymous reviewer #1 for this valuable comment.

Acknowledgements

I sincerely value the suggestions of Dr Sergiu Gherghina from the University of Glasgow for his reviews and valuable comments. His thorough assessment and kind ideas helped to improve the general description of the experiment.

I am indebted to the Open Society Foundation as the deliberative experiment was partially financed by its generous grants (grant numbers IN2013-08541, IN2014-15554) and to the Graduate School for Social Research for enabling the accomplishing of my research.

Moreover, I would like to thank the two anonymous reviewers for their many insightful comments and suggestions.

Finally, I would like to thank the Head of the Bucovinian Agency for Regional Development, not only for helping me to undertake the survey in Chernivtsi, but also for giving me the opportunity to attend various public meetings during participatory budgeting and meet so many interesting people.

Disclosure statement

No potential conflict of interest was reported by the author.

Funding

I am indebted to the Open Society Foundation as the deliberative experiment was partially financed by its generous grants [grant numbers: IN2013-08541, IN2014-15554].

References

Almond, G., & Verba, S. (1963). *The civic culture*. Princeton, NJ: Princeton University Press.

Amnå, E., & Ekman, J. (2013). Standby citizens: Diverse faces of political passivity. *European Political Science Review*, *6*(02), 261–281.

Armingeon, K., & Ceka, B. (2013). The loss of trust in the european union during the great recession since 2007: The role of heuristics from the national political system. *European Union Politics*, *15*(1), 82–107.

Asen, R. (2013). Deliberation and trust. *Argumentation and Advocacy*, *50*(1), 2–17.

Cabannes, Y. (2004). Participatory budgeting: A significant contribution to participatory democracy. *Environment and Urbanization*, *16*(1), 27–46.

Chiru, M., & Gherghina, S. (2012). Does the confidence in the EU spill over to the national level? A longitudinal analysis of political trust in Central Europe. *Perspectives on European Politics and Society*, *13*(2), 226–245.

Farrell, D., O'Malley, E., & Suiter, J. (2013). Deliberative democracy in action Irish-style: The 2011 we the citizens pilot citizens' assembly. *Irish Political Studies*, *28*(1), 99–113.

Festenstein, M. (2005). *Negotiating diversity: Culture, deliberation, trust*. Cambridge: Polity Press.

Fishkin, J. (2011). *When the people speak. Deliberative democracy and public consultation*. New York, NY: Oxford University Press.

Fishkin, J., & Luskin, R. (2005). Experimenting with a democratic ideal: Deliberative polling and public opinion. *Acta Politica*, *40*(3), 284–298.

Font, J., & Blanco, I. (2007). Procedural legitimacy and political trust: The case of citizen juries in Spain. *European Journal of Political Research*, *46*, 557–589.

Fung, A. (2005). *Democratizing the policy process. The Oxford handbook of public policy*. New York, NY: Oxford University Press.

Geissel, B., & Joas, M. (Eds.). (2013). *Participatory democratic innovations in Europe. Improving the quality of democracy?* Leverkusen Opladen: Barbara Budrich Publishers.

Gherghina, S. (2017). Direct democracy and subjective regime legitimacy in Europe. *Democratization*, *24*(4), 613–631.

Gherghina, S., & Miscoiu, S. (2016). Crowd-sourced legislation and politics. The legitimacy of constitutional deliberation in Romania. *Problems of Post-Communism*, *63*, 27–36.

Giddens, A. (1990). *The consequences of modernity*. Stanford, CA: Stanford University Press.

Habermas, J. (1994). Three normative models of democracy. *Constellations*, *1*(1), 1–10.

Hauser, G., & Benoit-Barne, C. (2002). Reflections on rhetoric, deliberative democracy, civil society, and trust. *Rhetoric and Public Affairs*, *5*(2), 261–275.

Hetherington, M. (2005). *Why trust matters: Declining political trust and the demise of American liberalism*. Princeton, NJ: Princeton University Press.

Hooghe, M., & Kern, A. (2017). The tipping point between stability and decline: Trends in voter turnout, 1950–1980–2012. *European Political Science*, *16*(4), 535–552.

Keane, J. (2009). *The life and death of democracy*. London: Simon and Schuster Publisher.

Khutkyy, D. (2017). Participatory budgeting: An empowering democratic institution. *EUROZINE*. Retrieved from http://www.eurozine.com/participatory-budgeting-an-empowering-democratic-institution/

Kumlin, S. (2013). Dissatisfied democrats, policy feedback and European welfare states 1976–2001. In M. Hooghe & S. Zmerli (Eds.), *Political trust. Why context matters* (pp. 163–187). Colchester: ECPR Press.

Landemore, H. (2015). Inclusive constitutional-making: The Icelandic experiment. *Journal of Political Philosophy*, *23*(2), 166–191.

Meny, Y. (2003). De la democratie en Europe: Old concepts and new challenges. *JCMS: Journal of Common Market Studies*, *41*, 1–13.

Moravcsik, A. (2002). Reassesing legitimacy in the European Union. *JCMS: Journal of Common Market Studies*, *40*(4), 603–624.

Morlino, L. (2009). Are there hybrid regimes? Or are they just an optical illusion? *European Political Science Review*, *1*(2), 273–296.

Morrell, M. (2005). Deliberation, democratic decision-making and internal political efficacy. *Political Behavior*, *27*(1), 49–69.

Newton, K. (2018). Social and political trust. In M. Uslaner (Ed.), *Social and political trust* (pp. 37–57). New York, NY: Oxford University Press.

Norris, P. (2000). *A virtuous circle: Political communications in postindustrial societies*. New York, NY: Cambridge University Press.

Norris, P. (2011). *Democratic deficit: Critical citizens revisited*. New York, NY: Cambridge University Press.

Parkinson, J. (2006). *Deliberating in the real world: Problems of legitimacy in deliberative democracy*. New York, NY: Oxford University Press.

Ross, C. (2011). *The leaderless revolution: How ordinary people will take power and change politics in the twenty-first century*. New York, NY: Blue Rider Press.

Rothstein, B., & Stolle, D. (2008). The state and social capital: An institutional theory of generalized trust. *Comparative Politics*, *40*(4), 441–459.

Siaroff, A. (2009). The decline of political participation: An empirical overview of voter turnout and party membership. In J. DeBardeleben & J. H. Pammett (Eds.), *Activating the citizen* (pp. 41–59). London: Palgrave Macmillan.

Swaner, R. (2017). Trust matters: Enhancing government legitimacy through participatory budgeting. *New Political Science*, *39*(1), 95–108.

Sztompka, P. (1999). *Trust: A sociological theory*. New York, NY: Cambridge University Press.

Tormey, S. (2015). *The end of representative politics*. Cambridge: Polity Press.

Uslaner, E. (2002). *The moral foundations of trust*. New York, NY: Cambridge University Press.

Van Biezen, I., Mair, P., & Poguntke, T. (2012). Going, going, . . . gone? The decline of party membership in contemporary Europe. *European Journal of Political Research*, *51*, 24–56.

Van Ryzin, G. (2011). Public participation, procedural fairness and evaluations of local governance: The moderating role of uncertainty. *Journal of Public Administration Research and Theory*, *21*(4), 745–760.

Worthington, R., Rask, M., & Minna, L. (2013). *Citizen participation in global environmental governance*. London: Routledge.

Zmerli, S., & Hooghe, M. (2013). *Political trust: Why context matters*. Colchester: ECPR Press.

Attrition in long-term deliberative processes. The neighbourhood consultative councils in Timisoara

Adrian Schiffbeck

ABSTRACT

In 2003, the neighbourhood citizen councils in Timisoara (Romania) were founded, with the aim of involving inhabitants in the decision-making process. This mini-public has been rewarded several times on European and national level for its innovative components, but has gradually become weaker and fewer citizens got involved. While much research investigates the determinants of public engagement and the linkage between participation and the quality of decision-making, little attention is paid to an analysis regarding attrition. The paper addresses this void in the literature and aims to explain the reasons for which citizens pulled out from this deliberative process. The analysis is qualitative and relies on primary data collected through personal participatory observations, interviews and document interpretation. Findings mainly indicate towards the self-selection procedure, an unlimited duration accompanied by the decrease in innovative components, perceptions of a low impact on the decision-making process and weak connections between politics and community.

Introduction

While much research investigates the determinants of public engagement and the linkage between participation and the quality of decision-making, little attention is paid to attrition in deliberative settings. Research focused extensively on arguments determining people to refuse taking part or retreat from short-time deliberative procedures (e.g. Jacquet, 2017; Karjalainen & Rapeli, 2015; Mutz, 2006; Neblo, Esterling, Kennedy, Lazer, & Sokhey, 2010; Ulbig & Funk, 1999). Attrition has predominantly been studied in the recruitment and organization phases of deliberative experiments (see also Caluwaerts & Ugarriza, 2012; Hansen, 2004). Scholars further set their attention on non-response in survey research (Fitzgerald, Gottschalk, & Moffitt, 1998; Uhrig, 2008; Voogt & Van Kempen, 2002). People already involved and who become demotivated in the course of a longer process of participation (not by means of electronic communication, but in the form of live meetings and debates) were far less taken into account. Long-term deliberative projects – i.e. different variants of participatory budgeting – were mainly observed in their structure, way of functioning and organization (e.g. Drouault, 2007; Smith, 2009), without particularly approaching attrition.

The article addresses this void in the literature and aims to explain the reasons for which active citizens pull out from long-term deliberative practices. Answers to this question are important for bringing an added value to existing theories on democratic innovations – by taking arguments for attrition in deliberative processes (rather than experiments) into account – and for providing practitioners with a supplement of knowledge and understanding when building sustainable participation setting.

Our analysis is qualitative, presenting the way of functioning and evolution of the neighbourhood consultative councils in the Romanian city of Timisoara, from the time of their creation, in 2003, to 2017. It is based on personal observations, primary documents and group discussions and interviews, the last ones conducted between 2015 and 2017.

We first look at popular assemblies and mini-publics and then focus on the neighbourhood organizations, which embrace both forms of democratic innovations. The next section outlines the arguments in the literature related to non-attendance (refusal to participate) and attrition (dropout from an ongoing process), as different, but strongly related aspects of a deliberation mechanism. Both involve rejection of participation and only occur at different stages of the process. Due to limited rationale on attrition – having been researched only with respect to short-term experiments and to their recruitment and organization phases – we look at the more general argumentation for the refusal to participate, too. After the theoretical part, we specify the methods used for gaining and interpreting our data and, finally, particularize the results and compare them to the existing argumentation.

Mini-publics vs. open assemblies

As instruments having been 'specifically designed to increase and deepen citizen participation in the political decision-making process', democratic innovations are divided into four main functioning structures: popular assemblies, mini-publics, direct legislation and e-democracy (Smith, 2009, p. 1, 28). Popular assemblies (participatory budgeting projects among the best-known) are 'forums open to all citizens. (…) arguably the most basic of democratic designs' (Smith, 2009, p. 28). They are generally functioning over longer periods of time, up to several years (Abers, 1998, pp. 54–55). The neighbourhood assembly open to all inhabitants, which we are particularly interested in, is the 'fundamental building block of Benjamin Barber's vision of strong democracy' (Barber, 1984, pp. 267–273; Smith, 2009, p. 30). Referring to basic functions of open assemblies, theoreticians first of all mention monitoring the administration and permanently holding it to account; second, people would establish certain priorities for their region and third, they would be represented in administrative councils where they can state their opinion (Smith, 2009, p. 36). The first two functions apply to the neighbourhood councils in Timisoara.

The second category of democratic innovations, the mini-publics, comprises educative forums, advisory panels, participatory problem-solving collaboration and participatory democratic governance (Fung, 2003, pp. 340–342). The organizations we look at most properly fit in the third category, as they were created to collaborate with the administration and politicians for solving concrete problems in different areas of the town.

Mini-publics are implemented over short periods of time, generally a few days (Smith, 2009, p. 97), using the random type of selection 'to open the door of deliberation to a larger public, beyond the circle of already active citizens' (Fung, 2007; Jacquet, 2017, p. 3). They attempt to make room for 'politically excluded social groups and their opinions' (Karjalainen & Rapeli, 2015, p. 408). Otherwise, 'the "usual suspects" do always prevail' (Geissel & Gherghina, 2016, p. 6). In the case of popular assemblies, by contrast, not all affected interests are presumably represented, because 'the relevant population from which citizens are drawn is typically related to the political boundary of the sponsoring public authority' (Goodin, 2007; Smith, 2009, p. 80). Other researchers concluded that, due to a broad representation of the population, popular assemblies (i.e. participatory budgeting) can be inclusive and representative, too, 'despite the absence of random selection' (Drouault, 2007, pp. 34–35).

The neighbourhood consultative councils are a form of open or popular assemblies, as defined by their organizational and structural features, and can be assimilated to mini-publics in the sense of their mission, as we will see in the following. The project in Timisoara was not related to the other two forms of democratic innovations – direct legislation and e-democracy.

The neighbourhood consultative councils

In the local community we look upon – although it was argued that similar political affiliations with the administration`s leaders prevailed in the sampling process, the opportunity to become active was offered to everyone. As local regulations were stipulating, potential members would have to be inhabitants of Timisoara at least 18 years of age, reside or work in the area they are opting for. 'Every consultative council will be formed of minimum seven people, citizens who express their will to commonly debate diverse aspects of collective life – representatives of education, health, culture, services and commerce, residents` associations etc.' (Consiliul Local Timisoara, 2005, I-2). Leaving citizens the choice to exclusively 'express their will' about taking part in the consultative process made room for a predominant self-selection mechanism: middle-aged and mostly older inhabitants, with particular needs in their areas (public works and investments), or people simply interested in community problem solving, eventually chose to use this newly created tool for communicating to the local administration. It was perhaps a form of 'participatory innovations open to all who wish to attend, where already active citizens are over-represented' (Fung, 2007; Jacquet, 2017, p. 1). The aim of the initiative in Timisoara was less to ensure inclusiveness, pursuing to build a constructing dialogue frame between administration and virtual representatives of inhabitants.

These citizens' non-political, non-profit organizations, formed by volunteers acting to improve the quality of life in their communities (Consiliul Local Timisoara, 2005, I-2) have been introduced at the end of 2003, with the aim of involving inhabitants in the decision-making process. The project was rewarded several times on European and national level for its elements of innovation. However, starting 2011, many citizens decided to step aside, up to the point where almost no participatory activity took place in the neighbourhoods. We have selected this specific case for our study for both reasons: the success of the deliberative practice – taken several times as a model by other administrations, and the subsequent radical attrition associated with it.

The project started with specifications from a French model of the twinned Alsace city of Mulhouse, taking the form of an administrative decision to be adopted by the Local

Council in Timisoara, within a top-down type of initiative. A permanent dialogue with the local administration, by making proposals regarding infrastructure, traffic, public transportation, environment, playgrounds, public illuminating, schools etc., was seen as the main mission of neighbourhood councils. This dialogue was to be put into practice by regular meetings between the two sides (at least once every three months in each of the 19 neighbourhoods in town) and by a permanent (direct, electronic and over the phone) communication to a City employee appointed to keep contact to these organizations and intermediate their relationship to the mayor and vice-mayors. The constituting act from 2003 mentions some potential advantages on both sides, among them, the fact that citizens can 'become more active in formulating solutions for the problems they are confronting' (Consiliul Local Timisoara, 2003). People were supposed to monitor the way requirements were being solved and results of this consultation mainly appeared in terms of investment works in the neighbourhoods.

At the beginning, the implementation of different infrastructural facilities was primarily pursued. In time, people also focused on social and media-related activities – organizing cultural and entertaining events in the neighbourhoods, setting up own websites and editing local newspapers – as well as on developing and maintaining contacts with local NGOs and international partners.

Commissions or groups of discussion on different thematic areas, such as street works, traffic issues, green areas, health or cultural events, have been constituted inside the organizations. In order to avoid conflicts of interests or discussions about certain privileges, employees of local administration could not become members; instead, in order for inhabitants to have their interests more efficiently represented, there were attempts to attract politicians from the Local Council and determine them to take part at the sessions: citizens would thus 'feel they are being listened by the elected ones' – yet another potential advantage mentioned by the administration (Consiliul Local Timisoara, 2003). In this respect, there was one major difference compared to the partner city in France: Timisoara had citizens running for and being elected by their co-inhabitants in leading functions (president, vice-president, secretary), thus pursuing a direct representativity at neighbourhood level. Coming to vote for these persons was not compulsory and only some dozens of inhabitants took this opportunity each time a particular council was constituted. This permanent freedom of choice stood for a relative inclusiveness and representativity of these organizations at the community level. Compared to the Romanians, the French partners preferred one of the vice-mayors to coordinate the organization. As we will see in the following, this direct connection between politics and community, or the manner in which mini-publics are linked to decision-makers, is actually seen by theoreticians as one of the main factors influencing attrition.

Theoretical framework

What we attempt to find out is why people stop getting involved in community matters: what are the reasons for a process of participatory democracy set on a long-term basis to be radically affected by attrition? Did citizens and civil society in Timisoara become increasingly discontent with the route on which the project slipped after a number of years? How can this complex evolution in time be described and explained?

Generally, it has been verified that 'only a small circle of the population is active in the political arena, especially in demanding forms of action like party activism or community groups' (Barnes & Kaase, 1979; Jacquet, 2017, p. 3). Jacquet speaks about six main 'logics of non-participation': concentration on the private sphere; internal inefficacy; public meetings avoidance; conflict of schedule; political alienation and mini-public's lack of impact (Jacquet, 2017, p. 9). People declaring themselves 'too busy' because of their work tend to focus on their private sphere (Neblo et al., 2010); families with small children are in the same situation, except participation in survey responses, where women spending more time at home are willing to get involved (Uhrig, 2008). Conflict of schedule intervenes especially in short-term experiments, when people have other events planned during a particular day or weekend (Jacquet, 2017, p. 11). Public meetings (especially conflict) avoidance was found to have a significant effect on the willingness to participate in general (Mutz, 2006; Neblo et al., 2010; Ulbig & Funk, 1999). Other factors approached in the literature include the connections between politics and community, social categorization (differences in terms of age, income, education), the element of self-selection, financial stimulation, duration of the process, satisfaction towards the community, rootedness in the community and the personal orientation and attitude (altruism vs. individualism). We have taken a look at all these reasons, except concentration on the private sphere, conflict of schedule and public meeting avoidance (shortly described above), as they have too little to do with our findings. The element of moral rewards, derived from the interviews, comes to complete our scheme (see Table 1).

To begin with, the factor of random selection has proven to have an important influence on participation: 'when you leave the participants too many moments to change their minds and decide not to participate' (Caluwaerts & Reuchamps, 2013, p. 25), self-selection is fostered and beneficiaries ultimately determine your structure.

Organizers should also take the duration of the process into consideration: 'Studies of political participation provide ample evidence of the fact that the larger the personal investment, the less likely citizens are to take part' (Brady, Verba, & Schlozman, 1995; Caluwaerts & Reuchamps, 2013, p. 11). If events are organized for periods longer than one single day, dropout becomes noticeable (Smith, 2009, p. 146). Length of the project inevitably influences peoplès capacity to remain focused: 'only the "diehards", i.e. most motivated citizens (...) will commit or continue to commit' (Caluwaerts & Reuchamps, 2013, p. 11).

People would remain focused if they see concrete results of their activity, too. What would be the point of investing your time and energy in an uncertain goal? 'With no guarantee of effectiveness, it is not worth spending time deliberating' (Jacquet, 2017, p. 14). On the other hand, if people show up on a large scale at meetings, chances for opinions (in terms of investment priorities) to be taken into account raise considerably (Smith, 2009, p. 43).

For attrition to be maintained at a low level, the connection to the political level is to be taken into account. Places where people are in close relations to politicians and/or administrators are more likely to become and remain scenes of efficient participatory mechanisms. Such connections are a premise for the success of deliberative events, which become able to capture 'the public imagination' (Groenlund, Baechtiger, & Saetaele, 2014, p. 79; Niemeyer, Felicetti, & Ruggero, 2012).

The relation to the community itself is a further influencing factor for the degree of participation. Even with a critical voice towards things that do not work, 'being satisfied with onès community may give residents a greater sense of community and collective efficacy and may result in more neighbouring behaviour, all of which are predicted to lead to greater collective participation' (Perkins, Brown, & Taylor, 1996, p. 91).

The attitude with respect to the community is related to the one developed towards the one next to you, the so-called civic virtue. Tocqueville referred to it as a 'self-interest properly understood': people may keep their orientation towards themselves and their individual needs, but not in an egoistic manner, rather as an 'enlightened self-love', which he saw as a stimulus for helping others and devoting to the community (Smidt, 2008, p. 177). Essentially, studies confirm that, when it comes to participation, 'the greatest benefits are in making a contribution and helping others, rather than in self-interest or personal gains' (Wandersman, Florin, Friedmannn, & Meier, 1987, p. 551). Satisfaction towards the community and personal attitude are both related to the development of civic spirit, or civic virtue, as it was described in the literature, which in turn significantly influences participation.

Regarding the categories of people inclined to take part in deliberative processes, gatherings 'tend to attract middle-aged and older citizens' (Zimmerman, 1999, p. 170), whereas e-democracy is rather popular among young people. From a socio-economic point of view, persons with 'higher than average income, wealth and education' are more likely to become involved (Smith, 2009, p. 40). Although very poor people tend not to participate, marginalized social groups will be willing to do so, mostly when it comes to participatory budgeting (Abers, 1998, p. 54). Theoretically, enrooted inhabitants of a particular place are also more likely to participate at gatherings: studies revealed that 'living in an area longer, intending to stay longer and having more children can be seen as embedding an individual within a community, increasing both the opportunities and incentives to participate' (Wandersman et al., 1987, p. 550). Jane Mansbridge speaks in this context about the 'interesting dynamics (…) between «old-timers» and «newcomers»' (Smith, 2009, p. 41). She mentions 'friendly joking and informality, the attempts to cover up embarrassing incidents, and the unanimous votes', meant to create a pleasant and familiar atmosphere: participation is thus made 'easier for established members of the community' (Mansbridge, 1980, p. 68; Smith, 2009, p. 41).

People also tend to remain on board when they are materially rewarded, as the cases in Ireland (the project called 'We the citizens', 2009) and Belgium (G1000 Citizens' Summit, 2011) have proven. Random selection 'should be combined with a financial incentive for participation, otherwise the drop-out will be great' (Caluwaerts & Reuchamps, 2013, p. 25).

On the other hand, a 'generalized rejection of political activities, with a feeling of powerlessness', determines people to refuse taking part in deliberations; participation is often perceived as 'an elite-driven manipulation' (Jacquet, 2017, p. 9). This idea of alienation or psychological estrangement dates back to Karl Marx, who was putting it in conjunction to the act of work, to the product of the labourer and finally to his own human nature. Work was not supposed to offer satisfaction in the capitalist system, due to imposed circumstances. Participation would similarly not attract (even remunerated) citizens, if they feel manipulated by politicians.

Developing a more trustful relation to the authority goes hand in hand with communication – designing consultative procedures, setting and respecting 'constitutive rules of reciprocal interaction': without co-operation between people involved, refraining from physical and verbal violence and from speaking at the same time with other participants, internal inefficacies will inevitably be reached and one can then little point to a veritable deliberative forum (Groenlund et al., 2014, p. 79). To this extent, 'high quality deliberation can only develop with clear rules and a moderator or facilitator' (Groenlund et al., 2014, p. 6, 8). Like we have observed ourselves when taking part at meetings respectively tracking the process in Timisoara, 'the larger a group and the more controversial the issue at hand is, the more challenging and the more important keeping the rules of procedure becomes' (Groenlund et al., 2014, p. 79).

The methods

To gather and interpret our data, we have chosen a qualitative approach, based on document analysis, process tracking with personal participatory observations in the field and presenting ideas from one group discussion and five interviews. These were carried out with representatives of neighbourhood councils and of civil society, as well as young people who were involved in public engagement projects in Timisoara. With the alternative method of standardized questionnaires, the subject can be extensively explored; on the other hand, the quantitative research does not offer respondents the chance to come with details and explicitly express their opinions: potentially relevant information can 'practically not come up for discussion' (Struebing, 2013, p. 92).

To help us in our approach, we used an interview guide (see Appendix 1); several questions were developed then again along the way, during the face-to-face discussions. The question guide should be regarded not as a 'scenario for the course of the interview, but rather a support for your memory' (Struebing, 2013, p. 92). An exclusive use of pre-formulated questions may leave important data aside, turning to 'an instrument for blocking the information' (Hopf, 1978, p. 102).

We have looked for the most active persons in the social practice to talk to. These had the quality of experts for our subject, fulfilling three necessary conditions: the capacity to look into decisional processes, experience in that particular field and knowledge for developing the process (Struebing, 2013). The group discussion and two of the interviews were performed at the respondents` places of work or study and lasted between 50 min and two hours. These were recorded and transcribed. The other three interviews have been carried out per e-mail.

The reduced number of people we have spoken to can be interpreted as a limitation of our approach; compensation comes from the relevance of the obtained data, respectively quantity and quality of knowledge attributed to the interlocutors. 'As usual for qualitative research, the aim is not to reach a representative sample of the population, but rather to collect the diversity of views and experiences with regard to the analysed topic' (Ritchie, Lewis, & Elam, 2003). The principle of data saturation requires that no further discussion or documents should be taken into account if 'no additional information' is provided (Jacquet, 2017, p. 7).

In the phase of data analysis, we made use of situation maps, in order to establish connections between relevant elements and, more importantly, figure out what the 'nature of that relationship' looks like; the instrument is described as an 'analytical exercise', meant to open up the data for interpretation (Clarke, 2005). There are generally two types of situation maps proposed to the researcher: the 'messy' plan of elements, with ideas sketched on paper before drawing some lines between them, and the ordered situation map (Clarke, 2005, p. 87), where new elements are added to each category, for coming to a conceptual image.

Our situation was related to a long-term deliberative process and we had the main situational element of attrition which needed to be analysed. The process of drawing the ordered map (Appendix 2) began with describing the particular situation and its components: 'Who and what matters in this situation? What elements «make a difference» in this situation?' (Clarke, 2005, pp. 86–87). The main components, identified as the neighbourhood consultative councils, had to be explained and understood. The corresponding situational element of attrition had also to be connected to its constituent parts (the resulted reasons), creating a systhematic picture of the social practice.

A selection of all initial factors was challenged, for restricting the map to what was relevant to the research question. Self-selection, the unlimited duration of the process, lack of impact and weak connections between politics and community were found to have the highest degree of influence on attrition; they are followed by the rest of the factors, with a less significant weight in the process. The nature of the indicated relations between elements is being reffered to in different parts of this paper.

The algorithm of a situation map requires a balance between freedom of creation and a procedural approach. The goals of drawing it are, for one, to foster a better understanding of the phenomenon by the analyst himself (by organizing his thinking process); secondly, to provide the research question with a solid structure, and, third – to clarify the context, objectives and/or (in our case) results of the investigation.

The same principle applied when coding our information. Extracting specific elements from a text helps coding the information, as well as encoding it (Struebing, 2013, p. 118): by encrypting your phrases, you actually uncover their meanings. There are three types of coding, according to Struebing (2013) and to earlier research (Strauss & Corbin, 1990): the open, or general procedure; the axial coding – focusing on a certain category, and selecting and re-deciphering – where the researcher 're-codes' his information and tries to build a coherent 'red wire' of argumentation from the relevant elements which had been discovered. We have used the axial procedure (see Appendix 3), encrypting the most significant factors resulted from collecting our data, in order to analyse and interpret them.

The qualitative instruments described above are of help in understanding how and why certain practices come to life and develop in time. After collecting the data from the field by means of interviews, group discussions and participatory observations, the researcher returns to his desk and analyses the information through a double hermeneutical approach: he attempts to explain the way people around him understood their environment. Analytical notes, situation maps and codes are there to assist in organizing and structuring the interpretative work. The (often) vast amount of data is being deciphered and selected within a constant comparison process. The 'red wire' of argumentation thus heads towards theoretical sub-concepts and, later, towards the results in the form of the final conceptual entity.

The basic principles for ensuring 'trustworthiness and possible replicability of findings' had also to be taken into account: transparency, systematic comparison and peer review

(Jacquet, 2017, p. 8; Miles & Huberman, 1994). Discussions are recorded and our personal analytical notes are kept in an archive. Peer review was essential for avoiding 'any bias related to the researcher's analytic preconceptions' (Jacquet, 2017, p. 8). We discussed a paper configured previously to this article and based on the same subject and available information at an international workshop, with fellow participants and direct discussants. Peer suggestions provided later to draft versions of the article have also been taken into account.

Last but not least, the researcher has to develop his information creating connections to available theoretical knowledge, if not for other reasons, than just for 'not discovering the wheel again' (Struebing, 2013, p. 112). Let us accordingly present our findings in the following paragraphs, with reference to the theoretical elements described earlier.

Results

The first factor, of self-selection, was obvious in the case of consultative councils: having the opportunity to drop out at any stage, more and more citizens made this choice over time. Documents of the administration (member lists, recorded meetings) show that, at the beginning, there were at least 25–30 people registered in each of the 19 town districts (and, often, much more people were present at gatherings). Their number reduced considerably: 'Citizens do not come to meetings anymore' (I.K., interview, March 20, 2017). According to releases on the City's website and in the local media, the intervals between public discussions also increased significantly: from sessions being convoked almost weekly in one neighbourhood or the other, one could hear about such events every several months starting with 2014–2015.

The argument of duration proved essential in our case, too. The decrease in participation is indeed related to a growing degree of saturation within a participatory mechanism with no limit in time. Innovative activities in the first years (the aforementioned local and international cooperation, cultural festivals, own websites and newspapers) were not replaced by new kinds of initiatives, except the development of an isolated project involving young students. Due to repetitive actions, people lost their focus and interest in these entities. 'After 2012, the activity inside our neighbourhood council reduced significantly. We had only a few concrete meetings, for mediating the problems of some groups of inhabitants' (C.S., interview, April 20, 2017). Another president of a neighbourhood organization says that 'it is almost like the only ones left are the leading committees; there are no members anymore or they do not cooperate with us anymore' (I.K., interview, March 20, 2017).

Unfulfilled expectations

Our empirical evidence further shows that people primarily remain involved in a deliberative practice if they obtain something concrete. Otherwise, scepticism turns to a veritable 'source of non-engagement' (Jacquet, 2017). Basic human needs were brought into question by our respondents: 'Neighborhood councils are suffering from this point of view, because their problems are not being solved. It is simple: we will attract people towards us by demonstrating that we do something for them' (I.K., interview, March 20, 2017).

The personal contacts

Withdrawal was basically caused by the decrease of cooperation with neighbourhood councils on the part of local politics, too. Meetings and communication between the two sides have diminished considerably. Political leaders have apparently chosen other participatory mechanisms. 'If the constructive role of neighbourhood councils – dealing with real problems of inhabitants – would be understood, and citizens would see a feedback from the administration, people would definitely turn their attention (anew – N/A) towards these organizations' (C.S., interview, April 20, 2017). Our interlocutor makes the suggestion that each politician in the Local Council should be responsible and permanently communicate to a certain district, a rule which had actually been implemented for several years. Not putting this existing regulation into practice anymore led to discontent among members of neighbourhood councils. In the model twinned city of Mulhouse, the administration allocated an annual budget for the neighbourhood councils, used by citizens for implementing own projects; in Timisoara, direct financial allocations limited to cultural events in the neighbourhoods. However, there were meetings with the mayor and leaders of technical departments organized every three months, where major works were discussed and monitored together: 'We were being asked to present a list of investment proposals coming from citizens each year, when the annual local budget took shape, and it was reviewed with the City Hall leaders' (C.S., interview, April 20, 2017). The fact that this direct communication on budgeting issues has not been carried on was yet another reason for the activities to decline.

To the same extent, of weak connections between politics and community, respondents told us that their relation to the moderator of the process, to the intermediary, played an essential part. Representatives of the Department of Communication at the City Hall, together with leaders of neighbourhood councils, moderated debates in the districts; apart from that, they met and discussed regularly. 'After 2011, meetings have been gradually eliminated and our relationship to the administration continued rather inertially; it reduced basically to the organization of neighborhood festivals' (G.S., interview, March 27, 2017).

Civic spirit and social responsibility

A further important factor to be brought up by our respondents was satisfaction towards the community. People in Timisoara would have developed a rather 'contrary attitude towards their neighbourhood. They did not love the place they were living in and found it important to talk about yourself and your house, but to hate your community' (Z.P., interview, March 12, 2015). Our interlocutor, Orthodox priest and leader of a citizens' council, found it necessary to explain to members of his organization that 'denigrating our neighbourhood means denigrating each and every one of us' (Z.P., interview, March 12, 2015). Residents could actually be satisfied with the place they live in, even when they are critical towards community problems (Perkins et al., 1996, p. 91).

If denigrating the neighbourhood means denigrating the other, respecting the area you live in means respecting your co-fellow, too. From the establishment of these structures, it has been specified that 'members of neighbourhood councils (…) will work only for the good of the community'. Developing this kind of attitude seems an idealistic aspiration. Our personal participatory observations at the meetings indicated that many people followed the accomplishment of certain needs in their area (modernizing a street, a water or sewerage network, renovating a park or a playground, improving public transport etc.) and dropped out after these were finally solved. A further dialogue partner – member in a neigh-bourhood council, teacher and psychologist – describes the meaning of voluntary work and mentions personal advantages of the positive attitude towards the other: 'When you make a good deed, there is a little egoism in the substrate … the good feeling, given by the thought that you are acting well' (Group discussion, March 10, 2015). A professor of Journalism, writer and head of an organization closely involved in civic education projects, further says that people are not sufficiently aware 'of what freedom means. It is about understanding and assuming social responsibility' (M.O., interview, March 6, 2015). Without an approach oriented less towards onés own interests and more towards the community and the one next to you, drop-out is only a matter of time.

Acknowledging participation

People who develop such a positive approach deserve to be recognized. Otherwise, their personal satisfaction – not in terms of material outcomes, but on the moral level – will be compromised. One of the projects initiated in Timisoara in 2009, called 'Young people decide!', included groups of students supposed to work with neighbourhood councils and launch different ideas of improving life in their communities; the ideas were to be put into practice together with the administration and other local institutions. The project was abandoned after several years. As a determining factor for not wishing to take part anymore, the element of moral rewards has often been mentioned by teachers, supervisors and adolescents in the course of our discussions. This time, it was not about concrete impacts of initiatives on the field; what was bothering this age category was that they were offered too little attention from adults organizing deliberative forms of activities with them. Pupils with very good ideas of implementing something for their neighbourhood felt 'betrayed' by adult supervisors trying to take advantage of their work and build their own image upon it: 'There is no place for arrogance here (…) Suffering is profound and the effect will be horrible. When you build democracy, you are not allowed to make mis-takes. The second time, people wont get involved anymore' (M.O., interview, March 6, 2015). One pupil speaks about the importance of the way they are treated by educators: 'I think, when you are blocking his freedom of expression, the person will have this problem all his life; inside a group of people, he will be scared and ashamed to state his opinion' (Group discussion, March 10, 2015).

   The perception of not being sufficiently appreciated was one of the factors causing the interruption of this cooperation, respectively a higher degree of attrition.

Who stays on board

At regular neighbourhood sessions, young people were actually a rare presence; middle-aged and mostly older people formed the majority – a fact revealed by our personal parti-cipatory observations, with presence at the meetings. The process tracking – including document analysis and several informal discussions with many members of neighbourhood consultative councils – showed on the other side that people with 'higher than average income, wealth and education', and, from the other extreme, marginalized social groups (those with Roma ethnic origin, for instance) were less present at debates. Participants mainly came from the middle class, with average levels of income and education.

Attrition was less related to the level of income and the same applies to the element of rootedness – the 'old-timers' and 'newcomers' from the community. 'Before 1989, the spirit of this city meant a lot of respect towards the place we live in. Neighbourhoods at the edge of the town, even rural, looked gorgeous, people were preoccupied by the way the street, the garden or the backyard looked like', told us the civil society representative. He further underlines the efforts of the administration to modernize and transform marginal neighbourhoods into residential areas. However,

> because of people who came (from outside the region – A/N), that housekeeping spirit got lost. Going along with young people to monitor marginal districts, we have observed that egoism, isolation, autarchy become stronger and stronger: everyone is preoccupied by his own house, but only between its walls; beyond them, to the street, this housekeeping spirit has vanished. (M.O., interview, March 6, 2015)

Rootedness was seen as a general social factor able to influence community involvement by our respondents, rather than a direct reason for attrition from the deliberative practice itself.

Does money matter?

Would the situation have looked otherwise if participants were remunerated? Members of neighbourhood councils 'are volunteers, they do not benefit from remuneration or other facilities (free travel on public transportation, badges etc.)' (Consiliul Local Timisoara, 2005, II.-4). On the other hand, as a part of civil society, but with no legal personality, they were offered the opportunity 'to cooperate with other institutions, organizations, associations and foundations, for achieving the objectives they aim to' (Consiliul Local Timisoara, 2005, III.-2). This was to be put into practice with the annual neighbourhood festivals, which remained one of the fewest visible forms of manifestation of consultative councils. Partner associations were the ones being directly sponsored in these cases and citizens did not benefit directly from financial support. Although financial stimulation is highlighted in the literature as a significant factor determining people to remain involved in deliberative practices, the idea was brought up at no point during this case study.

Powerless in front of the elite

When talking about the decline of this process, frustration was an element to be often noticed at our respondents:

> We now have to sadly realize, after 25 years, that things move in a negative direction. Social implications occur from this point onward, the collective mind, peoplés participation tends to diminish, because trust in what happens around them, as well as trust in the political class and in structures of administration has been lost. (M.O., interview, March 6, 2015)

(Re)-building a bridge of communication is necessary:

> What happens now is the expression of a crisis – crises are usual in the evolution of a society, they are part of a sort of normality. The problem is to find solutions for overcoming these crisis stages as quickly as possible. (M.O., interview, March 6, 2015)

Political alienation is put in connection to the 50 years of communist regime in Romania – a part of history which cannot be eliminated: 'People speak about a return to capitalism – in my opinion we cannot talk about this at all (…). Eastern Europe is endowed with a totally different structure of perception, of conception and of social reaction' (M.O., interview, March 6, 2015). After coordinating common civic engagement projects of neighbourhood councils and young students, the teacher we have spoken to also refers to political alienation and states that 'things come from this communist structure; this is the fundament for our mentality' (Group discussion, March 10, 2015). Estrangement in the sense of powerlessness in front of the 'elite-driven manipulation' is also finally seen as a general social feature, much less as a reason explaining attrition.

The informal organization

The important feeling of trust in the authority can be regained by a proper communicational process. Professional mediation and clear rules of discourse with moderate speech (all in one, an appropriate design of debates) were not among the strong points of neighbourhood councils. There were few elements in the official regulations to determine how meetings between citizens and representatives of the administration should be conducted, so it was all based on a rather informal algorithm. According to our personal observations and to written reports of the meetings – what was to be tracked down in Timisoara were rather non-conformist types of debates, common in societies closer to passionate and emotional behaviours, than to standardized and normative ones. The factor of internal inefficacies appeared less during our empirical research, hardly proving to bother participants and stand in the way of the process.

Table 1. Reasons for attrition in long-term deliberative processes.

Argument	Description	Occurrence during the empirical research
Self-selection	The opportunity to drop out at any stage of the process	Predominantly
Duration of the process	A longer project tends to eliminate active people; only 'diehards' continue	Predominantly
Lack of impact	The administration's capacity to respond to demands by converting ideas into public policies	Predominantly
Politics and community	Close relations between authority and beneficiaries create efficient participatory mechanisms	Predominantly
Satisfaction towards the community	Collective content leads to neighbouring, which produces higher levels of participation	Often
Personal orientation/ attitude	Accent on social contribution, rather than self-interest, increases participation	Often
Moral rewards	Appreciation / recognition of voluntary efforts	Often (especially with respect to young people)
Age differences	Young people tend to stay aside; older and middle-aged citizens form the majority of participants	Often
Social differences	Persons with higher income and education are more likely to participate	Less often
Rootedness	Higher probability for 'old-timers' / enrooted inhabitants to participate	Less often
Financial stimulation	Remuneration	Not the case
Political estrangement	Inveterate lack of trust and the feeling of manipulation reduce public engagement	Less often
Internal inefficacies	Appropriate design of debates as a condition for 'successful participatory procedures'	Less often

Conclusion

Most of the research on non-attendance and attrition has been performed on reasons for declining to take part in deliberations ex ante (e.g. Jacquet), respectively for dropping out from innovative experiments organized for a limited period of time (e.g. Caluwaerts, Reuchamps). The scientific added value of this paper comes with the analysis of withdrawal from participatory practices on community or neighbourhood level (to be more specific), from the side of long-term active citizens.

Several lessons can be learned from this case study: given the element of self-selection, citizens will certainly use this pre-established opportunity to drop out whenever they perceive their efforts as useless or certain other conditions as inappropriate. After all, 'participation is never compulsory' (Jacquet, 2017, p. 2). A constant investment in terms of time and energy in a long-term process is then again hard to imagine without permanently developing and maintaining innovative elements, able to attract and keep people involved. Equally important – through citizens` perception of a limited impact on public policies and weak connections between politics and community, a successful democratic innovation can definitely be compromised: even within imperfect organizational frames, if the citizen does not perceive his effort to be acknowledged by concrete accomplishments of his needs, he will not be motivated to stay on board of the process. On the other hand, if personal relations between the two sides suffer, this leads to a decrease in trust and consequently to withdrawal.

Secondly, the relation to the other and to the community are not to be neglected: if, indeed, when it comes to civic engagement, 'the greatest benefits are in making a contribution and helping others', following these benefits can provide the idea of social responsibility with a sustainable application. And the 'work only for the good of the community' should be acknowledged, for offering a moral satisfaction especially to young volunteers, thus motivating them to remain attracted to participation. Otherwise, attrition threatens to compromise any kind of democratic innovation: people simply 'won't get involved anymore'.

Acknowledgements

I would like to express my sincere thanks to Mariano Barbato and to Sergiu Gherghina, for providing valuable guidance and feedback during the entire process of constructing this paper. The international workshop at Södertörn University in 2017, hosted by Joakim Ekman and Olena Podolian at CBEES, was a great opportunity to discuss the piece in its early stages and receive important suggestions from the participants. Special thanks to the teachers and representatives of NGOs, members of neighborhood councils and students who agreed to be interviewed, as well as to the municipalities of Timisoara and Mulhouse. I am also grateful to the two anonymous reviewers of this paper and the editors of Contemporary Politics, for their precious recommendations.

Disclosure statement

No potential conflict of interest was reported by the author.

References

Abers, R. (1998). Learning democratic practice: Distributing Government Resources through popular participation in Porto Alegre, Brazil. In M. Douglass & J. Friedmann (Eds.), *Cities for citizens* (pp. 39–65). Chichester: Wiley.

Barber, B. (1984). *Strong democracy: Participatory politics for a New Age.* Berkeley: California University Press.

Barnes, S. H., & Kaase, M. (eds.). (1979). *Political action: Mass participation in five Western democracies.* London: Sage.

Brady, H., Verba, S., & Schlozman, K. (1995). Beyond Ses: A Resource model of political participation. *American Political Science Review, 89*(2), 271–294.

Caluwaerts, D., & Reuchamps, M. (2013, August). *Generating Democratic Legitimacy through Citizen deliberation.* Paper presented at the APSA annual meeting, Chicago, IL.

Caluwaerts, D., & Ugarriza, J. E. (2012). Favorable conditions to epistemic validity in deliberative experiments: A methodological assessment. *Journal of Public Deliberation, 8*(1), Article 6.

Clarke, A. E. (2005). *Situational analysis. Grounded theory after the postmodern turn.* London: Sage.

Consiliul Local Timisoara. (2003, September 16). Hotararea Consiliului Local 195/16.09.2003 privind Constituirea Consiliilor Consultative de Cartier [Decision of Timisoara Local Council 195/16.09.2003, regarding the Establishment of Neighborhood Consultative Councils]. Retrieved from https://www.primariatm.ro/hcl.php?s_nr=195&s_year=2003

Consiliul Local Timisoara. (2005, February 22). Hotararea Consiliului Local 29/22.02.2005 privind modificarea Regulamentului orientativ de funcţionare a Consiliilor Consultative de Cartier [Decision of Timisoara Local Council 29/22.02.2005, regarding the Amendment of the Advisory Functioning Regulations of Neighborhood Consultative Councils]. Retrieved from https://www.primariatm.ro/hcl.php?s_nr=29&s_year=2005

Drouault, S. (2007). Participatory budgeting: A developing country process? A comparative analysis of the experiences of PB in Brazil, France and Spain (Thesis). Political Science. University of Sydney.

Fitzgerald, J., Gottschalk, P., & Moffitt, R. (1998). *An Analysis of Sample Attrition in Panel Data: The Michigan Panel Study of Income Dynamics.* Cambridge, MA: NBER Technical Working Papers 0220, National Bureau of Economic Research, Inc.

Fung, A. (2003). Survey article: Recipes for public spheres: Eight institutional design choices and their consequences. *Journal of Political Philosophy, 11*(3), 338–367.

Fung, A. (2007). Minipublics: Deliberative designs and their consequences. In S. W. Rosenberg (Ed.), *Deliberation, participation and democracy: Can the people govern?* (pp. 159–183). Basingstoke: Palgrave Macmillan.

Geissel, B., & Gherghina, S. (2016). Constitutional deliberative democracy and democratic innovations. In M. Reuchamps & J. Suiter (Eds.), *Constitutional deliberative democracy in Europe* (pp. 75–92). Colchester: ECPR Press.

Goodin, R. E. (2007). Enfranchising all affected interests, and its alternatives. *Philosophy and Public Affairs, 35*, 40–68.

Groenlund, K., Baechtiger, A., & Saetaele, M. (2014). *Deliberative mini-publics. Involving citizens in the democratic process.* Colchester: ECPR Press.

Hansen, K. M. (2004). *Deliberative democracy and opinion formation.* Odense: University of Southern Denmark.

Hopf, C. (1978). Die Pseudo-Exploration - Überlegungen zur Technik qualitativer interviews in der Sozialforschung [The Pseudo-Exploration - Thoughts on the techniques of qualitative interviews in social research]. *Zeitschrift für Soziologie, 7*(Jg., Heft 2), 97–115.

Jacquet, V. (2017). Explaining non-participation in deliberative mini-publics. *European Journal of Political Research, 56*(3), 640–659.

Karjalainen, M., & Rapeli, L. (2015). Who will not deliberate? Attrition in a multi-stage citizen deliberation experiment. *Quality and Quantity, 49*(1), 407–422.

Mansbridge, J. J. (1980). *Beyond Adversarial democracy.* Chicago: University of Chicago Press.

Miles, M. B., & Huberman, M. A. (1994). *Qualitative data analysis: An expanded sourcebook.* London: Sage.

Mutz, D. C. (2006). *Hearing the other side: Deliberative versus participatory democracy.* Cambridge: Cambridge University Press.

Neblo, M. A., Esterling, K. M., Kennedy, R. P., Lazer, D. M. J., & Sokhey, A. E. (2010). Who wants to deliberate - and why? *American Political Science Review, 104*(3), 566–583.

Niemeyer, S. J., Felicetti, A., & Ruggero, O. D. (2012). *Valsamoggia citizens initiative review (Prelimary report).* Canberra: Centre for Deliberative Democracy and Global Governance – The Australian National University.

Perkins, D. D., Brown, B. B., & Taylor, R. B. (1996). The Ecology of Empowerment: Predicting participation in community organizations. *Journal of Social Issues, 52*(1), 85–110.

Ritchie, J., Lewis, J., & Elam, G. (2003). Designing and selecting samples. In J. Ritchie & J. Lewis (Eds.), *Qualitative research practice* (pp. 77–108). London: Sage.

Smidt, C. E. (2008). *Pews, prayers and participation. Civic responsibility in America.* Washington, DC: Georgetown University Press.

Smith, G. (2009). *Democratic innovations: Designing institutions for citizen participation.* Cambridge: Cambridge University Press.

Strauss, A., & Corbin, J. (1990). *Basics of qualitative research.* Newbury Park, CA: Sage.

Struebing, J. (2013). *Qualitative Sozialforschung. Eine komprimierte Einführung* [Qualitative social research. A compressed guide]. München: Oldenbourg Wissenschaftsverlag.

Uhrig, N. (2008). *The nature and causes of attrition in the British Household Panel Study.* ISER Working Paper Series, No. 2008-05. Colchester: University of Essex, Institute for Social and Economic Research (ISER).

Ulbig, S. G., & Funk, C. L. (1999). Conflict avoidance and political participation. *Political Behavior, 21*(3), 265–282.

Voogt, R. J. J., & Van Kempen, H. (2002). Nonresponse bias and stimulus effects in the Dutch national election study. *Quality and Quantity, 36*(4), 325–345.

Wandersman, A., Florin, P., Friedmann, R., & Meier, R. (1987). Who Participates, Who does not, and why? An analysis of voluntary neighborhood organizations in the United States and Israel. *Sociological Forum, 2*(3), 534–555.

Zimmerman, J. F. (1999). *The New England town meeting: Democracy in action.* Westport: Praeger.

Appendix 1. Interview guide

- You were a very active person, who engaged in voluntary activities in the neighbourhood. How do you think things evolved after 2011-2012?
- What is your perception on the activity of your neighbourhood consultative council and of the other ones in the city, during the past years?
- What are the negative points in the evolution of neighbourhood councils in the last years and why?
- What are the positive things, what do you think changed for the better, regarding the cooperation between citizens` councils and the administration?
- What solutions and what means of improvement do you see, regarding the problems you identify in the activities of citizens` organizations? I refer to organizational and communicational disfunctions inside the council and in the cooperation with the administration.
- How could people be motivated to participate more in the activities of neighbourhood consultative councils?

Appendix 2. Situation map

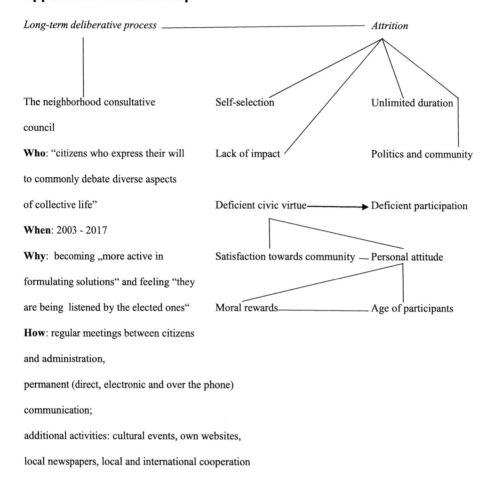

Long-term deliberative process ————————————— *Attrition*

The neighborhood consultative council

Who: "citizens who express their will to commonly debate diverse aspects of collective life"

When: 2003 - 2017

Why: becoming „more active in formulating solutions" and feeling "they are being listened by the elected ones"

How: regular meetings between citizens and administration, permanent (direct, electronic and over the phone) communication; additional activities: cultural events, own websites, local newspapers, local and international cooperation

Self-selection   Unlimited duration

Lack of impact   Politics and community

Deficient civic virtue ——————▶ Deficient participation

Satisfaction towards community — Personal attitude

Moral rewards ——————— Age of participants

Appendix 3. Coding scheme

Self-selection	Opposed to random selection
	Characteristic for popular assemblies
	Structure determined by beneficiaries
	Freedom of 'expressing your will'
	Freedom of 'changing your mind' anytime
Duration of the process	Loss of focus and interest
	Lack of innovative elements
	Repetitive actions
	Saturation
	'Diehards' – the only ones to commit
Lack of impact	Effect on public policies
	Relevance of investments
	Complexity of public investments
	Credibility
	Unfulfilled expectations
Politics and community	Decision-makers and beneficiaries
	Communication
	Trust
	Responsibility
	Importance of the moderator

Democratic innovations in Serbia: a misplaced trust in technology

Ivana Damnjanović 🅳

ABSTRACT
This article compares the results of three projects from Serbia, which share the assumption that the power of information and communication technologies (ICTs) can improve communication between the government and the citizens, and increase, to a limited extent, citizens' participation. Using interviews and document analysis, it investigates the intended objectives and actual results of the projects. The key findings are that none of these projects can be unequivocally seen as a success, although they fail in different ways and to the various degrees. These results will primarily contribute to the underdeveloped body of knowledge about democratic innovations in Eastern Europe, but will also help to identify the factors of success (or failure) of this type of technologically-based democratic innovations.

Introduction

The abundance of innovative practices and institutions sprouting around the world in the last decades has provided enough data for attempts of more generalized and/or comparative studies of democratic innovations (such as Geissel, 2012; Smith, 2009, 2005). While a number of these works study innovations that involve information and communication technologies (ICTs), their theoretical conceptualization is less clear, and the criteria for the assessment of their success are somewhat underdeveloped compared to more widespread forms of democratic innovations. One point of interest in social sciences was the relationship between ICTs and democracy, which resulted in a number of works, scattered across different disciplines (see Margetts, 2013). Different approaches have contributed to conceptual confusion, with terms such as e-democracy, e-government, internet-based/ICTs based/ICTs enabled democratic innovation. The issue is further complicated by the fact that practically all instances of democratic innovations in the twenty-first century have made some use of the available ICTs. Therefore, the first question to be addressed in this paper is when, and under which circumstances, the use of ICTs can be qualified as a democratic innovation.

Another important issue is a certain optimistic bias present in the literature on democratic innovations. It stems from the observation that the success of democratic innovations, especially their impact, is hard to assess, due to their diversity, lack of reliable data and abundant problems that riddle the research (Newton, 2012a). Researchers have thus focused on cases that have had a measurable impact. Even then, as Geissel (2012) noted, studies tend to overstate the impact of democratic innovations. This optimistic bias is sometimes built in the very design of the research, like in Newton's (2012a, p. 4) definition of democratic innovation, which excludes any unsuccessful democratic experiment. As Spada and Ryan (2017) recently demonstrated, this optimistic bias is both measurable and striking, since most papers present democratic innovation as best practices, with a noticeable absence of research on failures. However, if best practices can teach us what it takes for an innovation to succeed, failures can also provide insights into which pitfalls to avoid in the designing process.

The intention of this paper is to address these gaps in the literature by comparing three micro-cases from Serbia, which qualify as democratic innovations. With its complicated, and, arguably, not quite completed democratic transition, as well as its strategic commitment to European Union (EU) accession, Serbia is an illustrative case, representative of similar (post-communist, non-EU) countries where democratic innovations are seen as another means to increase participation of the citizens and bring the democracy closer to EU standards. Selected micro-cases differ in their immediate objectives, design and initiators, but share some basic similarities. Firstly, they all strive to enhance certain aspects of Serbian democracy: transparency, participation and accountability. Secondly, they rely on information and communications technologies to accomplish these objectives. The aim of the comparison is to assess the success of these projects over a period of four years (2010–2014) and to identify the drivers of their success (or failure). Findings indicate that while none of the projects meets the standards of success, they failed to differing degrees. The relevance of the findings is not exclusively scientific, since the reasons behind the failures could serve as lessons for the designers of similar future projects. In the following sections I shall briefly review the literature on democratic innovations and ICTs, present the rationale behind the case selection and analytical framework, outline the three cases from Serbia and compare their success.

Democratic innovations and ICTs

Scholarship on democratic innovation has yet to reach an agreement about its basic concept. Reasons, as Newton (2012a) explains, lie in the elusiveness of the two constituent terms. Furthermore, given the wide variety of innovative democratic experiments, it is hard to provide a definition that is both sufficiently comprehensive and operationalized. Nevertheless, there seems to exist a tendency towards broader definitions (see, for example, Saward, 2000, p. 4). Described as institutions (Smith, 2009), or processes and practices (Geissel, 2012), innovations refer to new ways for citizens to engage in democratic politics. Leading scholars in the field seem to share a similar position on the issue of the innovative component of democratic experiments – it does not have to be truly new. Saward (2000) and Newton (2012a) agree that it can mean revitalizing or reintroducing institutions and practices that were once present, but had fallen out of favour. It can also be the adaptation and implementation of solutions developed elsewhere (Geissel, 2012). Finally, most of the research on democratic innovations seems to be rooted in participatory (e.g. Geissel, 2012; Smith, 2009) and deliberative (e.g. Fung & Wright, 2001; Saward, 2000; Spada & Ryan, 2017) strands of democratic theory, and definitions reflect this. But it is worth pointing out that improvements of various aspects of representative democracy should not be discounted (see Pausch, 2016; Smith, 2005; Subirats, 2002). This may be especially important in 'new democracies', where the quality of democracy is not yet on the level termed in the literature as a substantive democracy (Pridham & Lewis, 1996), full poliarchy (Coppedge & Reinicke, 1990) or, simply, liberal democracy (Diamond, 2002).

Conceptual issues are further complicated in the case of democratic innovations relying on ICTs. In the first place, there seems to be a lot of terminological confusion. While in this paper they will be referred to as ICTs-based innovations, terms used to denote this category of innovations include e-democracy (|Smith, 2009, 2005), cyber democracy (Barth & Schlegelmilch, 2014; Bryan, Tambini, & Tsagarousianou, 2002; Ferber, Foltz, & Pugliese, 2007; Poster, 1997), innovations via ICTs (Subirats, 2002), ICTs-enabled innovations (Smith, 2009), technologically mediated innovations in political practices (Hoff, Horrocks, & Tops, 2003). Moreover, the terms themselves are not consistently used or very clearly defined. The definitions tend to include 'the use of ICTs' in some form, but what exactly is meant by *ICTs* and *use* is seldom elaborated on. It has already been observed that while definitions of ICTs used in social science research are frequently tacit, their most common feature is 'that they are related to technologies that facilitate the transfer of information and various types of electronically mediated communication' (Zuppo, 2012, p. 19). This, as Smith (2005) duly noted, includes radio, television, telephone, as well as computer mediated communication. The scholarly discussion about possible uses of new communication technologies and democracy started long before the wide adoption of the internet in the late 1990s. As Margetts (2013) points out, concepts of electronic democracy and teledemocracy had been introduced and studied since the 1970s. In the twenty-first century, though ICTs are by no means synonymous with internet technologies, this is usually the meaning implied in research on e-government, e-democracy, and ICTs-based democratic innovations.

Sound theoretical conceptualization of the role of ICTs in democratic innovations is further hindered by at least three other factors. Firstly, the relations between ICTs and democracy are studied within different disciplines with almost no overlap (Margetts, 2013). The second is the burden of technological determinism, which dominated the first studies in the field (see Barber, 1998; Hand & Sandywell, 2002), and has lead to distinctly techno-optimistic and techno-pessimistic evaluations of the potential impact of ICTs on democracy. High expectations in the exploration of the concept have only recently been replaced by more temperate observations based on empirical studies. Finally, given the diversity of ways ICTs can be used to enhance democratic practices, it is difficult to identify the features that are common enough to constitute a discrete category of democratic innovations.

These problems are reflected in research: when such innovations are treated as a separate category, the justifications for such classification are rather vague. Newton (2012a) provides three key reasons: ICTs cut across all other categories as a tool; their use in this manner attracts a lot of interest; and their potential for transformation of the political sphere is, as seen by some authors at least, very strong. Smith (2009, p. 29) argues that 'the family resemblance rests on the use of information and communication technology (ICT): other design features can and do vary quite dramatically'. He distinguishes between cases where ICTs are merely used to improve the effectiveness of innovations and those where ICTs are fundamental to the very design of the innovations. Based on the forms of engagement mentioned in his own work (Smith, 2005) – e-mail contact with officials, online access to information, for example – as well as those studied by others (i.e. Wright, 2012), the mere introduction of ICTs-based communication channel can count as an innovation *per se* if it enhances, broadens, complements or replaces previously existing opportunities for engagement.

One issue that seems to be recurring in the literature is the distinction between e-government and e-democracy, and their respective relations with democratic innovation. Innovative uses of ICTs by political actors, especially governments, were used more often to promote 'good management' than 'good democracy' (Musso, Weare, & Hale, 2000). The difference between them is somewhat contentious, since 'it is not always possible to place some facts only within the framework either the former or the latter' (Rodotä, 2007). There seems to be a consensus that e-government is more concerned with service delivery, while e-democracy focuses on participation (i.e. Netchaeva, 2002; Shane, 2012; Smith, 2009). Still, the improved delivery of services, access to government information and other e-government features can contribute to increased trust in the democratic system and improve some aspects of democratic governance, such as transparency and accountability. Newton (2012b) considers at least some e-government projects to be democratic innovations.

The most comprehensive theoretical framework for studying ICTS-based democratic innovations is the one proposed by Subirats (2002). The use of ICTs in democratic innovations, he argues, can be conceptualized within the framework based on two broad criteria: (1) is the innovation applied in the field of policies or in the field of polity, meaning relations between institutions and the citizens; and (2) does it intend to improve and innovate existing constitutional and political framework or to introduce alternatives to it. This second criterion is labelled as the degree of democratic innovation. Subirats identified four political strategies/discourses on how to relate ICTs and democratic systems: (1) consumerist mechanisms (policy, low degree of innovation); (2) changes in democratic elitism (polity, low degree of innovation); (3) pluralist networks provision of services (policy, high degree of innovation); and (4) direct democracy (polity, high degree of innovation). While the first two strategies are striving for improvements within the representative/liberal democracy, third and fourth strategies are going beyond it. In relation to ICTs, the first two strategies, according to Subirats, emphasize the use of their communicative elements, while the other two are primarily utilizing their relational elements. It should be noted that although Subirats claims that the consumerist mechanisms and changes in democratic elitism may reinforce the most elitist aspects of representative democracy, he nevertheless places them within the range of democratic innovations. Distinction, developed by Kakabadse, Kakabadse, and Kouzmin (2003), between four models of electronic democracy: (1) electronic bureaucracy; (2) information management; (3) populist model of direct democracy; and (4) civil society model, roughly corresponds to Subirats's framework.

Research design

The paper will address the gap in the literature on democratic innovations in Serbia. As a new democracy, Serbia is representative of the post-communist countries striving to join the European Union. This strategic commitment is reflected in the efforts of both the state and the civil society to bring all aspects of democratic politics closer to the EU standards. This had lead to the explosion of innovative democratic experiments, including various instances of participatory budgeting, participatory planning and other projects, frequently inspired by similar EU practices. There is, however, another strong commitment on the part of the political elite in Serbia, consistently promoted by all governments since the beginning of the century: digitalization of public services and advancement of the information society. This is the main reason why in this paper I shall explore three micro-cases that rely on the use of ICTs. The first of these cases is *e-Participation*, part of the e-government portal dedicated to discussion of bills and policy documents. The second is *Ask Your MP/Local Representative*, an effort of non-profit organizations to build online tools for communication between citizens and their representatives, and the third is *Networking of Local Communities*, where ICTs were used by local government to improve service delivery and, potentially, participation.

I will consider the design and results of these micro-cases in the period from 2010 to 2014. While all of the projects are ongoing, data was collected for this specific time frame. Most of the data was gathered by a qualitative content analysis of public sources. The official websites of organizations implementing the projects were the primary source of information on the project design, objectives, target population, initiators/implementers and results. These websites often featured other relevant documents, such as reports and promotional brochures, describing the objectives, implementation process as well as the context in which the project was embedded and prerequisites for their success. Additional data, primarily regarding the legal framework, and the social and political context, were retrieved from the relevant legislation and media reports. The descriptions of media strategies of the projects rely on self-reporting (reports from the implementers and interviews), while the data on media coverage were generally limited to the Serbian national media covered by the EBART media archives (http://www.arhiv.rs).

In addition to desk research, interviews were conducted in 2014 with implementers of two projects: *Ask Your MP/Representative* and *Networking of Local Communities*. Semi-structured interviews were used to collect data on project implementation and results. In addition to the facts about projects, informants were asked about their impressions on the success of the projects, rationale behind the projects and the most pressing problems regarding their implementation. In total, eight interviews were conducted. Three of them were with the informants on *Ask Your MP/Representative*: two from the civil society organization (CSO) implementing the national project and one from the local CSO implementing the project in Kraljevo. The remaining five interviews, involving the *Networking of Local Communities,* were conducted with four informants from the local government in Užice, all of them middle management level civil servants, including the representative of the IT department, and the fifth informant from the consulting company partnering on the project. Although the number of informants was small, all of them were directly engaged in the design and implementation of the projects and were able to provide relevant information.

These cases were selected because they are sufficiently similar in some respects so that comparison is possible. They all rely on the use of ICTs to promote some form of communication between the citizens and the government, in order to improve or enhance some aspects of liberal/representative democracy. Thus they can be described, within Subirats's framework, as democratic innovations, albeit of low degree. If we follow Smith's (2005) classification, two of them are electoral innovations, while the third, *Networking of Local Communities*, contains mostly e-government features. All three innovations do have a minor participatory component. They are also based on a top-down approach, not in terms of being institutionalized (although two of them are), but regarding their design, which was devised and implemented with little input from the citizens. Another common element is the underlying assumption of technological determinism: the belief of the initiators and designers of the projects that intrinsic properties of ICTs are sufficient to bring about a certain extent of social change. This attitude was either explicitly expressed in the interviews, or at least implied in the project materials. Finally, since they are all taking place in the same state, variables related to the political system and political culture can be safely disregarded in the explanation of their success or failure. That being said, one must bear in mind that the general political context in Serbia is not conducive to extensive participation. The potential impact of the projects is therefore significantly limited due to systemic constraints.

The success of the cases will be compared according to the criteria proposed in the previous empirical and comparative works on ICTs-based democratic innovations. Most comprehensive analytical frameworks developed by Smith (2009)[1] and Geissel (2012) seem to be too ambitious for the assessment of ICTs-based democratic innovations. However, two criteria seem to emerge as the most adequate for the evaluation of their success, and seem to be repeatedly used for this purpose (see Newton, 2012b; Shane, 2012; Smith, 2009). The first is reach: how successful the innovation is in mobilizing citizens, especially those who are otherwise not engaged or are underrepresented in the political process. The second is the impact on policy: to what extent, if any, does the innovation affect policy outcomes. After comparing the three micro-cases according to these criteria, I shall propose some possible explanations for the results based on the empirical findings.

ICTs-based democratic innovations in Serbia

After brief examination of systemic constraints stemming from Serbian institutional framework and political culture, this section will present three cases: *e-Participation, Ask Your MP/ Local Representative* and *Networking of Local Communities*. The overview will focus on the actors behind the projects, the design of the projects, their self-defined objectives, and their results.

Systemic constraints: institutional framework and political culture

Serbia falls into the category of new democracies, where democracy is fairly consolidated in terms of being 'the only game in town'. During the observed period (2010-2014), it was consistently rated as such in relevant surveys and reports, although the lack of deliberative and participatory components in Serbian democracy was noticed (see Democracy Index, 2014, 2015; Freedom in the World, 2015; Kaufman & Kraay, 2014). Voter turnout for two parliamentary elections held in 2012 and 2014 was 57.80% and 53.09%, which is slightly below EU average. However, opportunities for other forms of citizens' participation are very few. Instruments such as a referendum or popular initiative are permitted by legislation, but are very rarely used, although more frequently on local than on regional or national level (see Klačar, 2011; Narodna inicijativa, 2018).

Reasons for deficiencies in participation are twofold: they follow either from the institutional framework or from political culture. Regarding the former, the main problem seems to be the design of the electoral system, which is extremely party-centric. It is a proportional system with the single electoral unit, with relatively low 5% threshold.[2] Only the names of the parties, and, sometimes, their leaders, appear on the ballot. The parties, usually meaning the party leadership, are also in complete control over the choice of candidates. Therefore, elected officials are completely dependent on their parties and their loyalties tend to lie with them, rather than with the voters. There is no incentive for individual representatives, either in the Parliament or in the local assemblies, to take initiative or regularly and directly communicate with the citizens, even when channels for such communication do exist.[3]

Another institutional issue, mentioned repeatedly in the EU Commission reports, is extensive use of the urgent procedure in the Parliament (see Serbia Progress Report, 2014). This procedure allows for laws to be passed without public debate. It was conceived as a means to quickly pass the bills that have to be implemented immediately. In practice, it is used almost as a default, especially for bills proposed by the government. This seems to be a structural problem, since the same mechanism was used by whichever party that was in power during the observed period.

Dominant political culture in Serbia is generally seen as dominantly authoritarian, collectivistic, and patriarchal, burdened by the lack of democratic traditions and by the legacy of communism. As such, it does not encourage political participation. Furthermore, it is viewed by some authors as incompatible with established democratic institutions, or even actively opposed to them (Bešić, 2016; Pantić & Pavlović, 2009). The empirical data seem to, at least to some extent, corroborate these claims. Results of a survey from 2014 are illustrative for the period observed in this paper. Only 23% of subjects stated that they are interested in politics, and 21% of them have engaged in some sort of political activity apart from voting. The knowledge about political issues was also lower than in the previous years (Audit of Political Engagement in Serbia, 2014). Therefore, every attempt to engage citizens would be severely limited in its reach. It is, however, important to note that in a new and somewhat fragile democracy as Serbian, even small and incremental steps could, in the long term, potentially contribute to increase of trust in the democratic system.

e-Participation

e-Participation (*e-participacija*) is part of the national e-government (*e-uprava*)[4] project launched in 2010. It provides a platform for citizens to comment on bills and proposals of strategic policy documents before they are passed. The website's main page defines e-Participation as 'the use of ICTs in the processes of public administration and government', primarily aiming to improve the quality of the relationship between citizens on one side and government and administration on the other. While various Web 2.0 technologies (wiki platforms, social media, blogs) were mentioned as possible tools of the e-Participation, so far there are only three ways of communication: e-Participation function of the e-government portal, an all but defunct online forum[5] and e-Government social media (Facebook, Twitter and Google+) accounts. However, the only institutionalized way to discuss legislation and policy documents is through the e-Government portal. The idea is simple and straightforward: the documents are posted on the platform, and within given time-frame citizens can post their comments, and/or upload the files.

The e-Government portal was defined in the corresponding strategic documents as 'the single access point and the pathway for communication with other portals and systems of government agencies providing e-services' ("E-government Strategy," 2015). This allows all state agencies and local governments to post their documents for public discussion in an easy and uniform manner. For every posted document, the portal provides the text of the document, the time frame of the public discussion and a list of possible ways to participate in the discussion, including the comments section of the website. There is, however, no information on follow-up procedures (for example, how the comments are meant to be processed, are the institutions proposing the documents obligated to respond to comments).

In order to use the portal, including its e-participation segment, citizens must register on the website. The registration procedure is easy, but it is necessary to use an electronic certificate or provide personal information. The electronic certificate is tied to a biometric identity (ID) card with an inbuilt microcontroller,[6] available on request, and allows automatic registration to the portal, since the primary purpose of the electronic certificate is to facilitate the use of various e-government services. According to the Ministry of Internal Affairs, from March 1st 2010 to June 2016, there were only 152,060 certificates issued, which is barely more than 5% of valid ID cards (Vukosavljević, 2016). For those who do not have the certificate, registration to the portal requires full name and Unique Master Citizen Number. It is a unique 13-digit identification code that, being part of all identifying documents, allows the state authorities to verify the citizen's identity. Its use as the means of registration is justified, as stated on the website, by the need to prevent registration of multiple accounts.

However, the public interest in using this feature seems to be very low. During the observed period (2010–2014) there were 50 documents posted for public discussion. They include all proposed bills that were not subject to the urgent procedure, national strategic documents, and some local policy documents. Yet, only nine of those were commented on, and the total number of comments is 22. Four documents have only one comment each, and the highest number of comments on a document is seven. Furthermore, not all of the comments were made by individual citizens, but rather by companies (9 comments) or civil society organizations (4 comments). There were no responses to the comments on the website by any of the state organs or agencies.

Ask your MP/Local representative

Two very similar projects started in 2012 and 2013. Both were implemented by CSOs (CRTA[7] from Belgrade and PRODOR[8] from Kraljevo) and aimed at improving communication between elected representatives and their constituencies. The first project focused on the national Parliament, while the other provided a similar service for the City Assembly in Kraljevo. The idea was to provide an easy and user-friendly interface and open a channel for communication, and was implemented through online forms, allowing the citizens to send their questions to the representatives. Questions are then screened and forwarded to the representatives.

In January 2012 the Open Parliament website was launched. The 'Ask MPs' section is only one among the services this website provides, in addition to statistics, searchable session transcripts, educational materials about the legislative procedure and other materials related to parliamentary practices. Questions for Members of Parliament (MPs) are filtered in order to eliminate spam, insults, and questions regarding MPs' private life. Between 2014 and 2015, up to 50% of all inquiries were dismissed for these reasons. A similar question form does exist on Parliament's official website, but according to information provided by the Press Service the questions are automatically forwarded to MPs' emails, and there are no archives or data on them, so it is impossible to know to what extent the system is actually used. The implementers of the 'Ask MPs' project have noted in an interview that awareness about the importance of internet communication is steadily rising among MPs. Since 'Open Parliament' project's main interest is transparency, 'Ask MPs' insists on open communication on both ends: the full name of the person or organization asking the question is required, and there is profile page for every MP on which questions and answers are archived. In the period between the project's inception in 2012 and 2014 25% of forwarded questions were answered. The organization behind the project maintains regular communication with MPs, reminding them occasionally how many questions they have left unanswered. In addition to regular activities, the online platform was also used for two major civil society campaigns, 'Rights for Moms' and 'Convention on Violence against Women', which were very successful.

The online question form for the 'Ask Your Representative' project became operational in June 2013. It was designed as a part of the larger public advocacy project aiming to improve communication between the citizens and local assembly representatives. The project also tried to engage citizens and representatives through other means and channels, such as 'mailboxes' in local communities.

Unlike the national Parliament, the official website of Kraljevo does not have a contact form for representatives in the city assembly, nor a list of their e-mail addresses, with the exception of City Assembly Speaker and City Assembly Secretary. Through the 'Ask Your Representative' page citizens can ask questions of any representative, which are then, having been screened, forwarded electronically or in print, according to the representative's preferences. Questions are filtered using the same criteria as in the 'Ask MPs' project.

In the beginning, 5–6 questions were received monthly through the online form, with numbers rising to 20–30 a month during the campaign in the local media. However, a couple of months after the campaign ended, the number of questions nearly dropped to zero. The representatives were generally willing to cooperate, and about 40% of the questions were answered. It is important to note that CSOs behind this project had, through other activities and projects over the years, already established the relationship of mutual trust with the local government. Again, in the interviews, informants emphasized the need for permanent engagement with both sides.

Networking of local communities

The Užice city authorities implemented the 'Equipping and Networking the City of Užice and Local Communities' project in 2008–2011. The term 'local community', as it is used here, refers to *mesna zajednica,* a form of self-government specific for Serbia. Geographically, it is closest to a neighbourhood. For a while it served as an important feature of the socialist political system (Milosavljević, 2015). It was introduced as a legal entity in the 1963 Constitution. Its status as a form of a bottom-up democracy unit within the self-management system was further strengthened by constitutional changes in 1974 ("Ustav SFRJ," 1974, Articles 114–115). The local community was conceived as a form of direct democracy, along with the referendum and voter assemblies. In 1982, a *Law on Local Communities* determined their organization, finances and jurisdiction (Milosavljević, 2015). While not explicitly dismantled, in the 1990s local communities have lost their legal status as units of self-government as well as that of a democratic instrument, and became optional, depending on the will of the local authorities.

The main objective of the *Networking in Local Communities* project was to bring administrative services delivered by the city closer to the citizens residing in the remote local communities, some of which are hardly accessible in winter, thus providing equal access to services to all citizens. With the territory of 666.7 square kilometres, and almost 30,000 out of 83,000 citizens living outside the metropolitan area, the goal was to create an environment that would allow for better communication between citizens, especially those from rural areas, and the City Administration.

The first step to be taken, and the one most dependent on political support from the elected officials, was to provide an appropriate legal framework. Bridging the gap in the existing legislation, the City passed regulations that transformed local communities into offices of the City administration, allowing them to deliver the services provided by the City. The next prerequisite was to develop a modern and efficient model for service delivery. This was achieved by developing a unified IT network for all City administration departments, and by digitalizing the data available in the city registries. This step also increased transparency and accountability, since citizens are now able to follow the processing of their requests online. The necessary infrastructure was then put in place, in cooperation with the telecommunications company, which provided a fast internet connection between the central City Administration and the offices in local communities. They were then integrated into the unified City Administration IT system. This process was conducted in parallel with the personnel training. By the end of 2010, the system was fully functional in all 33 local communities. Along with these activities, a promotional campaign was carried out. It comprised advertisements in the local media as well as posters and guidebooks explaining the work of the new Service Centres. The service delivery was the focus of the project, as well as of the media campaign, but an improvement of other aspects of democracy in local self-government was also among the stated objectives. The establishment of Service Centres was seen as a precondition for more effective engagement of citizens in the decision making and the work of the local government, through public discussions on proposed regulations, popular initiatives and referenda.

Quantified data about the use of the network during the following three years were not available. Yet, in the interviews, informants have expressed their dissatisfaction with the reach of the project, emphasizing that the vast majority of citizens still prefer to take their business directly to the central City Administrations instead of using the Service centres. When asked about the potential reasons for this state of affairs, they were unable to provide a clear answer beyond the inefficiency and insufficiency of the promotional campaign.

Success or failure: limited reach and slim impact on policies

Interestingly, none of the considered projects is self-described as a democratic innovation. While the main page of *e-Participation* website states that e-participation is strongly correlated with both e-government and e-democracy, the concept of e-democracy is not elaborated on. *Open Parliament*, part of which is the *Ask Your MP* project, stresses its contribution to transparency, information access and regular communication between the citizens and MPs. Regarding the *Networking in the Local Communities* project, it was described by political actors involved as both a contribution to the improvement of democracy and an 'innovation in the area of local governance' ("The Citizens Service Centres," 2012), but this aspect was not emphasized by the informants. The first two projects are trying to replicate the innovations already tried in other countries, while the *Networking in the Local Communities* is more tied to specifically local context. All three cases, nevertheless, fall within the first two of Subirats's (2002) strategies, with *Networking of Local Communities* primarily aimed at service delivery, and *e-Participation* and *Ask Your MP/Representative* more concerned with improved communication between citizens and government and enhanced access to information. They are all introducing new, hitherto non-existing ways for citizens to engage with the government and promote certain democratic qualities. Their participatory component is, however, weak. *E-Participation* allows for participatory inputs, but not for deliberation. *Ask Your MP/Representative* can be, and was used for public advocacy/lobbying but there is no clear or formal connection with the decision-making process. *Networking of Local Communities* lists as one of the achieved results 'creating conditions for the more effective use of mechanisms for the inclusion of citizens in the decision making process' ("Užice Networking," n.d.), but the records show that those mechanisms were not used during the observed period.

The first criterion for assessment of success of the micro-cases is their reach. Our analysis will focus on the following questions: (1) how many citizens used the projects during the observed time-frame; (2) do they successfully mobilize inactive citizens; (3) do they facilitate easier engagement of active citizens; (4) do they remedy or alleviate existing disbalances in representation and participation?

The number of citizens involved in all three projects is low, whether measured in absolute numbers or compared to the potential pool of users. The *Ask Your MP/Representative* project was the most successful in this respect, considering that the observed period was shorter than for the other projects (2012–2014 for *Ask Your MP*; 2013–2014 for *Ask Your Representative*). During this period, *Ask Your MP* received a total of 753 questions, while *Ask Your Representative* received 124 questions. However, these numbers are still quite low, given that the projects' target groups are potential voters – over six and a half million on the national level and nearly 110,000 in the city of Kraljevo.[9] The number of users for *Networking of Local Communities* project is not available, but according to informants, it was not high. It is, nevertheless, presumably higher than the total of nine citizens, not counting comments by various organizations, who commented on the *e-Participation* website during a four year period. In this respect, the *e-Participation* project is by far the least successful, especially when its other features are taken into account, namely that it is implemented by the national government and conceived as a single entry point for online public discussion on the proposed laws, regulations, and policy documents. A low total number of citizens using the projects consequently leads to a negative answer to the second question. None of them was successful in the mobilization of inactive citizens, but the failure of the *e-Participation* project is again the most striking. The data for *Networking of Local Communities* concerning the third question is unavailable. The *Ask Your MP/ Representative* and *e-Participation* projects did to a certain extent facilitate engagement for active citizens, since both were used by CSOs.

Regarding the fourth question, *Networking of Local Communities* was conceived as a tool for providing equal access to the City Administration services to all citizens. In this respect, it does, at least potentially, alleviate existing disbalances, providing the residents of remote local communities with new means of communicating with the local government. Yet, since the participatory component of the project has had no effect thus far, it is hard to assess to which extent this potential will be realized. The design of the other two projects ignores, as Margolis (2007) puts it, 'the proverbial elephant in the room' – the digital divide. As a result it reinforces existing differences rather than diminishing them, since the use of ICTs in Serbia follows the usual pattern, being much higher in urban than in rural populations, and is also strongly correlated with age, level of education and income. The users of both projects are thus self-selected among those who have both access and skills to use the online platforms.

The second criterion is the impact on policy. The main question here is to what extent, if any, the innovation affects policy outcomes. *Networking of Local Communities* had no impact on policy, since the participatory instruments were not utilized. The impact of *e-Participation* is harder to assess, since it was available not only to citizens but also to companies and CSOs. Even if some impact could be detected, it would remain unclear whether it was the direct consequence of online participation or some other form of lobbying/ public advocacy. The same is the issue with the success of the *Ask Your MP/Representative* project. Two campaigns lead by CSOs were marked as a success, and they did have some impact. *Rights for Moms* obtained general support from the MPs for a change in legislation, but the law in question has not yet entered the parliamentary procedure. Furthermore, the online platform was only one way used to reach MPs, in addition to the face-to-face campaign. The second campaign, for Serbia to ratify the Istanbul Convention (Action against violence against women and domestic violence) of the Council of Europe, was also a success – the convention was ratified on October 31st 2013. But again, the use of the *Ask Your MP* platform was part of the wider effort, so it is impossible to discern to what extent it contributed to this outcome.

It seems clear that, during the observed period, none of the three innovations was very successful. *Ask Your MP/Representative* can be termed as a moderate success; the success of *Networking of Local Communities* is hard to discern due to a lack of quantifiable data; *e-Participation* was almost not used at all during the observed period. It is somewhat harder to determine the reasons for this outcome, but previous research provides some guidelines. Newton (2012a) argues that the lack of impact of democratic innovations may be caused by their design, or they can be blocked by other interested parties, while Smith (2009) finds that ICTs-based innovations succeed or fail primarily due to their design. Following this line of reasoning, I will try now to point out to some of the design features that may have contributed to the projects' underperformance.

The most serious flaw in the design, more pronounced for *Ask Your Representative* and *e-Participation* projects, seems to be lack of sensitivity to specific local context. While similar innovation may be successful in other countries, systemic constraints present in Serbia are limiting their potential. *Ask your Representative* was modelled primarily on the British experiences. However, differences in both electoral systems and political culture severely impact the success of the project in Serbia. For example, when the representatives are elected from party lists, it is hard to identify to whom the questions should be addressed – the citizens are confused who represents *them* specifically. In the case of *e-Participation* project, the project seems to be an afterthought, and addition to the delivery service. There was, so far no sign of strong commitment on the part of Government to make full use of this feature.

Projects' visibility was related primarily to their media presence. *Open Parliament*, of which *Ask Your MP* is a part, attracted lots of media attention. Its launch in 2012 was extensively covered by the press, and during that year there were 25 articles about the project's activities in the national newspapers. The project was presented in the cities across Serbia, and that also contributed to the visibility, since these events were also covered in the daily press. The trend continued in the next two years, with 27 articles in 2013 and 35 in 2014. While only two articles from 2012 were about the launching of the *Ask Your MP* feature, the high visibility of the *Open Parliament* made the feature easier to discover. *Open Parliament* is also very active on social media, with over 15,000 followers on Facebook and over 7000 on Twitter. *Ask Your Representative* was focused on the local media and, according to the informant, the campaign had a very strong, but not a long lasting effect on the number of citizens engaged with the platform. However, the same strategy did not work well enough for the *Networking of Local Communities* project, and failed to generate the expected response. The *e-Participation* web-page is practically invisible. There was a series of articles in the national press in 2010 announcing the launch of the e-government portal, but e-participation was mentioned in only two of them, in one sentence, as one of the available features. It was not reported on again during the observed period. Government's focus was on service delivery, which is reflected in the media reports: e-government was the keyword found in 70 articles from 2010–2014. E-government also has a social media presence, and the announcements about public discussions are posted there, although inconsistently. However, their outreach is relatively small: little over 7000 followers on both Facebook and Twitter.

As Smith (2009) has observed, the ICTs-based innovations do not need to take place entirely in the cyberspace. Judicious combining of online platforms with offline opportunities for engagements has produced results for the *Ask Your Representative* project. The same was attempted within the *Networking of Local Communities*, but the results were not so positive. The *e-Participation* platform could be used simply as an information delivery service, so it is possible that interested parties are using it to find out about opportunities for face-to-face participation, but there are no data available that would support this assumption.

The failure of *e-Participation*, an institutionalized national project, to engage citizens, merits additional analysis. The project design seems to be seriously flawed in some respects. First of all, since it is tied to the e-government portal, the registration requires disclosure of sensitive personal information, making users easily and instantly identifiable. This could present a significant barrier to participation, since, as Smith (2009) has observed, anonymity can be conducive to sincere and productive deliberation. This problem is even more pronounced when some aspects of the economic situation in

Serbia are taken into account. The unemployment rate during the observed period was relatively high – over 20%, and the state is the largest single employer in Serbia.[10] Lack of anonymity could thus be especially discouraging for many whose living depends on the state. Secondly, the project suffers from the usual problem of ICTs-based innovations – a lack of responsiveness on the part of the government and of established procedures regarding the translation of expressed preferences into policies. This can be due to organizational reasons: while the e-government department is responsible for the portal's maintenance, they only provide a venue for other institutions to post documents. It is therefore unclear who should respond to comments. Finally, the promotion of the e-participation feature has been very weak, compared to the service-delivery. Hence it shows all the signs of a reform designed to fail (Newton, 2012b).

Conclusions

This article analysed the extent to which three different Serbian cases of ICT-based democratic innovations were successful, and the causes behind this. The analysis shows that all three instances failed to engage a significant number of citizens and influence policy outcomes. Bearing in mind the differences in their institutional status, scope and ambition, the *Ask Your MP/Representative* produced the best results within the given time-frame, while *e-Participation's* failure is the most striking. These findings support the conclusions of previous research, namely that careful design of ICTs-based innovations, cognizant of the social and political context, is crucial for their success. Within the polity where citizens' participation is already low, a top-down approach seems to be insufficiently adjusted to the needs of the citizens, neglecting the specific characteristics of the target groups and relying instead on deterministic assumptions about 'the power' of the ICTs to achieve mobilization on its own. Therefore, stronger and more creative efforts to reach out to the citizens are necessary. A combination of online and offline participation can improve a project's performance, as can the savvy media approach.

Overall, these projects suffer from, as Coleman (2001) put it, 'apparent irrelevance to the 'real' world of policy and politics', and confirm Newton's observation that '[t]he impact of electronic notice boards, electronic consultation, various forms of e-democracy and online government also seems to be fairly slight' (Newton, 2012b, p. 150).

Finally, research presented in this study provides assessment of the results within a relatively brief period of time. Given that all of the projects are still ongoing, future research is needed to properly assess the projects' current status and achievements. Especially important would be to include the perspective of the end users, surveying their experiences and satisfaction with the accessibility of the projects they used, as well as with the scope of services and/or opportunities they provide. The choice of interviewees should, in this future endeavour, also be expanded to include the decision-makers, primarily elected officials, involved in the projects.

The ultimate impact of the ICTs-based projects, especially in terms of mobilization, is bound to remain low in the absence of more comprehensive structural reforms which depend on the commitment of the top-level decision-makers. Within these constraints, similar future projects would benefit if they take into account the design-related issues observed in this analysis.

Notes

1. Although Smith's framework was used for this purpose by Wright (2012).
2. The system is the same on both national and local levels. For further information on Serbian electoral system, see (Jovanović, 2011).
3. Clientelism, patronage and other features of partitocracy in Serbia are discussed in more detail in (Damnjanović, 2016).
4. https://www.euprava.gov.rs/eParticipacija.
5. http://eparticipacija.euprava.gov.rs/.
6. Citizens can opt out and have a biometric ID card without the microcontroller instead. Information regarding the number of citizens who opted out is unfortunately unavailable.
7. http://www.crta.rs/.
8. http://prodor.org/.
9. There were 6,767,324 voters registered for 2014 general elections and 109,597 registered in Kraljevo for the 2012 general and presidential elections.
10. In 2014, there were about 1,705,000 formally employed individuals, 780,000 of them working either in public administration or in state-owned companies, according to National Statistical Office (http://www.stat.gov.rs) and media reports (Ćirković, 2014).

Disclosure statement

No potential conflict of interest was reported by the author.

ORCID

Ivana Damnjanović ⓘ http://orcid.org/0000-0002-8553-492X

References

Barber, B. R. (1998). Three scenarios for the future of technology and strong democracy. *Political Science Quarterly, 113*, 573–589.

Barth, T. D., & Schlegelmilch, W. (2014). Cyber democracy: The future of democracy? In E. G. Carayannis, D. F. Campbell, & M. P. Efthymiopoulos (Eds.), *Cyber-development, cyber-democracy and cyber-defense* (pp. 195–206). New York, NY: Springer.

Bešić, M. (2016). Građanska politička kultura - Srbija u Evropi [Civic political culture: Serbia in Europe]. *Sociološki pregled, 50*, 299–326.

Bringing local self-governments closer to citizens: The citizens service centres network in Uzice (2012). Kraljevo: Swiss Agency for Development and Cooperation (SDC). Retrieved from http://www.msp.co.rs/biblioteka/MSP%20Priblizavanje%20lokalnih%20samouprava%20gradjanima.pdf

Bryan, C., Tambini, D., & Tsagarousianou, R. (2002). *Cyberdemocracy: Technology, cities and civic networks*. London/New York, NY: Routledge.

Coleman, S. (2001). The transformation of citizenship. In B. Axford, & R. Huggins (Eds.), *New media and politics* (pp. 109–126). London: Sage.

Coppedge, M., & Reinicke, W. H. (1990). Measuring polyarchy. *Studies in Comparative International Development, 25*, 51–72.

Ćirković, R. (2014, June 17). Ko je na listi od 780.000 zaposlenih u javnom sektoru. [Who is on the list of 780,000 employees in the public sector]. *Dnevni list Danas.* Retrieved from https://www.danas.rs/

Damnjanović, I. (2016). Increasing transparency and accountability with ICTs: A case from Serbia. In A. Balthasar, B. Golob, H. Hansen, R. Mueller-Toeroek, A. Nemselaki, J. Pichler, & A. Prosser (Eds.), *Multilevel (e)Governance: Is ICT a means to enhance transparency and democracy* (pp. 41–52). Vienna: Austrian Computer Society.

Diamond, L. J. (2002). Thinking about hybrid regimes. *Journal of Democracy, 13*, 21–35.

European Commission. Serbia Progress Report. (2014). Retrieved from https://ec.europa.eu/neighbourhood-enlargement/sites/near/files/pdf/key_documents/2014/20140108-serbia-progress-report_en.pdf

Ferber, P., Foltz, F., & Pugliese, R. (2007). Cyberdemocracy and online politics: A new model of interactivity. *Bulletin of Science, Technology & Society, 27*, 391–400.

Freedom House. (2015). *Freedom in the World 2015.* Retrieved from https://freedomhouse.org

Fung, A., & Wright, E. O. (2001). Deepening democracy: Innovations in empowered participatory governance. *Politics & Society, 29*, 5–41.

Geissel, B. (2012). Impacts of democratic innovations in Europe. In K. Newton, & B. Geissel (Eds.), *Evaluating democratic innovations: Curing the democratic malaise?* (pp. 163–183). London: Routledge.

Government of the Republic of Serbia. 2015. *Strategy for development of e-government in Republic of Serbia 2015-2018 and the action plan for implementation of the strategy 2015-2016.* Retrieved from http://www.gs.gov.rs/english/strategije-vs.html

Hand, M., & Sandywell, B. (2002). E-topia as cosmopolis or citadel: On the democratizing and de-democratizing logics of the internet, or, toward a critique of the new technological fetishism. *Theory, Culture & Society, 19*, 197–225.

Hoff, J., Horrocks, I., & Tops, P. (2003). *Democratic governance and new technology.* London/New York, NY: Routledge.

Jovanović, M. (2011). The designing of Serbia's electoral system. *Serbian Political Thought, 3*, 63–86.

Kakabadse, A., Kakabadse, N. K., & Kouzmin, A. (2003). Reinventing the democratic governance project through information technology? A growing agenda for debate. *Public Administration Review, 63*, 44–60.

Kaufman, D., & Kraay, A. (2014). *Worldwide governance indicators.* Retrieved from World Bank website: http://info.worldbank.org/governance/wgi/index.aspx#home

Klačar, B. (2011). Istraživanje obima i intenziteta neposrednog učešća građana kroz referendume, građanske inicijative i zborove građana [Research of scope and intensity of citizens' participation trough referenda and people's initiatives]. In M. Mićić, P. Nikolić, & J. Božanić (Eds.), *Neposredno učešće građana u upravljanju lokalnom zajednicom* [direct participation of citizens in local governance] (pp. 40–52). Belgrade: OSCE Mission to Serbia.

Margetts, H. (2013). The internet and democracy. In W. H. Dutton (Ed.), *The Oxford handbook of internet studies* (pp. 421–440). Oxford: Oxford University Press.

Margolis, M. (2007). E-Government and democracy. In R. Dalton & H. D. Klingemann (Eds.), *The Oxford handbook of political behavior* (pp. 765–782). Oxford: Oxford University Press.

Milosavljević, B. (2015). *Dva veka lokalne samouprave u Srbiji: razvoj zakonodavstva 1804-2014* [Two centuries of local self-government in Serbia: Legislative developments 1804-2014]. Belgrade: SKGO.

Musso, J., Weare, C., & Hale, M. (2000). Designing web technologies for local governance reform: Good management or good democracy? *Political Communication, 17*, 1–19.

Narodna inicijativa u fioci: Analiza kolektivnog učešća građana u procesu donošenja odluka [People's initiative in the drawer: Analysis of collective citizens' participation in the decision-making process]. (2018). Retrieved from CRTA website: http://crta.rs/wp-content/uploads/2018/03/Finalno_03-narodna-inicijativa-NOVO.pdf

Netchaeva, I. (2002). E-government and e-democracy: A comparison of opportunities in the north and south. *International Communication Gazette, 64*, 467–477.

Newton, K. (2012a). Curing the democratic malaise with democratic innovations. In K. Newton & B. Geissel (Eds.), *Evaluating democratic innovations: Curing the democratic malaise?* (pp. 3–20). London, NY: Routledge.

Newton, K. (2012b). Making better citizens? In K. Newton & B. Geissel (Eds.), *Evaluating democratic innovations: Curing the democratic malaise?* (pp. 137–162). London: Routledge.

Opremanje i umrežavanje Grada Užica i mesnih zajednica [Equipping and networking of the City of Užice and local communities]. (n.d.). Retrieved from MSP Consulting website: http://www.msp. co.rs/sr/programi-i-projekti/program-podrske-opstinama/104-opremanje-i-umrezavanje-grada-uzica-i-mesnih-zajednica

Otvoreni Parlament. (2014). *Audit of political engagement in Serbia*. Retrieved from http://www. otvoreniparlament.rs/

Pantić, D., & Pavlović, Z. M. (2009). *Political culture of voters in Serbia*. Belgrade: Institute of Social Sciences.

Pausch, M. (2016). Input, output and political communication. Fields of democratic innovations along different democratic theories. *Comunicazione Politica, 3*, 373–392.

Poster, M. (1997). Cyberdemocracy: Internet and the public sphere. In D. Porter (Ed.), *Internet culture* (pp. 201–218). New York, NY: Routledge.

Pridham, G., & Lewis, P. G. (1996). *Stabilising fragile democracies: Comparing new party systems in southern and Eastern Europe*. London: Routledge.

Rodotä, S. (2007). Democracy. Innovation, and the information society. In P. Goujon, S. Lavelle, P. Duquenoy, K. Kimppa, & V. Laurent (Eds.), *The information society: Innovation, legitimacy, ethics and democracy in Honor of Professor Jacques Berleur s.j* (pp. 17–25). New York, NY: Springer.

Saward, M. (2000). Democratic innovation. In M. Saward (Ed.), *Democratic innovation: Deliberation, representation and association* (pp. 3–13). London: Routledge/ECPR.

Shane, P. M. (2012). Online consultation and political communication in the era of Obama: An introduction. In S. Coleman, & P. Shane (Eds.), *Connecting democracy: Online consultation and the flow of political communication* (pp. 1–20). Cambridge: MIT Press.

Smith, G. (2005). *Beyond the ballot: 57 democratic innovations from around the world*. London: The POWER Inquiry.

Smith, G. (2009). *Democratic innovation: Designing institutions for citizen participation*. New York, NY: Cambridge University Press.

Spada, P., & Ryan, M. (2017). The failure to examine failures in democratic innovations. *Political Science & Politics, 50*, 772–778.

Subirats, J. (2002). The dillemas of an inevitable relationship: Democratic innovation and communication technology. In J. Jacint (Ed.), *Governing telecommunications and the new information society in Europe* (pp. 228–250). Cheltenham: Edward Elgar.

The Economist Intelligence Unit. (2015). *Democracy Index 2014*. Retrieved from https://www.eiu.com

Ustav Socijalističke Federativne Republike Jugoslavije [Constitution of Socialist Federal Republic of Yugoslavia], (1974). Belgrade: Savremena administracija.

Vukosavljević, D. (2016, June 20). Digitalni potpis malo ko koristi [Digital signature rarely used]. *Politika*. Retrieved from http://www.politika.rs/

Wright, S. (2012). Assessing (e-)democratic innovations: 'Democratic goods' and downing street e-petitions. *Journal of Information Technology & Politics, 9*, 453–470.

Zuppo, C. M. (2012). Defining ICT in a boundaryless world: The development of a working hierarchy. *International Journal of Managing Information Technology, 4*, 13–22.

Index

Alliance for Family 19, 20, 37–38; *see also* 'Family' referendum (Slovakia)
Alsace city of Mulhouse 96–97
Antal, A. 64, 75
anti-corruption protests, in Budapest 5
Ask Your MP/Local Representative projects 115–116, 118–119, 121; impact on policy 122; lack of sensitivity to specific local context 122–123; number of citizens involved in 121; success level 122; visibility of 123
attrition: and civic spirit 103–104; in deliberative settings 94; and duration of process 98, 101, 102; and financial stimulation 98, 99, 103, 105; and informal organization 106; and internal inefficacies 98, 100, 106; and lack of impact 101; and moral rewards 98, 104, 107; and participants 104–105; and personal observations 95, 98, 99, 100, 103, 104, 106; political level 98; and politics–community weak connections 97, 98, 101, 103, 107; and powerlessness 105–106; and rootedness, in the community 98, 99, 105; and satisfaction towards the community 99, 103, 104, 107; and self-selection 96, 98, 101, 102, 107; and social responsibility 103–104; and socio-demographic differences 96, 98, 99, 104–105; and unfulfilled expectations 102
authoritarian backlash 3

Barber, Benjamin 95
Basescu, Traian 57
Benoit-Barne, C. 81
'Black Protest' marches (Poland) 4–5
Blanco, I. 81
Borges, W. 14
Bozóki, A. 63
Brexit referendum 13, 32
Bucovinian Agency for Regional Development (BARD) 87, 91n3
Budapest: anti-corruption protests in 5
Bühlmann, M. 13
Bulgarian referendum (2016) 30; access to information 40; government support 41; non-party actor's initiation 35–36; pre-campaign opinion 40, 42; responses to 39; socio-demographics 40
Butler, D. 3

chauvinism 3
Chirtoacă, Dorin 50–58; *see also* Moldovan referendum (2017)
Chişinău, Mayor of *see* Moldovan referendum (2017)
citizen behaviour 5
citizen-initiated referendums 4
citizen involvement 2–3, 5; with technological aid 7 (*see also* information and communication technologies (ICTs))
citizen juries 81
civic virtue 99
civil society model, of e-democracy 114
Clarke, H. D. 14
Coleman, S. 124
Coman, R. 62
community, and participation 99; and civic virtue 99
conflict of schedule, and non-participation 98
consumerist mechanisms, and ICTs-based democratic innovations 114
corruption 3
Creswell, John M. 50
Croatian Referendum on the Constitutional Definition of Marriage (2013) 14

deliberative democracy 2, 4, 6–7, 79, 90–91, 112; advantages 80; citizens withdraw from 7; future research 91; in hybrid regime 79; participatory budgeting (*see* participatory budgeting); and trust 80, 81
democracy, effective 78
democracy in crisis 62
democratic backsliding 3
democratic elitism, and ICTs-based democratic innovations 114
Democratic innovations (Smith) 3
democratic innovations, definition and overview 1–2

direct democracy 2, 3, 5, 74–75; in Bulgaria 35; and consensus 65; contradictory effects 65; definition of 64; governmental 65–66; and ICTs-based democratic innovations 114; instruments 64–65; majoritarian democracy 65–66; oppositional 66; and populism 114; and recall procedure (see recall referendums); referendums (see referendums); and representative democracy (see representative democracy); Western and Eastern Europe, compared 3–4
direct democracy, legislation in Hungary 66–67; Act on Referendum and Popular Initiative 68; constitutional changes of 1997 68; instruments 67–68; plebiscite 67; popular agenda initiative 67; popular initiative 67; procedures 68
direct legislation 95
Dodon, Igor 52

e-democracy 4, 95, 99, 113; and e-government, distinction between 114; models of 114
e-government 114, 123
electronic bureaucracy 114
elite populism 75
e-Participation project 4, 115–116, 117–118, 121; anonymity, lack of 123–124; and government responsiveness 124; impact on policy 122; number of citizens involved in 121; sensitivity to specific local context, lack of 122–124; success level 122; weak promotion of 124
Estonia, E-participation in 4
Euroscepticism 3
Evaluating democratic innovations (Geissel and Newton) 3

'Family' referendum (Slovakia) 12, 16–18, 37–38; access to information 40; and Catholic Church 38; compliance to constitutional law 19–20; context of 19–24; informative campaign 40; non-party actor's initiation 16, 19; partisan cues, clarity and impacts of 12, 16, 17, 21–23; political parties' stance 16, 20; pre-campaign opinion 40, 42; responses to 39–40; and socio-demographics 17–18, 22, 40
Festenstein, M. 81
Folscher, A. 4
Font, J. 81

Gastil, J. 3
Geissel, B. 3, 112, 116
Gherghina, S. 3, 4
Ghimpu, Vasile 51
Glaurdić, J. 14
governmental direct democracy 65–66
government-initiated referendums 65
Grozavu, Nistor 52
Gyurcsány, Ferenc 70

Hauser, G. 81
Hegedûs, D. 63
Hobolt, S. B. 15
Hornig, E.-C. 64
Hug, S. 16
Hungarian Helsinki Committee 73–74
Hungarian political system 6
Hungary: abolition of fees referendum campaign 71; Alliance of Free Democrats (Szabad Demokraták Szövetsége – SZDSZ) 69; Christian Democratic People's Party 63; consolidated democracy, referendums in 69–70; deconsolidation and the struggle for power 70–71; democracy in 62–63; democratic transition 63; direct democracy in 71–75; and European integration 69; Fidesz Party 63–64, 69, 70, 75; and financial crisis of 2008 63; health insurance and health care referendum 71; Hungarian Socialist Party's (Magyar Szocialista Párt – MSZP) 69, 70; Kúria (administrative court) 68, 72; migrant quota, referendum against 73–74; National Consultations 73, 75; National Election Commission (NEC) 68, 72; National Electoral Office (NEO) 68; national referendum 67; opposition, role of 72–73; parliamentary power 66–67; populism in 64; referendum campaigning 73; shop opening hours referendum 71–72; System of National Cooperation (Nemzeti Együtmüködés Rendszere) 63–64; transition-related referendums in 1989/1990 69; two-party system 63
hybrid regime: deliberative democracy in 79; externally constrained 63; and political trust 80–81; Ukraine 82–83

illiberal democracy 63, 75
individual determinants, and partisan cues 14
information and communication technologies (ICTs) 7, 111, 112–114; e-democracy (see e-democracy); future research 124; in Serbia (see Ask Your MP/Local Representative projects; e-Participation project; Networking of Local Communities project); terminologies 113; theoretical conceptualization 113–114
information management 114
informative campaign 34, 39–40, 41–42, 43
Iniciatíva Inakosť 38; see also 'Family' referendum (Slovakia)
institutional determinants, and partisan cues 15–16
internal inefficacy, and non-participation 98
intra-campaign 29, 30
Ireland 80
issue-voting 30

Jacquet, V. 98
Joas, M. 3
Jobbik 73

Kakabadse, A. 114
Kakabadse, N. K. 114
Kaufmann, B. 3
Kiska, Andrej 19
Kleindienst, P. 4
Knobloch, K. R. 3
Komorowski, Bronislaw 36
Kouzmin, A. 114
Kriesi, H. 13
Kukiz, Pawel 36, 37

Listhaug, O. 16
long-term deliberative projects 94–95

majoritarian democracy 65–66
Mansbridge, Jane 99
Margetts, H. 113
Margolis, M. 122
Marx, Karl 99
mayors recall, referendums for see recall
    referendums
media: and project visibility 123; and
    referendum campaigns 31, 32, 36
mini-publics 95–96, 97, 98
Moldovan referendum (2017) 50–53, 57–59; and
    citizens' will to prevention of concentration
    of power 54, 56–57, 58; and geopolitical
    stake perception 54, 57, 58; and perceived
    decisive importance of the capital's control
    nationwide 53, 55–56, 58; and popular
    mistrust of institutions and parties 53,
    54–55, 58

neighbourhood assembly 95
neighbourhood consultative councils 96–97,
    101, 104
Networking of Local Communities project 115,
    116, 119–120, 121; alleviation of existing
    disbalances 122; impact on policy 122;
    number of citizens involved in 121–122;
    success level 122; visibility of 123
new democracies 113
Newton, K. 3, 112, 113, 114, 122
non-participation, logics of 98; conflict of
    schedule 98; internal inefficacy 98; and
    mini-public's lack of impact 98; political
    alienation 98; private sphere 98; public
    meetings avoidance 98; see also attrition
Nyakó, István 72

obligatory referendums 65
open assemblies 95
Open Parliament 119, 121; visibility of 123
oppositional direct democracy 66
opposition-initiated referendums 65
optimistic bias, in democratic innovations
    studies 112
Orbán, Viktor 63, 70

participatory budgeting 6–7, 112; and political
    trust 81, 86–89

Participatory democratic innovations in Europe
    (Joas) 3
participatory innovations 1–2
partisan cues 5–6, 33, 34; and decision to
    abstain from voting 11; future studies 25
partisan cues, influence on voter behaviour
    11, 14, 24–25; clarity 15; and clarity 15, 16,
    17, 21; and individual determinants 14–15;
    and institutional determinants 15–16;
    uniformity 15
Petro, Gustavo 47–48
Pierce, R. 16
Plahotniuc, Vladimir 51–52, 54, 56–57
Plevneliev, Rosen 36
pluralist networks provision of services, and
    ICTs-based democratic innovations 114
Poland: 'Black Protest' marches in 4–5
Polish referendum (2015) 36–37; access
    to information 40; pre-campaign
    opinion 40, 42; responses to 40; and
    satisfaction with government 40–41;
    socio-demographics 40
political alienation, and non-participation 98
political participation: decline in 1;
    state actors and non-state actors,
    cooperation between 2
political trust see trust in political systems
politics–community weak connections, and
    attrition 97, 98, 101, 103, 107
popular assemblies 95, 96
prejudices and voting, link between 14, 32
pre-referendum discourse 13, 40, 42
private sphere, and non-participation 98
process duration, and attrition 98, 101, 102
public meetings avoidance 98

Qvortrup, M. 3

radical right populism 3
Ranney, A. 3
recall referendums 5, 47–48, 57–59; and citizens
    conviction of national/international stake of
    the recall 49; and citizens' empowerment 58;
    and citizens tendency to overrate city's
    importance 49; citizens' views on the
    significance of 58; degree of legitimacy,
    assessment of 48; future research 58; key
    roles of 47–48; and lack of trust in political
    systems 48–49; mayor's political orientation
    and government, difference between 49;
    Moldovan referendum (2017) (see Moldovan
    referendum (2017)); reasons for failure of
    48–49; see also Moldovan referendum (2017)
referendum campaigns 29, 43; access to
    information 33, 34, 40; agenda setting 32;
    Bulgarian referendum (see Bulgarian
    referendum); and citizens' attitudes 31;
    effect on the voting behaviour 32;
    and election campaigns, differences
    between 29; framing and priming of
    events 32; government support 33–35, 40;

hypodermic model 31; information delivery 31, 42; informative campaign 39–40; mechanisms of influence voters' preferences 31–33; and media 31, 32, 36; minimal-effect hypothesis 31; opposers the referendum proposals 33; partisan cues 33, 34, 40; pre-campaign opinion 33, 34, 40; promoters of the policy 32–33; resonance model 32; simplification of choices 32; socio-demographics 33, 34, 40; and uncertainty reduction 32
referendums 3–4, 5, 11; Brexit referendum 13, 32; Bulgarian referendum (see Bulgarian referendum); campaigns 6; citizen-initiated 4; complexity of the topic 13; Croatian Referendum on the Constitutional Definition of Marriage (2013) 14; 'Family' referendum (Slovakia) (see 'Family' referendum (Slovakia)); government-initiated 65; obligatory referendums 65; opposition-initiated 65; partisan cues 5–6 (see partisan cues, influence on voter behaviour); and political stance 24–25; and popular demands 13, 24–25; same-sex marriage referendums in the USA 14; as second-order national elections 30; second-order perception 15, 33; and voting decision 6, 12–13
Referendums and representative democracy (Setälä and Schiller) 3
representative democracy 5, 78
Republic of Moldova 5, 6, 50; Communist Party (PCRM) 50–51, 52; corruption scandal 52; corruption scandals 51; Democratic Party (PDM) 51, 52; Liberal Party 54; parliamentary elections 2009 51; parliamentary elections 2015 52; Socialist Party (PSRM) 51, 52; see also Moldovan referendum (2017)
Rights for Moms 122
Romania 80; deliberative democracy 4
Romanian referendum (2012) 11
rootedness, in the community 98, 99, 105
Ryan, M. 112

Sager, F. 13
same-sex marriage referendums (USA) 14
Sandu, Maia 52
Dos Santos government 48
Saward, M. 112
Schiller, T. 3
Sciarini, P. 16
second-order voting 30
self-selection, and attrition 96, 98, 101, 102, 107
Serbia 112, 114–115; Ask Your MP/Local Representative 115–116, 118–119, 121–123; deficiencies in participation 117; e-Government portal 117–118; e-Participation 115–116, 117–118, 121–124; establishment of Service Centres 120;

institutional framework 116–117; Istanbul Convention, ratification of 122; Networking of Local Communities 115, 116, 119–120, 121–123; Open Parliament website 119; political culture 117; Rights for Moms 122
Setälä, M. 3
Silagadze, N. 3
Slovakia referendums: conditions for success of 19, 23, 38; 'Family' referendum (see 'Family' referendum (Slovakia)); support for government 41; turnout for 12
Smilov, D. 4
Smith, G. 3, 65, 113, 115–116, 122, 123
Spada, P. 112
Spain, citizen juries in 81
Struebing, J. 101
Subirats, J. 114, 115, 121

technological determinism 113
teledemocracy 113
Timisoara 95, 100; attrition in (see attrition); neighbourhood consultative councils 96–97; satisfaction towards the community 99, 103, 104, 107; 'Young people decide!' initiative 104
Timofti, Vasile 51
Tocqueville, Alexis de 99
Tomini, L. 62
Tomšič, M., 4
Trifonov, Stanislav 35–36; see also Bulgarian referendum
trust in political systems 78–79, 80–81, 84; and deliberative democracy 80, 81; lack of 48–49; at local level 81; and participatory budgeting 81–82, 86–89
two-dimensional political space, European referendums 30

Ukraine 7; Chernivtsi city 83; hybrid regime 79, 82–83
Ukraine, deliberative activities and citizens' political trust: change in trust level, evaluation of 89–90; deliberation during the public meetings 88; level of trust 82–83, 84; participatory budgeting process 82, 86–89; preparatory survey 84–86; reasons for lack of approval 88–89

Vágo, Gábor 72
Valen, H. 16
van Eeden, P. 75
Vospernik, S. 65, 66
voter's political awareness, and partisan cues 15
Vuković, V. 14

Waters, D. 3
World Federation of Hungarians 70

xenophobia 3